TRADEMARKED

A HISTORY OF WELL-KNOWN BRANDS
FROM AERTEX TO WRIGHT'S COAL TAR

DAVID NEWTON

SUTTON PUBLISHING

First published in the United Kingdom in 2008 by
Sutton Publishing, an imprint of NPI Media Group Limited
Cirencester Road · Chalford · Stroud · Gloucestershire · GL6 8PE

British Library Cataloguing in Publication Data
A catalogue record for this book is available from the British Library.

Hardback ISBN 978-0-7509-4590-5

Typeset in Iowan.
Typesetting and origination by
NPI Media Group Limited.
Printed and bound in England.

CONTENTS

ACKNOWLEDGEMENTS

Over a period of more than three years, and for many more years of gestation, the project to put together a book highlighting the history of trademarks that were registered in the early days of the Trade Mark Registry has been something of a passion (or perhaps obsession) for me. I would like to thank all those who have had to endure my preoccupation with this work.

I have used principally two libraries for my research: the British Library and Birmingham City Library. I am very grateful to these two institutions and especially to the staff of the British Library Business and IP Centre and others who have helped me but who are too numerous to name individually. In addition I have had help on the trademarks of specific firms from a number of other libraries, local studies departments and tourist information bureaux, especially Plymouth Central Library, Manchester Central Library, Oxfordshire Studies, Skipton Library and Malvern Tourist Information Centre.

In addition to the registered trademarks taken from the *Trade Mark Journal*, pictures and images have been supplied by the Bridgeman Art Library, the British Library, Britvic Soft Drinks Ltd (Idris), the Gordon Bunce Collection, Clarks International, Corbis, Dents, the Mary Evans Picture Library, Greene King plc, the Illustrated London News Picture Library, Leeds City Library Patent Information Unit, the Motoring Picture Library, the

National Archives Image Library, Science & Society Picture Library, Thornton & Ross (Ellimans), and the Worcester Porcelain Museum.

Special thanks are also due to Robert Opie for his help in finding so many relevant illustrations from the Robert Opie Collection (http://www.robertopiecollection.com) and providing them for use in this book. The photographs reproduced in the following pages are from a collection of over 500,000 items illustrating the story of Britain's consumer society, which is currently housed at Opie's Museum of Memories in the Museum of Brands, Packaging & Advertising at 2 Colville Mews, Lonsdale Road, Notting Hill, London, W11 2AR.

I would especially like to thank John Nelhams of ColArt Fine Art & Graphics Ltd (from whom I received a lot of help with the trademarks of Reeves and Winsor & Newton); Peter Marsh, Honorary Chairman and Curator of the Stephens Collection in Finchley, London (for information and images of trademarks for Stephens ink), David Harman of the Transport Ticket Society (for help with Bell Punch) and various staff of the UK Patent Office.

I have used many hundreds of websites in the course of the research for this book. They are far too numerous to mention individually, although I should point out the extensive use I have made of the Patent Office website and especially Trade Mark pages and other pages listed in the bibliography. For these I acknowledge my gratitude.

I should like to thank Sutton Publishing and its staff who have had faith in *Trademarked* from the outset and who developed it into the book you see today.

Finally I am especially grateful to my wife Jane, who has had to endure my preoccupation during the writing of this book over many long days.

Despite the many sources used and the lengthy research I have conducted, any errors and omissions that remain in this text are solely the responsibility of the author.

INTRODUCTION

THE ORIGIN OF MARKS

Trademarks probably originated in marks used to indicate ownership in the Stone Age or early Bronze Age. The branding of cattle was an early example of this. Then in about 2700 BC in China and later in the Roman Republic marks were put on pottery to indicate the maker. This kind of marking burgeoned in the Middle Ages when merchants would mark their goods. As trade developed in the seventeenth and eighteenth centuries many more makers of goods were putting their own marks on the items they sold and a few were taking action against others who tried to pass off their goods as those of the original manufacturer. At this time it was not easy for a trademark owner to obtain redress from another person who had used the rightful owner's mark.

In the nineteenth century goods were more and more made and packaged in central factories and distributed nationally and thus manufacturers needed to compete against locally produced goods.

REGISTRATION

In Victorian times counterfeiting became more of a problem at home and abroad and in 1862 a select committee was set up to determine whether Britain should have a system of registration of trademarks to stop this copying. Mr Jackson of the firm Spear & Jackson reported to the committee that registration systems were already in place in Prussia, France, Belgium and some of the states in America. Despite pressure for a similar law to be introduced in Britain, some manufacturers were against registration and it was not recommended by the committee at that time. By 1875, however, the demand for registration had increased and the Trademark Registration Act was duly passed by Parliament. Registration under the Act started on 1 January 1876 and from then on manufacturers could much more easily stop others using their trademarks.

The Trade Mark Registry was set up under the Commissioners of Patents in 1876 in London and after the passing of the Patents, Designs & Trade Marks Act of 1883 it was run by the Comptroller of Patents, Designs and Trade Marks, appointed by the Board of Trade. The first public notification of the whereabouts of the office which was to open for acceptance of applications was a notice hastily inserted in *The Times* on 29 December 1875, after a letter had been published on Christmas Day. In part it read, 'Having some important trademarks to register for various clients we have made enquiries at the Patent Office and at Stationers' Hall as to where the new office is situated but at both places there is utter ignorance of the matter. Has it been forgotten?' Nevertheless applicants were queuing at the door of the Registry before it opened on 1 January to obtain registration at the earliest opportunity. Although many applications were received in the first few weeks it was not until May 1876 that details started to be published in the *Trade Mark Journal*. By the end of 1876 over ten thousand applications had been made.

The process of registration has varied over the years as relevant pieces of legislation were amended but it essentially consists of filing an application for registration at the Trade Mark Registry, which then advertises the mark, if acceptable, by publishing it in the *Trade Mark Journal*. The advertisement gives notification that the mark is to be registered and allows anyone to object to it if they wish. If there are no objections, the trademark is registered. On registration, the owner of the trademark is given a certificate. (As an example, see the illustration of the certificate for Winsor & Newton's trademark number 630,436 on p. xii.) Once registered, it was easier for the owners to prevent others from using the mark.

To maintain a trademark on the register requires regular fees to be paid to the Trade Mark Registry; if they are not paid, the trademark simply expires. Some of the marks in this book are still registered exactly as they were when first submitted but many have lapsed or are no longer used. For those that are still maintained, you will see that although the ownership of the mark may have changed over the years, the mark itself, with very few exceptions, is unchanged. Each time a trademark logo is changed, as happened with the Shell symbol of Royal Dutch Shell, a new registration has to be made at the Trade Mark Registry.

SOURCES OF TRADEMARK INFORMATION

The early issues of the *Trade Mark Journal* in which the marks were advertised are a great source of information and they have provided much of the detail for this book. For each trademark an entry in the *Journal* shows the word or device that is being registered, the name and address of the applicant or his firm and often the type of business carried on. If a mark had been used before 1876 the number of years of earlier use was also given. Also listed is the type of goods for which the mark is to be used, say 'meat pies', and the trademark class into which the goods are placed, such as class 42 for 'substances used as food or as ingredients for food'. The classification system employed from 1876 until 1938 was derived in some haste from the scheme used to classify exhibits at the 1851 Great Exhibition!

Many other sources were used in compiling this book: the Internet, books, journals, law reports and so on. While the *Trade Mark Journal* is authoritative and other printed matter is generally reliable, web pages are variable in their quality and often provide information without provenance. Nevertheless, so much information about the early British manufacturers and traders is available on the Internet that it is impossible to ignore it as a source, even though the details provided are often difficult to check. Only the most reliable sources have been chosen in the compilation of this book – I hope! Important sources of reference are listed in the Bibliography but Internet sources have only been cited where they are unique and significant. Where recent

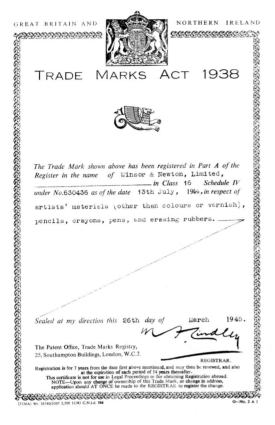

A trademark certificate of registration given to Winsor & Newton in 1945. (© *ColArt Fine Art & Graphics Ltd*)

information is given for a particular trademark it has generally been updated to 2005 unless otherwise noted.

The trademarks illustrated in this book only scratch the surface of the vast numbers of registered trademarks. They have been selected for a number of reasons. First, each trademark shown generally has some visual appeal. Trademarks can be words, graphical devices (logos) or a combination of both (or indeed much more recently even smells), but in this book every entry is illustrated by one or more devices, whether logos, illustrations, signatures or some distinctive writing. Secondly, the principal trademarks used here mostly originate from the nineteenth century, although a few are earlier or later. Thirdly, the trademark or the firm that owned it is still known or remembered today for some reason. In addition, others have been included to demonstrate variations or developments. In some cases advertising material has been included from other sources to show the trademarks in use, or even sometimes the lack of use of marks!

In this book the single word 'trademark' is used except where reference is made to the Trade Mark Registry or the like, when this older British style is applied. The symbols ™ and ® have not been used since it should be clear from the text that the trademarks cited are, or were, registered.

This book is about trademarks that have been registered in Britain but quite a few of them were and are owned by foreign companies. You may be surprised sometimes to learn of the foreign ownership of some apparently British products and the British ownership of apparently foreign trademarks. In a few cases illustrations of marks registered in America, France or Germany are shown for comparison.

TRADEMARKS AS BRANDS

In the nineteenth century little science was involved in creating trademarks. Most of them were simply the names of the company founders, although some were invented marks, such as Aquascutum coats, Camp coffee, HMV gramophones, Kodak cameras and Sunlight soap. For information on how many names originated I recommend the *Dictionary of trade name origins*. The device marks occasionally derived from the names of the firms, such as a fish for Chubb, a prancing horse for Colt, a camel for Cammell and stylised birds for Alfred Bird's later trademarks for custard powder.

Some trademarks derived their characteristics from the packaging or product to which they were applied. Cement was packed in barrels and the relevant mark applied to the circular top, and so the mark itself was often circular, as with Blue Circle and Rugby Portland Cement. Marks for paper sometimes took the form of a watermark, as in the case of Wiggins Teape number 14,900, and beer marks often had similar features because they were designed as oval labels. Some of the biscuit trademarks, such as those of Carr, Huntley & Palmer and Jacobs, show many similarities but this may have been because purchasers of these products expected the packaging of biscuits to have a traditional look rather than from any design necessity.

Of course, trademarks often reflected current styles. Lambert & Butler and Benson & Hedges both produced cigarettes with fashionable Egyptian themes. Lions were a recurrent theme to suggest connections with the British Empire to consumers, while Price's candles, for example, bore trademarks showing scenes from far-away parts of the world.

A few trademarks were themselves works of art, including those for Woodward's Gripe Water, His Master's Voice gramophones and Pear's soap. They were obtained from well-known artists and have subsequently become well loved by consumers. It is said that European culture shows an intuitive preference for supernatural symbols such as the sun, the eye, hands, female figures, crowns and horses, but only a few of these feature in this book, or indeed in trademarks in general.

Local landmarks or local connections were often used as symbols. Examples include the trademarks for Cash's name tapes (Coventry spires), Clark's shoes (Glastonbury Tor), Greene King's beer (Bury St Edmunds Gatehouse) and Wolsey woollen goods (the burial place of Cardinal Wolsey in Leicester). The associations were sometimes more general, as with the use of thistles for Callard & Bowser's butterscotch and Nairn's Scottish-produced linoleum.

The prerequisite for brands to stand the test of time is the survival of the firm, which generally results from successful management rather than from the specific creation of a strong name or image as the firm's trademark. It is often said that to be a strong mark the logo needs to be a simple visual statement: the symbols of Bass (a triangle), Schweppes (a fountain), Shell and Worthington (white shields) would seem to support this theory, as do Colman (a bull), Quaker and Nestlé (nests) although Marmite and Lyle's Golden Syrup have both survived as brands despite having more complex logos.

It should be apparent from the book that a brand can give rise to many instances of trademarks. A brand may evolve but the individual trademark cannot and so new trademarks have to be created within the brand. The entries for Shell oil and Reeves' artist's materials illustrate evolving logos which have resulted in many registered trademarks.

The reader is invited to browse through the trademarks illustrated in these pages to see if any reasons become apparent as to why some trademarks have become iconic while most have disappeared with little trace.

TRANSPORT

From Bikes to Cars and Other Things Vehicular

The introduction of the steam train in the nineteenth century brought mass public transportation and by 1900 a billion passenger journeys were made each year. It was the development of the bicycle in the second half of the nineteenth century, though, that brought the first mass-produced transport for which trademark protection was used. The bicycle became commonplace, especially after the introduction of the Rover safety bicycle which had pedals driving a chain to turn the rear wheel.

Companies like Humber, Rover, Singer and Triumph started out as manufacturers of bicycles and tricycles and then, as the internal combustion engine was developed early in the twentieth century, moved into motorcycle and car production. Other companies, like Austin, came directly into motor manufacture early in the twentieth century. Car manufacturers registered trademarks for their brand names and later for the names of individual models. Car and bike trademarks were often in the form of badges.

On the back of the use of the internal combustion engine in road transport came the growth of the use of petrol and the rise of the oil companies. Firms like Shell and Standard Oil (abbreviated to SO and later called Esso) started out selling oil for lighting and heating and only in the twentieth century sold it for transport use. Other manufacturers developed components needed for the motor car, like Joseph Lucas's lamps and Herbert Frood's brake blocks, which he called 'Ferodo' as an anagram of his surname (trademark number 286,194 of 1906).

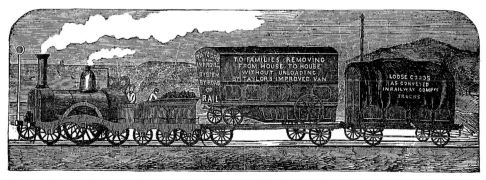

Despite Walter Taylor's attractive trademark (number 4,034) his firm did not survive.

In the railway business few companies bothered to take out trademarks, although the Cammell company, which manufactured steel products, took out early trademarks for their steel rails, railway carriages and other items. Other firms, like that of Walter Taylor, who took out a splendidly illustrated trademark for his railway vans and removals in 1876 (number 4,034), have disappeared.

AUSTIN CARS

Herbert Austin, the son of a Yorkshire farmer, was born in 1866 in Buckinghamshire. He went to Australia in 1882 but returned to England in 1893 to run Frederick Wolseley's sheep-shearing factory. He had already built some experimental cars when in 1901 he became the manager at the Wolseley Tool and Motor Car Company.

In 1905 Austin found a site at Longbridge outside Birmingham and set up his own Austin Motor Company. The following year the firm's first trademark, showing 'a winged wheel kicking up dust', was registered (number 286,069) and production was just 120 cars. Twenty years later 14,000 cars were being produced each year and in 1931 a 'flying A' replaced the first mark. The year 1932 saw the introduction of the best-selling 'Austin Ten'.

In 1952, eleven years after Herbert Austin's death, the Austin Motor Company merged with the Nuffield Group, which had earlier swallowed up the Wolseley company, and the British Motor Corporation was born. Another merger in 1968 formed British Leyland but by 1975 it had run into difficulties and was nationalised. In 1986 it became Rover Group and soon the Austin brand was dropped. Manufacture of cars at the Longbridge plant ended in 2005.

The Austin Motor Company's 'Winged Wheel' trademark (number 286,069).

CHANGE UP—TO AN

AUSTIN TEN

Above, left: Cover of the *Austin Advocate* magazine of 1912 showing the 'Winged Wheel' trademark. *Above, right:* A poster for the successful Austin Ten, which was introduced in 1932, does not display either the 'Winged Wheel' or 'Flying-A' trademark. (*The Robert Opie Collection*)

BELL PUNCH TICKETING

The Bell Punch Company was established in 1878 to acquire the patent rights of an American registering ticket-punch that was used in conjunction with a series of pre-printed tickets to check the receipt of money. In 1884 John Melton Black joined the board as managing director and soon afterwards began to develop a small rotary ticket-printing machine. In the same year the firm registered a trademark (number 40,471) and a site was acquired in Tabernacle Street in the City of London, where a factory was built. The trademark shows a ticket punch similar in design to those illustrated in some of Black's many patents.

The Bell Punch trademark (number 40,471) illustrates the product in miniature.

In 1891 the London General Omnibus Co. started to use the Bell Punch ticketing system and it was soon extended over all

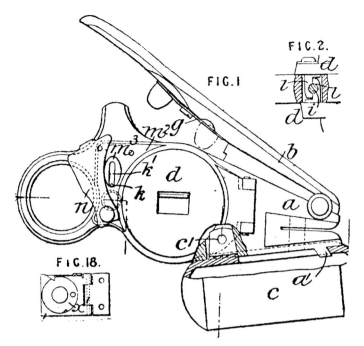

FIG.1

FIG.2.

FIG.18.

Patent for a ticket punch invented by John Melton Black, managing director of Bell Punch (GB 15,574 of 1893).

routes. The company had transferred to Uxbridge by 1922 to expand production and during the 1920s and 1930s it started to produced taxi-meters and ticketing systems for cinemas and horse-race betting.

Later Sumlock Anita Electronics Ltd was set up as an offshoot of Bell Punch to produce 'comptometers' and it made the world's first electronic desktop calculator, the 'Anita', in 1961. The Sumlock business was bought by the American firm Rockwell in 1973 but in 1986 its Portsmouth factory closed while the remainder of Bell Punch eventually became part of the German Höft & Wessel Group.

CAMMELL RAILWAY ENGINEERING

Charles Cammell's trademark number 10,807 uses a visual pun.

Charles Cammell was born in Hull, Yorkshire, in 1810, the son of a wealthy ship-owner. His first employment was as an apprentice ironmonger but he later set up the iron and steel business Johnson Cammell & Co. in Sheffield with Henry and Thomas Johnson. By 1854 the company had offices in London and America and in 1870 it opened a factory at Dronfield to the south of Sheffield, first making railway wheels and then steel rails.

In 1877, as Charles Cammell & Co., the firm applied for trademarks depicting a camel (numbers 10,807–10) for which it claimed use since 1855. The camel logo continued in use until 1972, when it was replaced by a CL monogram design. The goods covered by the trademark show the wide range of products manufactured, including iron and steel, boilers, weighing

4

machines, machine tools, files, tools, cannon, railway carriages, railway trucks and other carriages. In 1882 the Dronfield factory was closed and a new one opened in Workington on the Cumbrian coast.

Cammell & Co. merged with the Laird shipbuilding firm in 1903 to form Cammell Laird. The Laird shipbuilding business had been started in 1824 by William Laird, a Scot, who moved to the River Mersey and set up a boiler-making works which later expanded into iron shipbuilding. Later still the railway business became Metro-Cammell, based in Birmingham, and in the 1990s this merged with GEC Traction to form GEC-Alstom, now part of the engineering company Alstom. The shipbuilding business on Merseyside went into public ownership in the 1970s, was de-nationalised in 1983 and recently closed altogether.

COMMER VEHICLES

Commer began in 1905 as Commercial Cars Ltd and in December of that year the firm applied for its first trademark (number 278,012), in the form of a letter C made from a wheel, from its headquarters in Gracechurch Street, London. Soon it set up a factory in Luton, Bedfordshire, where it remained for almost fifty years, mainly producing trucks.

Commercial Cars' 'single wheel' trademark, number 278,012.

Military vehicles were built during the First World War but when peace came the firm declined and in 1926 was taken over by Humber, which was amalgamated the following year into the Rootes Group. Production of vans and trucks continued at Luton but after the Second World War a move was made to nearby Dunstable.

The American company Chrysler took a 30 per cent holding in Rootes in 1964 and bought the rest in 1967. The Commer name

The Commer 'two wheel' trademark, number 298,759 of 1908.

was dropped in 1976 and in 1979 Chrysler UK was sold to the Peugeot-Citroën group. The truck-making business was sold on to Renault.

CROSSLEY'S ENGINES

The firm Crossley Brothers was set up in 1867 by Francis (Frank) Crossley when he bought the engineering business of John M. Dunlop in Great Marlborough Street, Manchester. William Crossley, his younger brother, soon joined him, concentrating on business aspects at the firm. The brothers made machinery for rubber manufacturers, including the nearby firm of Macintosh for their raincoat fabrication.

In 1869 Crossley Brothers acquired the world rights to the patents of the German firm of Otto and Langden for their new gas-fuelled internal combustion engine and in 1876 rights were also acquired for the famous Otto four-stroke cycle engine. The firm moved to larger premises in Openshaw, Manchester, in 1880 and the following year registered a trademark for the Otto Gas Engine (number 26,000); by 1882 the brothers claimed to have sold over 8,000 engines. In 1898 the company built its first diesel engines and soon began to make petrol engines, which found their way into Leyland and other buses.

In 1904 cars started to be made and a separate company was set up to manufacture them in 1910 using a Coptic cross as its logo. In 1919 Crossley bought Premier Gas Engines of Nottingham, where large engines were built. In the 1960s the firm went bankrupt but was revived and joined Amalgamated Power Engineering, which later became part of Northern Engineering Industries, which in turn was taken over by Rolls-Royce plc in 1998.

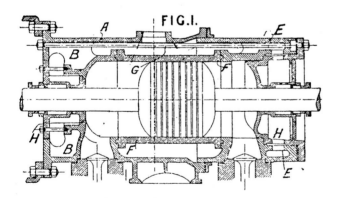

FIG.I.

Gas and like engines.—The cylinders of double-acting engines are constructed as shown in Fig. 1. The outer casing A, which encloses the liner F, is formed in one with the engine framing, and is closed at its ends by a separate casting E, and a casting B formed with the casing, respectively. The ends are provided with covers H, the whole arrangement being held together by bolts G passing through the water space.

HUMBER'S CARS

Humber & Company, better remembered for its cars, was set up as a cycle manufacturer in Beeston, Nottingham, by Thomas Humber in about 1869. Humber entered into a brief partnership with Marriott and and then also Cooper from 1875 but this later broke up, with Marriott and Cooper continuing to sell their own Humber bicycles. Thomas Humber registered four trademarks to distinguish his own company's 'Genuine Humber' bicycles and tricycles in 1885 and 1886 (including number 45,748 for the 'Cripper', named after Robert Cripps, who successfully raced Humber cycles). Two years later, after a fire in the Nottingham works, the company set up a factory in Wolverhampton and later moved to Coventry. Humber bicycles gained a good reputation throughout the world and the firm continued to prosper.

The very first Humber car, the 3hp Forecar, was built in 1896 and owed a lot to the firm's cycle origins – it even had pedals to help it up the hills! The Phaeton, driven by a mixture of belts and gears, was the next car and at the turn of the century Humber began making the Humberette (trademark 256,044 of 1903).

Humber took over Commer Cars in 1926 and the Hillman Motor Car Company, which had works in Coventry adjoining those of Humber, in 1928. The firm became part of the Rootes Group just as a slump hit car manufacturers and in 1932 the cycle business was sold to Raleigh. The Second World War saw the firm producing military vehicles and aircraft engines but it returned to manufacturing luxury cars after the war. American car maker Chrysler bought a stake in the Rootes Group in 1964 and later bought the whole business. By 1974 the well-known Snipe and Hawk models had been dropped and the only remaining Humber car in production was the Sceptre.

A 'Genuine Humber' trademark (number 43,856) showing 'Five figures with one head on a cycle wheel' (see colour plate 1 for an example of its use in advertising).

Thomas Humber's bicycle patent of 1884 (GB 6,767).

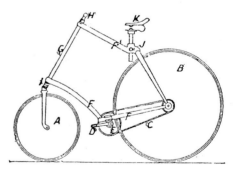

Bicycles with small front steering-wheel A and large rear wheel B driven through an endless chain C. The cranks D are carried on the frame F between the two wheels. The lower chain-wheel E can be removed and replaced by one of different size so as to vary the gearing as required. The head of the steering-wheel is prolonged up-wards, forming an inclined spindle G which is fitted with the usual transverse handles H. The annular cam and spring I, described in Specifi-cation No. 5583, A.D. 1883, may be used to keep the steering-wheel to its normal position when the handles are released. The saddle K is carried on the upper part of the frame F¹, its height being adjustable by means of the set-screw J.

Lucas's trademark number 22,822 makes reference to the Tom Bowling Lamp Works.

LUCAS LAMPS

Joseph Lucas was born in 1834 in Birmingham but it is not known whether he was related to the Joseph Lucas of London who took out patents for lamps in 1785 and 1793. As a youth he was apprenticed to a silversmith as an electroplater but in 1860 he started on his own selling paraffin and then hollow-ware (bowl or tube-shaped items of earthenware) from a basket skip on wheels. Later he started to make hollow-ware and then lamps. He continued to sell products made by other people, including the Tom Bowling lamps made by Isaac Sherwood. (The Tom Bowling was a ship's lantern named after a sea-shanty written by Charles Dibdin in 1789.)

In 1875 Lucas founded a factory in Little King Street which he called the Tom Bowling Lamp Works and here he manufactured lamps. He made his first cycle lamp in 1878 and by 1882 he had applied for his famous 'King of the Road' trademark for lamps and lanterns (number 22,822). The lamp business was very successful as cycling became increasingly popular. In 1872 Joseph's oldest son Harry had joined the business and after ten years he became a partner in Joseph Lucas & Son. About this time other lamp-makers started copying the Lucas product and in 1885 Lucas successfully took an infringer of his bicycle lamp patent (GB 2,493 of 1880) to the High Court. By this time the firm was also making saddles and other parts for bicycles and by 1897 they started to sell kits of components for cycle manufacturers.

In 1902 the firm started to produce oil lamps for cars but in the same year Joseph died of typhoid while on holiday in Naples. Acetylene lamps followed and later electric lamps were produced. By 1976 turnover was £719 million from vehicle equipment, aircraft equipment and industrial products. In 1996 Lucas Industries merged with the Varity Corporation of America to form LucasVarity plc; this was acquired in 1999 by the American company TRW. The earliest trademark still registered is the Pathfinder (number 34,783) for lamps made of tin or brass; this was first registered in 1884.

A Lucas advertisement has the slogan 'The King of the Road' on the signpost in the background. (*Gordon Bunce Collection*)

Premier's Kangaroo
trademark, number
45,791.

Hillman, Herbert &
Cooper's patented
bicycle chain
tensioning invention
for Premier (GB
1,775 of 1886).

PREMIER CYCLES

The bicycle manufacturing firm Hillman, Herbert & Cooper started in business in Coventry in 1875. Three years later the firm applied for a trademark for bicycles and tricycles (number 15,568) with Coventry cycle manufacturer Singer. In 1880 another trademark was registered by the firm at its Premier Works for Cooper's lamp (number 22,340).

In 1884 the firm applied for trademarks for Kangaroo and Premier cycles (numbers 36,402–3), and the following year a kangaroo logo was registered (number 45,791). The Kangaroo cycle had a smaller front wheel driven by a gear-and-chain mechanism, allowing the rider to sit further back but still reach the pedals. Soon this was being copied by other manufacturers.

The Premier, named after the cycle works in Coventry, was the first safety bicycle with a cross-frame design. Following the success of this cycle the firm was renamed the Premier Cycle Co. in 1891. The first motorcycles were manufactured in 1908 but in 1921 the firm was taken over by Singer.

An advertisement for Premier from *Cycling* in 1919, by then showing a royal appointment.

RALEIGH CYCLES

Frank Bowden was a lawyer and cyclist who in 1887 bought a small workshop in Raleigh Street, Nottingham, that produced diamond-frame safety bicycles. At the end of the following year the Raleigh Cycle Company began life as a public company and on 29 December 1888 it made an application for a trademark (number 84,260) for velocipedes, and Bowden lost control of the company. Within eight years he bought back the firm and it remained with his family for many years.

By the early 1920s the firm was producing 100,000 cycles each year, along with Sturmey-Archer gears and motorcycles. Humber cycles was acquired in 1932. Soon a three-wheeler car was in production. By 1951 production of cycles was over a million but cycling was in decline. Raleigh bought up Triumph cycles in 1954 and BSA in 1957. Raleigh was then taken over by Tube Investments (TI), which amalgamated its British Cycle Corporation into

The first Raleigh trademark (number 84,260).

A Raleigh advertisement from *Cycling* in 1919.

Rover trademark number 216,247 was apparently not much used.

Raleigh, but in 1987 TI sold the business to Derby International. In 2001 the management bought out the firm and recently revived the Chopper brand from its home at Eastwood in Nottingham.

ROVER CARS

The Rover car company began life as Starley & Sutton, when John Kemp Starley, a manufacturer of cycles with his uncle James, and William Sutton, a cycling enthusiast, became partners in cycle manufacturing. They set up a business producing penny-farthing bicycles and tricycles in the West Orchard factory in Coventry in 1877. George Franks, a retired diamond merchant who had put money into the business, suggested the name Rover for Starley's cycles and in 1884 the firm registered the name Rover as a trademark (number 35,242) for tricycles. Soon they were also producing Rover small-wheeled safety bicycles, which became a huge success. In 1888 the firm and the Rover name were taken over by Starley under the business name J.K. Starley & Company, but in 1896, five years before his death, Starley sold out for £150,000 and the firm became the

12

Steering-mechanism; frames.—The fork &c. carrying the front steering wheel or wheels is connected to the steering post or frame by links and springs forming an anti-vibration arrangement. The Figure shows the invention applied to a bicycle of the 'Rover' type. To the steering-wheel fork A are jointed at G, G¹ links D, D¹, the rear ends of which are pivoted at F, F¹ to collars E, E¹ clamped on the steering-post C. A coil spring I, arranged as shown, tends to keep the steering-wheel in its normal position. The handle-bar is sometimes mounted directly on the head of the steering-wheel fork, in which case the rear ends of the links are pivoted to the frame. The invention is also applicable to 'Cripper' type and rear-driving double front-steering tricycles. More than two links and more than one spring may be used if desired.

Rover Cycle Company. The company also used the trademark Meteor (for example number 216,247). After 1901 the company started to build motorcycles under the name Imperial Rover.

John Starley's 1886 patent for Rover (GB 12,586).

The first Rover car was sold in 1904 and in 1906 the firm became the Rover Company Ltd. Rover merged with the Leyland Motor Corporation in 1967 and the following year with British Motor Holdings to form the British Leyland Motor Corporation. For some years the Rover Group, as it became, was owned by British Aerospace and then, from 1994, by the German car maker BMW, but in 2000 BMW split the company and sold off MG Rover, which went out of business in 2005.

Advertisement for the Rover safety bicycle from the *CTC Monthly Gazette* of January 1886.

Shell trademark
(number 233,523)
from 1900.

SHELL BRAND.

The Shell scallop
trademark (number
263,277) appears a
little damaged.

SHELL PETROLEUM

Marcus Samuel set up a shop selling antiques and curios in East Smithfield, London, in about 1833. He was soon selling sea shells from Britain and abroad to natural history enthusiasts and his shop became known as the 'Shell Shop'. On a visit to the Caspian Sea Samuel's son, also Marcus, saw an opportunity to export illuminating and heating oil from Russia to the Far East and soon had tankers plying these routes. The name Shell first appeared in 1891, being used for

Unleaded
Litre **88.9**

Diesel
Litre **95.9**

Right: Still going strong! A Shell petrol pump still standing, but not in use, in Scotland.
Far right: The present-day Shell logo.

14

kerosene being shipped to the Far East by Marcus Samuel & Company.

Marcus Samuel Jr formed the Shell Transport and Trading Company in 1897 and three years later the firm applied for its first trademark (number 233,532) using a shell logo. Although this trademark is still on the trademark register, the logo depicting a shell has continued to evolve, with distinct redesigns in 1904, when the pecten or scallop shell was introduced, 1930, 1955 and 1999. In 1907 the Shell Group combined with Royal Dutch to create Royal Dutch Shell. Now the company operates in 145 countries and has sales of $23 billion. The Shell brand is valued at $3 billion.

SINGER'S CARS AND CYCLES

The Singer Co. car manufacturing business was started in Coventry by George Singer in 1874, at which time it built bicycles and tricycles. In 1878 the firm registered Challenge as its first trademark (number 14,618) for oil and cement for the repair of bicycle tyres. Singer also applied for a trademark (number 15,568) showing a Double Hollow Fork for a penny-farthing bicycle, and the letters DHF with Coventry cycle-maker Hillman and Herbert (later to become Premier Cycles). The following year the trademark 'The Xtraordinary' (number 21,031) was registered for bicycles and the firm followed this in 1882 with Apollo and the Tandem Tricycle.

Later motorcycles began to be built and the first cars were made in 1905. By 1929 Singer was the third biggest motor manufacturer behind Morris and Austin but in 1935 its sales slumped and the company recorded a £200,000 loss. Production continued at the Canterbury Street Works in Coventry until 1956, when it was taken over by the Rootes Group. Though Rootes was absorbed by Chrysler in 1964, Singer cars were still made until 1970, after which the remaining trademarks expired.

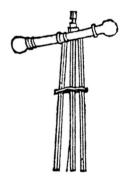

Singer & Co. with Hillman and Herbert registered this trademark in 1878 (number 15,568).

Singer's 1879 trademark (number 21,031).

THE

DEVOE M'F'G CO
NEW YORK.

65 POUNDS
OF OIL
DEVOE'S
BRILLIANT
OIL
IMPROVED
PATENT CAN

Standard Oil
registered this
trademark for the
Devoe
Manufacturing
Company in 1895
(number 188,897).

STANDARD OIL

The Standard Oil company was set up by John D. Rockefeller and partners in 1863 to refine oil for lighting. He borrowed large sums of money to buy five big refineries and by 1868 he headed the world's largest oil-refining business. In 1870 he formed the Standard Oil Company of Ohio and started buying up all oil-refining competition. By 1878 Standard Oil held about 90 per cent of American refining capacity.

The Standard Oil Company had been using the trademark Royal Daylight for illuminating oils in Britain since 1870 and registered this in 1880 (number 21,083). This trademark is still owned by the descendant of Standard Oil, Esso Petroleum Company Ltd. In America at least, the Standard Oil Company gained a reputation for dubious business practices but as oil was used increasingly as a fuel for cars the company's dominance grew. Rockefeller swore an affidavit in 1880 that he did not control a number of rival companies, including the Devoe Manufacturing Company, but later this was officially acquired and a British trademark for Devoe was registered by Standard Oil in the UK in 1895 (number 188,897).

Anti-trust action started against the firm in America in the 1890s resulted in the US Supreme Court declaring in 1911 there

US trademark
number 25,770 from
1894 showing the
Esso tiger.

16

was an unreasonable monopoly and the company was broken up. The right to use the well-known Standard brand name was divided up among the various Standard companies: Standard Oil of New Jersey marketed their petrol under the Esso brand, although in 1972 the name Exxon began to be used in America. Exxon took over Standard Oil of New York while other major Standard Oil companies have ended up as part of BP, Chevron Texaco and ConocoPhillips.

TRIUMPH CARS AND CYCLES

The Triumph Cycle Company was set up to manufacture cycles in London and Coventry in 1886 by German immigrant Siegfried Bettmann. A couple of years before he had started to import cycles into Britain under his own name. The firm applied for a trademark (number 150,867) for its cycles in 1890 and soon it started motorcycle manufacture at Coventry. It was not until 1923 that the company started car production but the firm ran into trouble following the stock market crash of 1929. The bicycle business was sold off in 1932 and British trademarks for Triumph bicycles are now owned by Swissbike Vertriebs.

Triumph's first trademark, number 150,867.

In 1935 Bettmann was ousted from the company and the car and motorcycle divisions were separated. In the 1930s Triumph produced some notable sports cars but by 1940 it had gone into receivership. At the end of the Second World War the car business was bought by the Standard Motor Company and soon sports cars like the TR-1 and TR-2 were produced. In 1960 Standard-Triumph was taken over by Leyland Motors but Triumph cars like the Sptifire and later TR models continued in production. The Triumph trademark for cars is now owned by German motor manufacturer BMW.

In 1904 the Triumph trademark became more elaborate (number 254,383).

The motorcycle business was sold off in the 1930s and renamed as the Triumph Engineering Co. In 1951 the BSA group bought the motorcycle firm and later merged it with other motorcycle manufacturers. A workers co-operative subsequently bought the Triumph motorcycle business but it went into liquidation in 1983. The Triumph marque was then bought by John Bloor and production was restarted at Hinckley in Leicestershire in 1988.

Leonard & Ellis
trademark, number
12,917.

VALVOLINE OIL

In the 1860s John Ellis, a doctor from Michigan, went to Pennsylvania to see if the crude oil that had been discovered there could be used for medicinal purposes. Instead, he ended up using it as a lubricant for steam engine cylinders and in 1865 patented the continuous refining of petroleum using a steam distillation process to produce the oil.

Ellis's company, the first to produce engine lubricating oil, became Leonard & Ellis and was later renamed Valvoline. This name was registered for the firm by Wilbur Dixon Ellis as a British trademark in 1877 (number 12,917). The company was still producing oil for medicinal purposes in 1905 when it registered Ucalyptum in Britain, for 'Eucalyptus and other oils prepared for use in medicine and pharmacy'. In 1949 another American company, Ashland Inc., acquired the Valvoline brand. Sales of Valvoline lubricants, anti-freeze, automotive chemicals and speciality products are now worth over $300 million.

An 1894 German
trademark for
Valvoline, registered
by Franz Sander.

Nr. 1057. S. 147. Franz Sander, Hamburg. Anmeldung vom 1. 10. 94/14. 4. 86. Eintragung am 11. 12. 94.

Geschäftsbetrieb: Vertrieb der nachbenannten Waare.

Waarenverzeichniß: Mineralschmieröl.

2

CLOTHING, FOOTWEAR AND TEXTILES
Outer and Under-wear, Fibres and Fabrics

Many of the clothing manufacturers that applied for trademarks in the early days of trademark registration no longer survive. Take Robert Heath, for example, who manufactured hats at Hyde Park Corner in London and whose trademark showed the careful fitting of 'hats of all kinds'. Hats have fallen out of fashion in recent times but, perhaps surprisingly, the 'Christy's' name has survived, although now as a mere shadow of its former self.

The few clothing manufacturers that we do retain from the nineteenth century were innovators in their day: Aertex with its warm cellular material for underwear, Aquascutum and Macintosh with their waterproof coats and Wolsey with its unshrinkable woollens.

Textile manufacturers had traditionally used marks before registration was introduced and there was a fear among these firms that marks which were commonly used in the industry to designate particular qualities, for example, would be registered by firms, so preventing the existing industry-wide use. As a result a Manchester Branch of the Trade Mark Registry was set up in October 1876 to consider the 60,000 existing marks and to decide which could be registered. The Branch was assisted by a committee of experts which sat until August 1879.

The twentieth century saw the closure of many of the textile mills that once produced nearly all of the fabrics for our clothes. Today most fibres and textiles are manufactured abroad. There has been a huge contraction in the names that were familiar in the past, such as Baldwin, Coats, Lister and Paton, to name but a few. Of the names in this chapter Liberty is one which continues to sell the same type of product successfully – art fabrics – that started to be sold in the nineteenth century.

Shoe manufacture was also once a thriving business in Britain but much

This early trademark (number 636) never became well-known despite Robert Heath's evident attentive fitting of hats.

manufacturing has now gone abroad. Three British brands from the 1800s are still very much in business though: Clark's, Church and K shoes. Lilley & Skinner, too, is still a name on our high streets though it has been swallowed up by another retailer and its factories have long since disappeared.

Aertex trademark number 87,821 showing a honeycombed shield and Latin motto.

AERTEX UNDERWEAR

In 1886 Lewis Haslam, a partner in the firm of John Haslam & Co. Ltd of Bolton and Manchester, designed a type of gauze fabric which was warm, allowed expiration from the skin and was ideal for use in making underwear. Three designs were registered for the fabric which was given the name Cellular. In 1888 the Cellular Clothing Company was set up to exploit the material and all the rights for the Cellular textile were assigned to it. The firm filed an application for a trademark for wearing apparel the following year (number 87,821) with the motto 'Ventus textilis – Calor Aequalis' which can be translated as 'Woven from air – even heat'.

Scottish weavers Maxton & Murray started to use the mark Cellular for their own cloth and in 1897 the Cellular Clothing Company took Maxton & Murray to court for 'passing off'.

A 1919 advertisement for Aertex.

Ultimately in 1899 the case reached the House of Lords, which decided that Cellular could be used as a trademark by anyone. So on 2 May 1899 the Cellular Clothing Company applied to register a new trademark (number 222,685) for the fabric and the name Aertex was born. The brand was later owned by Coats Viyella and in 2001 the Aertex business was bought out by Aertex Ltd, which still maintains the 1899 trademark.

AQUASCUTUM COATS

In 1851 John Emary opened a gentlemen's tailors shop at 46–48 Regent Street in London, where he developed waterproof fabrics, and later took out patents (GB 2,624 of 1864 and GB 1,128 of 1865) for improvements to capes and coats by attaching a supplementary band for securing the garment. In 1895 the firm, then Scantlebury and Commin, registered a trademark (number 184,663) for waterproof coats using the word Aquascutum from the Latin for 'water shield'. The mark had been in use since 1865 and is still registered today.

Aquascutum

The Aquascutum signature trademark (number 184,663).

Aquascutum trench coats became well known particularly after their issue to British army officers during the 1854 Crimean War, and in the First World War a new double-breasted gabardine wool coat with an oil-dressed interlining was produced. The business moved to 100 Regent Street in 1901 and this address is still the main showroom for Aquascutum Ltd. Their coats are now manufactured at a Northampton factory that opened in 1909.

Emary's patent cape from 1865, the year Aquascutum was introduced (GB 1,128).

Baldwin's first 'hand-in-hand' trademark (number 5,336). The meaning of 'LS' is not explained.

Baldwin's 'hand-in-hand' trademark of 1883 (number 33,104).

J. & J. BALDWIN'S WOOL

The worsted and woollen spinning company J. & J. Baldwin was set up in Malt Shovel Yard, Halifax, by John and James Baldwin in the early nineteenth century. John went on to be first mayor of Halifax in 1848 and, with his sons, was a benefactor in the town. In 1876 the firm applied for trademarks for yarns and threads made of wool or worsted (numbers 5,336–8). The first included the 'hand-in-hand' logo and the second the Baldwin's Beehive (BB), which is still registered. BB later turned into 'Britain's Best'.

In about 1920 J. & J. Baldwin merged with John Paton Son & Company, from Alloa in Scotland, to create Patons & Baldwins. After the Second World War the firm closed down its Halifax operations and moved to new premises in Darlington, County Durham, where the firm is still based, and soon became well known as publishers of knitting patterns. In 1960 the company became J. & P. Coats, Patons & Baldwins Ltd following a takeover by Coats, and in 2001 it became Coats plc.

TRADE MARK.

Baldwin's BB trademark of 1900 (number 227,383).

The Baldwin's Beehive trademark (number 5,337).

BALLY'S SHOES

Carl Franz Bally and his brother Fritz took over their father's business manufacturing suspenders and elastic in 1847 but Carl, after buying shoes which took his fancy on a trip to Paris in 1850, returned to Switzerland to begin shoe manufacture. The first shoes were made in the basement of their house but by 1854 a factory was built in their village of Schönenwerd. When Fritz left the business Carl continued and the firm became C.F. Bally. Soon shops were opened in the major Swiss towns and the factory was employing over five hundred staff.

In the 1870s Carl's son Edward travelled to Britain and America, from where he imported new machinery to improve production in their factory. Business was good and branches were opened in several European cities and in South America. In 1881

C.F. Bally's original but rather nondescript trademark, number 32,168.

A 1920s poster for Bally shoes. (*The Robert Opie Collection*).

the firm opened a store in New Bond Street in London and two years later Bally registered a British trademark (number 32,168) for leather, boots and shoes claiming use back to 1870. By 1892, when Carl's sons took over, C.F. Bally & Sons was producing two million pairs of shoes each year.

The family continued to run the business until 1977, when an investor bought the firm and sold it on to Oerlikon-Bührle, a Swiss armaments business, which sold it on again to American equity fund Texas Pacific Group in 1999. The company still has a number of trademarks registered in Britain: 'Maxbally', 'Scribe Hand-Made By Bally', 'Parawet', 'Bally', 'B – Switzerland Since 1851', 'Styleflex Sole' and 'Styleflex'.

BARBOUR'S LINEN THREAD

William Barbour & Sons has its origins as a flax spinning operation in Lisburn, Ireland, in 1785. The business was established by John Barbour, a merchant from Paisley in Scotland, who had been buying linen thread from Ireland for manufacturing back home. The firm was taken over by his son William and then by his grandson John Dougherty Barbour.

By 1831 the works had moved to nearby Hilden and employed over 1,500 workers. In 1864 the firm began manufacturing in the

A Barbour hand trademark, number 6,549.

The Barbour lion trademark, number 22,413.

United States in Patterson, New Jersey, and offices were soon opened across America. A series of Hand trademarks were registered in 1876 (numbers 6,549–52), two of which only expired in 2002. The firm also used a lion mark that was registered in Britain in 1880 (number 22,413); a similar mark was registered in Germany in 1895.

In 1898 John Dougherty Barbour formed the Linen Thread Co. by combining William Barbour & Sons with nine other thread manufacturers. The firm, now Barbour Threads Ltd, is owned today by Coats Ltd but Hilden Mill in Lisburn is set to close.

CASH'S NAME TAPES

John and Joseph Cash were the sons of a Quaker stuff merchant from Coventry who started to make silk ribbon in the 1840s. In 1857 they began to build a factory and workers' cottages on a site at Kingfield, Coventry, which the business occupied for 138 years.

Cash's Coventry Spires trademark (number 7,430) for cambric frillings.

In 1860 free trade spelled the end for many ribbon manufacturers in England but Cash's switched to narrow frillings, silk commemoratives and then woven labels for clothes manufacturers to use to identify their products.

In the 1870s Cash's first produced woven name tape on their Jacquard looms – a product that would make the firm familiar to parents and their children for years to come. In 1876 John Cash applied for a trademark on behalf of John and Joseph Cash, frilling manufacturers of Coventry and Kingfield (erroneously recorded as Ringfield in the *Trade Mark Journal*). The mark illustrates the three spires for which Coventry is famous. The firm still has trademarks registered for both Cash's and Cash's name tapes. Until 1976 the firm remained with the Cash family but then it became part of the Nottinghamshire textiles holding company Jones Stroud plc. Today the company is still weaving in Coventry and has three product lines: woven name tapes and personalised products; labels and badges; and gifts. It now uses the latest computerised design techniques alongside traditional weaving.

CHRISTY'S HATS

In 1773 Miller Christy and fellow Quaker Joseph Storrs started the Christy's felt-making business in White Hart Court off Gracechurch Street in London. In 1788 they moved to larger premises in Gracechurch Street. When Storrs retired in 1794, two of Christy's sons, Thomas and William, became partners, and were joined by a third son, John, in 1804.

Factories were opened in Bermondsey in London, Frampton Cotterell in Gloucestershire and Wray in Lancashire. Supplies were obtained from J. Worsley of Canal Street, Stockport, which was taken over by Christy's in 1826, after which Stockport became the main manufacturing centre.

In 1876 the firm, still a family business, applied for two heraldic trademarks for hats, caps, felts and helmets (numbers 3,088–9), the first of which is still owned by Christy & Co. Ltd. After the First World War demand for hats fell and felt-hatters gradually merged until in 1966 Associated British Hat Manufacturers Ltd was formed to absorb Christy's and the four other remaining felt-hat manufacturers. After 1980 the whole

Christy's trademark number 3,088 is a badge showing the British Royal Standard within a belt and buckle.

27

29,979. HATS, CAPS, AND HELMETS. CHRISTY & COMPANY, LIMITED, London, England. Filed Apr. 14, 1897.

Christy's American trademark of 1897 consists of a badge with helmets.

Essential feature.—A heraldic device comprising a garter with a buckle, the garter bearing the words "CHRISTYS' LONDON," a helmet surmounting the garter, and a shield within the garter, the shield being quartered by a saltire argent and having a helmet on each quarter. Used since January 1, 1897.

group traded under the name Christy & Co. Ltd but in 1997 all hat-making ceased in Stockport.

CHRISTY'S TOWELS

Henry Christy, one of William Miller Christy's sons, visited Turkey in the late 1840s and went to the palace of the Sultan in Constantinople. Impressed by some loop-pile towelling fabric, which was new to the West, he brought back a sample. His brother Richard managed to make similar cloth by machine and the Turkish Towel was created.

W.M. Christy & Sons' trademark number 4,686 for towels.

The first towels were shown at the Great Exhibition of 1851 at Crystal Palace in London. In 1876 the company W.M. Christy & Sons Ltd, then based at Fairfield Mills, Droylsden, and 14 Back Mosley Street, Manchester, applied for trademarks (numbers 4,683, 4,685–6 and 4,692) for towels and bath blankets. Trademark number 4,686 proudly announced 'Under the patronage of Her Majesty the Queen by royal letters patent'.

Though these earliest trademarks are no longer registered, a later one, trademark number 46,118 for 'Royal Turkish Towels' dating from 1885, is still on the trademark register. Christy UK Ltd is now the country's largest towel manufacturer and was bought in 2000 by its management in a £15 million deal.

CHURCH'S SHOES

Church's footwear business was started in 1873 by three brothers in Northampton, a traditional centre of the British footwear manufacturing industry. In 1882 the firm applied for its first trademark (number 29,195) for the Adapted Boot for broad or narrow feet, and the following year there were applications for other marks for the Easier Boot (number 31,860), the Premier Choix (number 33,054) and the Impervious Boot (number 34,001).

At the beginning of 2004 Church & Co. plc, under the chairmanship of John Church, manufactured 5,000 pairs of Goodyear welted men's shoes every week at their St James factory

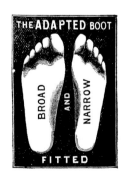

Church's first trademark (number 29,195).

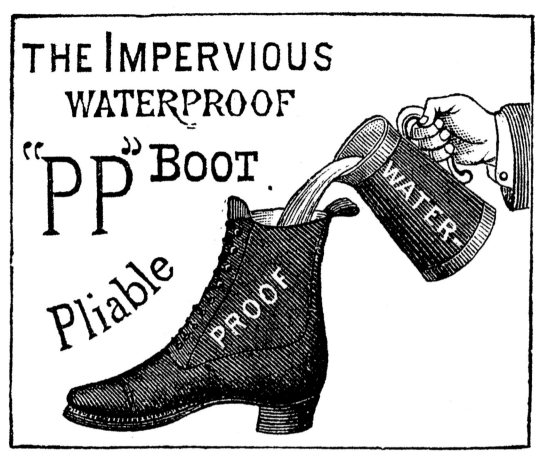

THE IMPERVIOUS WATERPROOF "PP" BOOT

Pliable

PROOF

WATER

Church's trademark number 34,001 demonstrates the testing procedure!

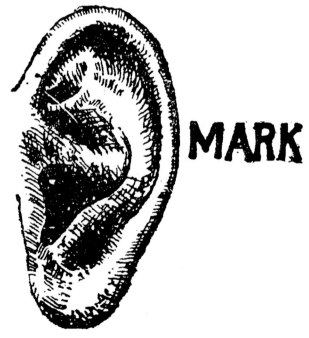

EAR MARK

It is not readily apparent that this Church's 1903 trademark (number 252,539) is for boots, shoes and leggings.

in Northampton. Later in the year the firm agreed to a £106m takeover bid from Italian luxury goods manufacturer Prada.

CLARK'S SHOES

Cyrus Clark started work in 1821 as an apprentice to fellow Quaker Arthur Clothier, who had opened a tannery in Middleleigh, Somerset, in 1810. In 1825 Clark started a tanning business of his own in Street, Somerset, and a few years later employed his younger brother James as an apprentice. He started producing sheepskin rugs and slippers from offcuts but later sold boots and shoes.

Clark's first factory was built in Street in 1829, though the stitching of the shoes was done by outworkers. James became a partner in the firm in 1833 and later James's son William took over. By 1842 some 12,000 pairs of shoes were made each year.

In 1879 C. & J. Clark & Co. applied for its first trademark (number 20,235), for which it claimed use for nearly fifty years. The trademark shows St Michael's tower, the remains of a fourteenth-century church that had long been a place of Christian pilgrimage, on the summit of Glastonbury Tor near Street. The town of Street is still the headquarters for the firm C. & J. Clark, although shoes are no longer manufactured there, the old factory having been turned into a factory retail outlet for the firm. Global turnover is £955 million and sales have reached almost 41 million pairs.

Clark's 1879 trademark showing Glastonbury Tor (number 20,235).

Clark's 1901 trademark is still using the Glastonbury Tor logo (number 235,965).

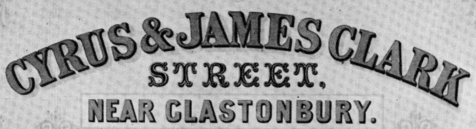

Clark's advertisement from about 1864. (*Clarks International*)

DENT'S GLOVES

In 1765 John Dent was apprenticed to a master glover in Worcester at the age of 14. He started making gloves on his own account in 1777. After his death in 1811 two of his sons John and William ran the business, which thrived until 1826 when the ban on imports into England was lifted and French gloves entered the country, forcing many manufacturers out of business. Dent's survived by improving the quality of their gloves.

In 1845 the company was purchased by John Derby Allcroft, the 21-year-old son of an employee at the firm, and in 1852 it became Dent, Allcroft & Co. In 1853 the firm moved to Warmstry House in Worcester, where a factory was built and used for leather glove production for the next 106 years. In 1881 the firm applied for trademarks for 'articles of apparel including gloves' (numbers 25,905–7) illustrating the

Dent's trademark (number 25,905) showing the Wildebeest, which it used for its leather.

Dent's Worcester factory in the nineteenth century. (*Dents*)

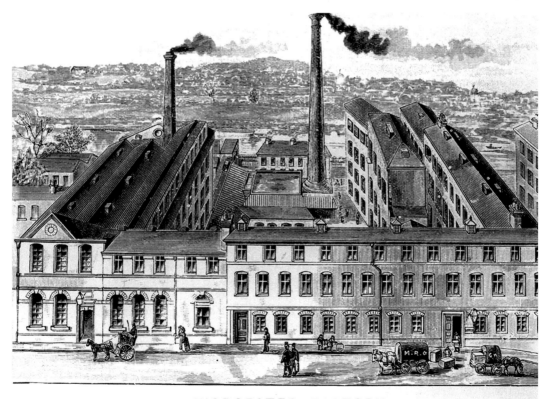

WORCESTER FACTORY.

animals from which the leather was obtained, Wildebeest and Springbok.

After the First World War Dent's introduced the phrase 'Dents hand in glove with the world' to highlight their export trade. In 1937 glovers A.L. Jefferies was acquired and the business moved to Warminster, Wiltshire, where it has stayed. The business survived increased competition from many parts of the world in the 1950s and bought out its main British rival in 1972. Dent's now sells gloves and a range of leather goods and is part of the Dewhurst Dent Group plc, which owns the Dents registered trademarks.

Dewhurst's Three Shells trademark (number 935).

DEWHURST'S SEWING COTTON

Open any sewing basket and you are likely to find Dewhurst's Sylko sewing cotton. The origins of the firm date back to about 1789, when Thomas Dewhurst acquired a building at Elslack outside Skipton, Yorkshire, which he converted into a watermill for spinning cotton. In the early nineteenth century other mills were bought or leased in North Yorkshire and in 1828 Belle Vue Mill was built in Skipton as a woollen mill. It burnt down in 1831 but was quickly rebuilt, this time as a cotton mill. In 1869 John Dewhurst & Sons started to manufacture sewing cotton alongside the cotton yarn for spinning.

In January 1876 John Bonny Dewhurst, on behalf of the company, was one of the first to register a trademark and this mark (number 935) has been maintained on the register ever since. Dewhurst's sewing cotton has often been referred to as the Three Shells brand from the trademark, which shows a shield with three scallop shells. By 1888, when the firm became a limited company, the mill had been greatly expanded and employed about a thousand people. In 1897 fourteen well-known English thread-makers, including Dewhurst's, consolidated as the English Sewing Cotton Co. Ltd with Algernon Dewhurst as its chairman. Through a series of mergers, particularly in the 1960s, the firm ended up as part of Coats plc.

Dewhurst's float showing the Three Shells brand at a Skipton Hospital Gala early in the twentieth century. (*Rowley Collection with permission of North Yorkshire County Council*)

EARLY'S BLANKETS

New Mill in Witney, Oxfordshire, had been in use since the late sixteenth century when, in 1818, Edward Early, his brother John and their brother-in-law Paul Harris started spinning and blanket-making there. After John's death in 1862 his share passed to his son Charles, who ran the blanket-making business Charles Early & Co. Edward's share of the mill passed to his son and then to his grandsons Thomas and Walter, who, as T. & W. Early & Co., applied in 1876 for a trademark (number 31,709). The mark shows the seal of the Witney Blanket Weavers' Company, the local trade guild, which was created in 1711 but stopped

Early's trademark number 31,709 uses the seal of the blanket-makers' guild (note the spelling of 'Weaver').

A group of women whipping (oversewing) the edges of the finished blankets at Early's mill in 1898. (*Henry W. Taunt/ Oxfordshire County Council Photographic Archive*)

regulating the industry in the first half of the nineteenth century, long before Early's trademark came into use.

Blanket-making prospered and at the end of the nineteenth century Charles Early & Co. employed about 400 workers at Witney. The business was hit by recession at the beginning of the 1930s but after the Second World War the town was producing about 700,000 blankets each year. In 1952 Early's was nearly bankrupted and in 1960 it merged with blanket-maker Marriotts, forming Charles Early and Marriott (Witney) Ltd.

A new production technique called fibreweaving was introduced in the 1960s and mechanisation meant a steady reduction in the workforce. The market for blankets declined again and in the late 1980s the firm went into receivership, followed by a management buy-out in 1991. The American firm Quiltex took over in 1999 but production was reduced to only 5,000 blankets a week. In 2002 Early's was put into liquidation again and the Witney factory was closed, with production being moved to Derbyshire. Two trademarks, but not the original, are now owned by Early's of Witney plc for blankets: Early's and Witney Point Blanket.

ENGLISH'S NEEDLES

In about 1750 Job English founded a needle business at Feckenham in the 'needle district' of East Worcestershire and West Warwickshire. Needles and fishing hooks were made from wire by outworkers in their cottages and sold by Job as he travelled the country on horseback. Job was succeeded in the business by his eldest son John, and in about 1823 John was succeeded by his son, John Jr.

The introduction of new and better roads, such as the Birmingham to Redditch turnpike, which opened in 1835, enabled wire to be brought easily from Yorkshire to Feckenham and the business prospered. In 1873 John Jr took over Eagle Mill in Studeley. The English male line ended in 1876 and the firm passed to J.J.W. Gutch, formerly the firm's London agent, who had married John's daughter.

English's trademark for sharps or needles (number 27,003).

Two trademarks were registered in 1882 (numbers 27,003–4) by John English & Son. Connections with Feckenham were ended in 1925. The business merged with Needle Industries Ltd, which was taken over by Coats Viyella but separated off again in 1991 following a management buy-out to become Entaco. The John English name is still used, especially for sales of sewing needles in America.

K SHOES

Robert Miller Somervell was very nearly 21 in 1842 when he opened a business as a 'Shoemaking Accessories Merchant and Leather Factor' in Kendal, Westmorland. He had learnt the leather trade with his brother William in London, where his family lived until the death of his father. In about 1845 he moved into larger premises at Netherfield in Kendal, where the head office and factory still operate. In 1848 Robert and another brother John became partners in the firm Somervell Brothers.

Some years later the firm started to manufacture shoes rather than just trading in leather. The firm's 'K' logo began in 1865 when

K's trademark number 5,767 covered boots, shoes, leggings, gaiters, uppers, belting, buckets and hoses.

The Somervell
Brothers' British
patent of 1901
(GB 14,274) for
'Fastenings for
leggings and gaiters'.

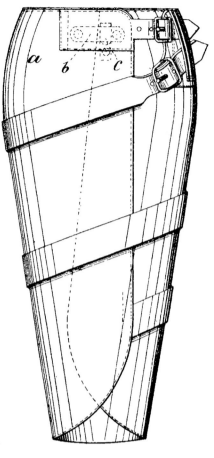

an employee picked up a leather punch with a K on it and used it to mark all the soles issued to outworkers. The mark quickly became associated with Kendal by customers and in 1876 Somervell Brothers applied for two trademarks (numbers 5,767–8), the first of which was K and the second SB Kendal. The registration of a single letter would not normally have been permitted but as the K mark had already been in use for ten years, registration was allowed in this case.

The brothers died at about the turn of the century and the next generation took over a thriving business producing about 175,000 pairs of shoes each year. By 1920 a factory had been built in Lancaster to satisfy the increasing demand. The firm became K Shoes Ltd in 1949 and production went up to one million pairs a year. In 1981 K Shoes and its biggest competitor, C. & J. Clark Ltd, merged. K is still registered as a trademark, but it is now owned by Clarks.

Liberty's stylish 1882 trademark number 28,520.

LIBERTY'S FABRICS

Arthur Liberty was born in Chesham, Buckinghamshire, in 1843 and from 1862 he worked at the Farmer and Rogers shawl and cloak emporium in Regent Street, London. In 1875 he took a £2,000 loan from his future father-in-law to secure the lease of half a shop at 218a Regent Street, just across the road from Farmer and Rogers. He was joined by William Judd, a colleague of his former employer, and they took on a young girl and a Japanese boy. The business sold ornaments, fabrics and articles from Japan

and it did well, and within eighteen months Liberty had acquired the other half of the shop.

In 1882 Arthur Liberty, now at 218–220 Regent Street, applied for a trademark (number 28,520) for Liberty's Art Fabrics, for which the store was becoming well known. He then acquired 142–4 Regent Street, which he called Chesham House after his home town, in 1885 to sell carpets and furniture. In the 1890s Liberty commissioned work from leading English designers in the Arts and Crafts and Art Nouveau movements. Arthur Liberty died in 1917, before the expansion of his store in the 1920s. Today Liberty plc still owns the original trademark, along with others, and continues to sell products designed by leading contemporary artists.

LILLEY & SKINNER'S SHOES

The firm of Lilley & Skinner has its origins as a shoe shop in Southwark in London, which was opened in 1835 by Thomas Lilley. By the middle of the nineteenth century Lilley had opened other factories in the shoe-manufacturing towns of Northamptonshire. In the 1870s more shops were opened and the firm's headquarters moved to Paddington Green, London.

It was only in 1881 when William Banks Skinner became a partner that the name of the firm became Lilley & Skinner. Two years later the firm applied for a trademark for Lady Dudley boots and shoes (number 32,833), and other trademarks followed. The firm continued to grow and by the end of the First

Lilley & Skinner's trademark number 32,833.

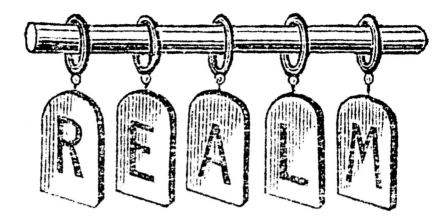

Lilley & Skinner's 1904 trademark for Realm (number 266,009).

Lilley & Skinner's 1906 trademark for The Combined – Fit, Style, Value (number 280,330).

Lister's Lion and Monogram trademark, number 2,725.

World War it had become one of the best-known British shoe brands. The company, along with other shoe firms, was taken over by the British Shoe Corporation in the 1950s but the latter was broken up in the 1990s. The name Lilley & Skinner is still registered as a trademark and is now owned by shoe retailers Stead & Simpson.

LISTER'S SILK

Samuel Cunliffe Lister was born in 1815 and in 1838 he set up Manningham Mills in Bradford to produce textiles. He was a prolific inventor and from 1844 onwards was granted well over a hundred patents connected with weaving and the preparation of cloth. Eventually Lister became one of the city's richest and most famous fathers. The original mills were destroyed by fire in 1871 but the replacement mills were the largest in the north of England. At its peak the firm employed over 11,000 people and ran a colliery and several other mills. The mills produced silk worsted, mohair, chiffon and other textiles and in 1876 the firm, describing itself as silk waste spinners, applied for two Lion and Monogram trademarks (numbers 2,725–6) for silk products. The monogram logo continued to be used by the firm for many years but the lion did not enjoy such a long life.

In 1890 the business declined as American tariffs were raised and Samuel Lister reduced wages by 30 per cent, leading to a bitter dispute with the workers. The business declined again in

40

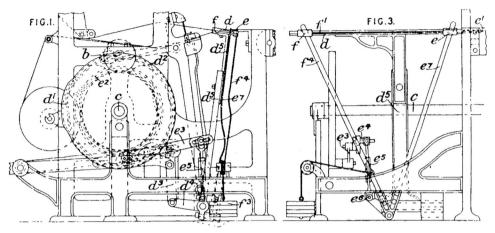

Looms, pile forming in.—In looms for weaving pile fabrics, the pile-forming wire c^1, Fig. 3, and its supporting trough f^1 are fixed to slides e, f, Figs. 1 and 3, capable of moving on a bar d for inserting and withdrawing the wire, and the bar is oscillated to move the wire, when withdrawn, opposite the open shed ready for insertion again. The bar d which is fixed to a pivoted bell-crank lever d^5, d^4 is oscillated, by a lever d^3, and bowl d^2, from a cam d^1 on a shaft c driven from the crank shaft b. The slide e is moved, to insert and withdraw the wire c^1 by a cam e^2 acting through levers and rods e^3, e^4, e^5, e^6, e^7. The trough f^1 is caused to travel into the shed with the wire, and then return rapidly before the beat-up, these movements being effected by arranging a spring catch on the slide e to engage a pin on the slide f on the withdrawal of the wire. The two slides are thus locked and move together during the next insertion of the wire, and near the end of the travel, a pin on the bar d moves the catch to release the slide f, which is then rapidly withdrawn by a weight f^3 acting on the lever f^4. A similar device is provided for each wire, some of the devices being pivoted above, and others below, the warp level. The trough f^1 is dispensed with when the wires are sufficiently stiff.

Loom shedding-motions. — According to the Provisional Specification, a more regular and even pile surface is produced by fixing the instruments for lifting the warp over the wires to form the loops to two bars so that only half of the pile warp is lifted at a time.

---

the later part of the twentieth century and now Manningham Mills are being converted into homes, shops and community facilities in a £100m project.

A Samuel Cunliffe Lister weaving patent from 1855 (GB 2,493).

MACINTOSH'S RAINCOATS

Charles Macintosh was born in 1766. His father George moved to Glasgow to manufacture a dyeing powder from lichens in 1777. Charles took an interest in chemistry and became a partner of Charles Tennant, who ran a cloth-bleaching business in Paisley near Glasgow. In 1799 Tennant and Macintosh invented a dry bleaching powder made from chlorine and slaked lime, and it was later claimed that Macintosh was principally responsible for this development.

In 1818 Charles Macintosh discovered that if two sheets of cloth were bonded together with a rubber solution the resulting material was rainproof. He went on to develop the fabric for use in coats and

Macintosh's first trademark, number 328.

A portrait of Macintosh forms this 1904 trademark (number 267,615).

other goods with chemist George Hancock, and set up a small factory in Glasgow in 1823. The following year he entered into a partnership with the Birleys, who owned cotton mills in Manchester, and they built a mill for Macintosh. The material produced was not, however, universally admired and the process of manufacture encountered problems that were only fully overcome when the rubber vulcanisation process was adopted from 1844.

After Macintosh's death in 1843 the factory was operated by Thomas Hancock, a partner in the company. A week after the Trade Mark

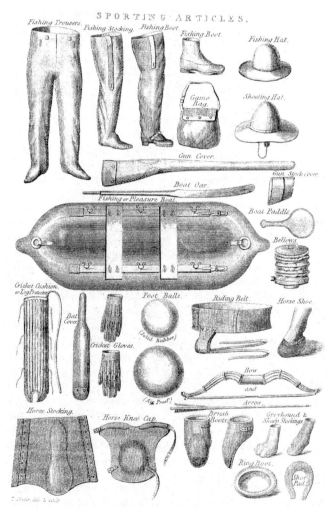

Illustrations from Charles Macintosh's 1853 *Trade Price List*.

ORIGINAL INVENTORS OF THE

OLDEST HOUSE IN THE TRADE.

GENUINE "MACINTOSH" WATERPROOFS

Established 1824.

To be had from all Respectable Houses in the Trade.

ODOURLESS.
STAND ALL
CLIMATES.

NEWEST AND MOST
ELEGANT DESIGNS
AND SHAPES.

BEST AND WEAR LONGEST.

Chas. Macintosh & Co.'s goods are known all over the world, and are always in demand, being EVERY GARMENT

**THOROUGHLY WATERPROOF,
UNAFFECTED BY CLIMATE,
MOST ELEGANT IN STYLE & DESIGN.**
AND IN ADVANCE OF ANY OTHER MAKE OFFERED TO THE PUBLIC.

TESTIMONIAL.

"Messrs. CHAS. MACINTOSH & CO., Limited, Manchester.
"ABERDEEN, January 5th, 1891.
"GENTLEMEN,—Referring to your memorandum of last month, *re* garment made for us, it was submitted to the following test by the writer :—
"On January 1st I crossed over from Spey Side to Dee Side by way of two of the highest peaks in Scotland (both over 4,000 feet). The temperature was below **freezing point**, and accompanied by **very thick driving mist**, which froze upon everything. In spite of this the coat kept its **flexibility**, and remained proof to the slowly melting ice, even **after an exposure of fifteen hours**, and looked **considerably fresher** than the wearer, as you may suppose, if you can appreciate the difficulty of such a journey through snow two to four feet thick on the rocks.
"Yours faithfully, "W. GLOVER."

BEARS THE NAME AND TRADE MARK.

The Genuine "MACINTOSH" Waterproofs being vulcanized by a perfect process of Dry Heat are infinitely superior to those vulcanized by any other method, and are perfectly FREE FROM ODOUR, without the aid of perfume or any similar device.

CHAS. MACINTOSH & CO. LTD.

CAMBRIDGE ST., **MANCHESTER.**
And 30, FORE ST., **LONDON, E.C.**

ORIGINAL PATENTEES OF VULCANIZED RUBBER.

London Retail Agents—SHOWERS & CO., 78, Westbourne Grove, W.

An 1891 advertisement showing the Hand and Cockerel trademark. (*Illustrated London News Picture Library*)

Registry opened its doors at the start of 1876, Hugh Birley on behalf of Charles Macintosh & Co. had registered the company's first trademark (number 328) for garments, rubber valves, etc. The trademark shows a cockerel on a hand, which might be the symbol of George Hancock. This trademark is still registered but is now owned by the Dutch company Macintosh Retail Group, although the word macintosh (or mackintosh) has passed into the English language as a synonym for a waterproof coat. Meanwhile the Dunlop Company used the mill to produce rubber goods from 1923 until February 2000, when it closed.

Paton's yarn
trademark number
12,037 of 1877.

Paton's more artistic
1900 trademark
(number 230,813).

PATON'S YARNS

John Paton formed a wool dyeing and spinning company in 1814
in Alloa, Scotland. When his father died he inherited Kilncraigs
House, on the site of which he built Kilncraigs Mill. John's son
Alexander joined the firm, which then became Paton & Son.
When John died in 1848 Alexander's brother-in-law and nephew
joined the firm.

In 1877 Paton & Son & Co. applied to register two trademarks
(numbers 12,037–8) that the firm had already used for over thirty
years for woollen and worsted yarns. Other trademarks registered
in the nineteenth century include Paton's rose, 'Virtute Viget' ('it
thrives by its goodness') and a White Heather and Bonnet device.
The business remained in family hands until it joined with textile
firm J. & J. Baldwin to create Patons & Baldwins in 1920. The

Kilncraigs Mill at Alloa at one time employed over 4,000 people producing wool and yarns but it closed in December 1999 with the loss of 240 jobs.

WOLSEY SOCKS

Henry Wood was born in Leicester in 1707 and, despite his humble beginnings, became a successful businessman. In his 30s he started producing hosiery and formed a partnership in 1748 with hosier Job Middleton, and two years later also with John Wightman, who put capital into the business of finishing knitted goods produced by outworkers. In 1755 the partnership dissolved but Wood's business grew. Wood died in 1768 and the business was run for the next ten years by his widow Ann, who was John Wightman's niece. Then their two eldest sons joined the business.

Wolsey's trademark number 208,354.

In 1842 Robert Walker, the son of a Glasgow retail hosier, became a partner in the firm with Richard Wood, a grandson of the founder, and when Richard retired in 1849 the firm became Robert Walker & Co. The business grew and by 1883, the year that Robert Walker died, it was the largest hosiery company in the region. The firm was very innovative and perhaps its most important development was the introduction of unshrinkable woollens. To herald this advance the trademark Wolsey was adopted and registered for knitted articles of clothing in 1897 (number 208,354). The mark was named after Cardinal Wolsey, who was buried without any

Wolsey's 1930s display featured Cardinal Wolsey. (*The Robert Opie Collection*)

tombstone in Leicester Abbey, close to the firm's offices, but it may also have been simply a pun on the word wool.

As the result of a merger in 1920 the firm became Wolsey Ltd and produced a range of sportswear and knitted clothing but by the end of the decade it was losing money. The firm survived but in 1967 was taken over by textile company Courtaulds, which continued to own the first Wolsey trademark until it expired in 1995. After becoming independent again in 1996 Wolsey was taken over by clothing retailer Matalan in 2002, when a contemporary Wolsey fox trademark was registered.

3

DRINKS

Whisky, Wine and Water; Lager, Liqueurs and Lemonade

The brewing of beer dates back many thousands of years and taverns selling beer are known to have been in existence in Roman times in Britain. Beer was generally consumed close to the brewery until the coming of the canals and the railways enabled it to be distributed to pubs far and wide. Many of the breweries whose names we still know originated in the eighteenth and nineteenth centuries and were able to expand, concentrating their brewing in towns where good water was available. The international trade in bottled beer grew, with British brewers sending beer to Europe and the Empire and foreign brewers, such as Carlsberg, dispatching beer to the UK.

A representative of Bass & Co. wrote to the Select Committee set up in 1862 to look into trademark law stating that the firm's ales were often counterfeited. The 'omission of the word "by" after export will enable those of you who are advised of it to detect it readily', he stated about counterfeit bottle labels. Bass was in favour of the new trademark law and was the very first brewer to register. Others such as Ind Coope, Tennent, Worthington and William Younger soon followed.

It is perhaps surprising that champagne makers were also applying for trademarks in the first few months of registration but champagne houses like Veuve Clicquot, Heidsieck, Mumm and Krug saw Britain as an important market for their wine and needed to protect their names.

Foreign producers of spirits and liqueurs were also early to apply for British trademarks: Chartreuse, Martell and Hennessy had all applied in the first month of 1876. Whisky distillers, perhaps more assured of their home market, were generally slower but Glenlivet was one Scotch for which an application was made in January 1876. At this time Gilbey's had not yet started distilling gin but the firm was already importing cheap wine for mass consumption when it applied for three trademarks.

Old Carlsberg Brewery trademark, number 31,065.

Allsopp's trademark number 2,945 with the hand logo.

Allsopp's 1900 trademark for lager (number 225,990).

ALLSOPP'S BEER

When bachelor Benjamin Wilson retired in 1805 he left the Wilson brewery in Burton upon Trent, Staffordshire, in the hands of his nephew Samuel Allsopp, then aged 24. Allsopp later married the heiress of one of the wealthiest families in Staffordshire. According to brewery legend, when Samuel Allsopp tasted the pale ale produced by Hodgson, the brewer at Bow Brewery, East London, in 1821 he called in his head brewer, Job Goodhead, and asked him to reproduce it. Hodgson's ale not only tasted good, it was able to survive long sea journeys. Goodhead succeeded in producing a similar brew in a large teapot and Allsopp was soon able to export his own pale ale. Within a decade the Burton brewers Allsopp and Bass were sending 6,000 barrels of ale a year to India. In 1897 Allsopps erected a 60,000-barrel lager plant at Burton on Trent but by 1900 the firm was in financial difficulties and went into receivership in 1913. In 1934 the brewer merged with Ind Coope & Co. Ltd to form Ind Coope & Allsopp Ltd.

ISSUED BY S. ALLSOPP & SONS, LIMITED.

Samuel Allsopp, on behalf of himself and his partners Henry Allsopp, Henry Townshend, James Finlay, Josiah Thomas Poyser, Walter Leith, James Young Stephen and George Higginson Allsopp, trading as Samuel Allsopp & Sons, applied for a series of trademarks in 1876, all of which featured a hand. These marks had already been in use for fourteen years and numbers 2,945, 2,949 and 2,950 were maintained in use until 2002. Newer trademarks owned by the Danish brewing giant Carlsberg now protect the Allsopp name and the Hand logo.

ANSELL'S BEER

Ansell's Brewery was set up by Joseph Ansell and his sons in 1881 at Aston Cross, Birmingham. It became a limited company in 1889 and bought out another large Aston brewer, the Holt Brewery Co., in 1934. Ansells was taken over by Ind

Ansell's squirrel trademark, number 14,295.

Ansell's advertising in around 1950 still featured the squirrel logo. (*The Robert Opie Collection*)

Coope in 1961, along with several other breweries, to form the Allied Brewing group, which in turn became part of Carlsberg.

Though Ansell's has been subsumed by Carlsberg, many of its early trademarks have been retained. The earliest trademark still registered is AA, with one of the letters inverted (number 4,126), first registered in 1876. Others still registered include 1882 and 1883 trademarks for AAA and Ansell's Aston Ales (numbers 21,510–11 and 31,405). Also still registered is number 14,295 from 1878, which depicts a squirrel, and is still to be seen on some old public houses in the Birmingham area. The squirrel was taken from the coat of arms of the Holte family, the gentry owners of Aston Hall; when Ansell's took over the Holt Brewery, the firm adopted the squirrel logo.

APOLLINARIS MINERAL WATER

In 1852 Georg Kreuzberg, a vintner from Ahrweiler in Germany, bought a vineyard at an auction for 15 thaler but found the vines would not grow there. On investigation, he found the soil had an exceptionally high concentration of carbonate. He began to dig to

Apollinaris's trademark number 2,077 showing the source of the water.

find the source and soon discovered a spring. By the following year he had obtained a sales licence and began filling clay jugs with the mineral water. The spring was named after the statue of St Apollinaris that stood at the bottom of the vineyard, and thus Apollinaris water was born.

In 1873 the Apollinaris Company Ltd was set up in Westminster, London, and the brand became internationally well known. The firm applied for British trademarks in 1876 (numbers 2,076–7 and 6,356–7). Trademark number 2,077 showing the Apollinaris spring was registered until 1988.

By 1881 10 million jugs and bottles of Apollinaris water were sold each year. The

A trademark registered in 1876 by Apollinaris for water imported from Hungary (number 6,357).

Nr. 518. A. 49. The Apollinaris Company Limited, London. Anmeldung vom 1. 10. 94. Eintragung am 24. 11. 94.

Geschäftsbetrieb: Verkauf von Mineralwasser.
Waarenverzeichniß: Mineralwasser.

In Germany a diamond was registered by Apollinaris in 1894 but the company is better known there today by its red triangle mark.

English hotel group Frederick Gordon acquired the Apollinaris companies in Germany and England in 1897 but in 1956 Apollinaris became a German company once more through its sale to the Dortmunder Union Brauerei. In 1991 Apollinaris and drinks firm Schweppes of Germany merged but then in 2002 the whole company was bought out by the British company Cadbury Schweppes.

BASS BEER

Bass trademark number 1, showing the triangle on a label.

The brewery started by William Bass had been in existence for almost a century when an employee of the firm spent a night on the steps of the newly established Trade Mark Registry so as to be first in the queue to register a trademark. It is said that the employee was a burly drayman who was well able to defend his pitch against all comers. Bass & Co. was rewarded for this effort by being given British trademarks numbers 1, 2 and 3. It is not recorded what reward the drayman received. Numbers 1 (a triangle) and 2 (a diamond) are still registered, and the logo of a red triangle continues to be synonymous with Bass ale.

William Bass was 60 by the time he established a brewery in 1777 in Burton upon Trent. Burton had been recognised since at least 1002 as a place where the water was ideal for making beer. The brewery thrived with much of the product being exported, especially to Russia and Eastern Europe. As the British canal system grew and improved, enabling easy shipment from Burton to the east coast port of Hull and elsewhere, so did the business of Bass & Co. In 1792 John Ratcliff became involved with the firm and later became a partner with Michael Bass, William's son. In 1835, after the death of John Ratcliff, another partner, John Gretton, joined in what was then Bass, Ratcliff and Gretton.

During the Napoleonic wars exports to Europe decreased but soon a new market opened up in India. East India Pale Ale (IPA) was developed for shipping by sea from Liverpool and Hull to the troops, civil servants and other Britons in the sub-continent. IPA was brewed with a lot of hops and continued to ferment en route, thus arriving in perfect condition in India.

Nr. 2656. B. 968. Baß, Ratcliff & Gretton Limited, Burton on Trent (England); Vertr.: Friedrich Emil Bärwinkel, Justizrath, Leipzig. Anmeldung vom 12.11.94/17.6.79. Eintragung am 12. 2. 95.

Geschäftsbetrieb: Bierbrauerei.

Waarenverzeichniß: Ale und Stout (Weiß= und Doppelbraunbier).

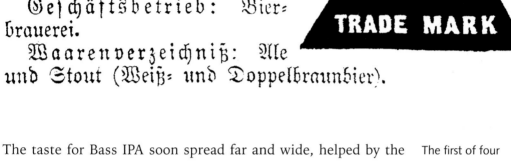

The first of four German Bass trademarks from 1895.

The taste for Bass IPA soon spread far and wide, helped by the auction in Liverpool of a cargo of 300 casks from a shipwreck in the Irish Sea. With the extension of the railways in England ingredients, supplies and finished beer were sent to and from Burton by rail. In 1868 the new terminus of the Midland Railway at St Pancras in London was opened. The huge St Pancras train shed designed by William Barlow was built with a 245ft clear span roof covering a passenger station at the upper level and enormous cellars beneath to store beer received from Bass & Co.

By 1999 Bass & Co. was the second largest brewer in the UK, with a turnover of £1.8 billion, but it was sold in 2000 to the Belgian brewer Interbrew, which had just acquired Worthington, to give Interbrew a third of the UK market. However, the UK government's Department of Trade and Industry forced Interbrew to split up and Bass was sold to the American brewer Coors at the end of 2001.

The extent of the fame of the Bass red triangle trademark can be judged from the painting *A Bar at the Folies-Bergères* by Edouard Manet, completed in 1882. In Manet's last great masterpiece bottles of Bass beer are clearly visible on the bar along with champagne and other drinks. It is the trademark red triangle which tells us the provenance of the beer.

BÉNÉDICTINE LIQUEUR

The Bénédictine *Deo Optimo Maximo* trademark (number 7,011).

Bénédictine is a sweet liqueur that has been prepared for centuries by Bénédictine monks at the Abbey of Fecamp in France since one of their number, Dom Bernardo Vincelli, created a concoction from twenty-seven plants and spices. During the French Revolution the recipe was almost lost when the manuscript describing it was sold and then left in a library.

In 1863 Alexandre Le Grand came across the secret recipe and decided to decipher it to re-create the liqueur. A decade later he was producing almost 150,000 bottles a year. In 1876 Le Grand set up the Bénédictine SA Company with capital of 2,200,000 francs and the same year applied for ten British trademarks (numbers 7,010–19). Trademarks 7,011 and 7,014 were registered until 2002 though now only newer, though similar, trademarks are used. Trademark number 7,011, which had been in use since 1864, shows the initials DOM, from the Latin *Deo Optimo Maximo* ('to God most good, most great'), which, to this day, are shown on every bottle.

Bénédictine trademark number 7,017 shows the St Bénédictus and Mitre logos.

VÉRITABLE BÉNÉDICTINE

LIQUEUR DE L'ABBAYE DE FÉCAMP

Toutes les Bouteilles de Véritable liqueur Bénédictine doivent avoir au bas une étiquette portant le fac-simile de la signature de Monsr A. Legrand Aîné, Directeur général.	Every bottle of the genuine liquor Benedictine bears on the lowest etiquette the fac-simile of the signature of the general-director A. Legrand Aîné.	Jede Flasche der ächten Benedictiner Liqueur trägt auf der untersten Etiquette das fac-simile der Unterschrift des General-Directors A. Legrand Aîné.	Tutte le bottiglie del Vero Liquore Benedittino debbono avere un' etichetta portando il fac-simile della firma del Signor A. Legrand Aîné, Direttore Generale.	Å nvarje fiaska veritabel Benediktiner likör finnes tecknadt å nedersta etiketten General-Direktören A. Legrand Aîné's fac-simile underskrift.
La plus large ligature du plomb qui entoure le col doit porter les marques et inscriptions suivantes :	The broadest leaden ligature surrounding the neck of the bottle bears the following marks and inscriptions :	Das breiteste Band von Blei, welches den Hals der Flasche umgiebt trägt folgende Marken und Inscriptionen :	La più larga legatura del piombo che attornia il collo, deve portare le marche, ed inscrizioni seguenti ;	Det bredaste blybandet som omgifver flaskhalsen har följande märken och inskriptioner ;
• VÉRITABLE ✠ BÉNÉDICTINE •	• VÉRITABLE ✠ BÉNÉDICTINE •	• VÉRITABLE ✠ BÉNÉDICTINE •	• VÉRITABLE ✠ BÉNÉDICTINE •	• VÉRITABLE ✠ BÉNÉDICTINE •
Le bouchon devra être marqué tout autour de :	The cork is marked all around with :	Der Pfropf trägt ringsum :	Il turacciolo dev'essere marcato tutt'all'intorno di :	Korken är märkt rundtomkring med :
• VÉRITABLE LIQUEUR BÉNÉDICTINE •	• VÉRITABLE LIQUEUR BÉNÉDICTINE •	• VÉRITABLE LIQUEUR BÉNÉDICTINE •	• VÉRITABLE LIQUEUR BÉNÉDICTINE •	• VÉRITABLE LIQUEUR BÉNÉDICTINE •
Enfin le dessous du bouchon portera :	At last on the under-side of the cork is to be found :	Ferner findet sich auf der Unterseite des Pfropfes :	Infino il disotto del turacciolo porterà ;	A korkens undersida finnes märket :
D. O. M. ✠	**D. O. M.** ✠	**D. O. M.** ✠	**D. O. M.** ✠	**D. O. M.** ✠

The liqueur is still manufactured in the distillery built in 1882 in the grounds of the old abbey. The exact composition of Bénédictine is a trade secret but it is probably made from lemon peel, cardamoms, hyssop tops, peppermint, angelica, thyme, cinnamon, nutmegs, cloves and arnica flowers.

JOHN BULL'S YEAST AND MALT

John Bull, originally a fictional character created by John Arbuthnot in the eighteenth century, has come to personify the British nation. He is always shown as an elderly gentleman, rather stout and wearing a full riding kit.

The John Bull Brand was registered as a British trademark (number 20,352) in 1879 by John McNish and William Paine, trading as Paine & Co. at St Neots in Huntingdonshire. Originally registered for food and fermented liquors and spirits, the trademark is still on the register for yeast, cereal preparations, hops, malt, malt extract and beer kits, syrups and other preparations for use in home brewing or making beverages. The trademark is now known worldwide principally for home beer brewing kits. The original owner, Paine's Malt Ltd, is still in existence but is now part of the International Diamalt Company Ltd.

The John Bull trademark, number 20,352 of 1879.

In 1936 a virtually identical trademark (number 571,578) was registered for fermented liquors and spirits by Ind Coope & Allsopp, with the proviso that trademark number 20,352 should be cancelled for these goods. Unusually a further restriction was placed on the mark, so that it could only be used on goods produced in England. The rights to the John Bull Brand trademark for beer have now ended up with the Charles Wells Brewery in Bedford.

The very similar 1936 version of the John Bull trademark now owned by Charles Wells (number 571,578).

New Carlsberg
Brewery trademark
number 29,358.

CARLSBERG'S BEER

In 1847 Captain J.C. Jacobsen set up the Carlsberg Brewery in Valby, outside Copenhagen in Denmark, where the firm pioneered steam brewing, various refrigeration techniques and, later, the propagation of a single yeast strain, *Saccharomyces Carlsbergensis*, which revolutionised the brewing industry. In 1868 the firm began exporting to Britain, with its first shipment landing at Leith in Scotland. The brewery was named after Jacobsen's son Carl, who went on to set up his own brewery in 1882; this was called the Ny (New) Carlsberg Brewery while the original became the Gamle (Old) Carlsberg Brewery.

In December 1882 the Old Carlsberg Brewery registered its British trademark in London, number 31,065, which they said had been in use for twelve years. A few months earlier, in October 1882, Leopold Damm & Co. of Copenhagen had registered a swastika logo as trademarks (numbers 29,358–9) for New Carlsberg Lager Beer. These original trademarks are no longer registered in the UK.

Old Carlsberg's 1889
trademark for Pilsner.

Today's Carlsberg logo was designed by the well-known Danish designer Thorvald Bindesbøll in 1904.

In 1887 J.C. Jacobsen died and the Carlsberg Foundation took over Old Carlsberg, and then in 1906 the New and Old firms were merged to form Carlsberg Breweries. In 1970 it merged with its rival Tuborg to form United Breweries, now known as Carlsberg AS. In Britain Allied Breweries merged with Carlsberg UK in 1992 but five years later Carlsberg AS took 100 per cent ownership of the merged firm.

CHARTREUSE LIQUEUR

The Chartreuse Order of cloistered monks was founded in 1084, when Bruno, later St Bruno, arrived in Grenoble, France, and met the local bishop, who saw Bruno and his companions as the living manifestation of a dream in which God built an abode in the heart of the Chartreuse Mountains. In 1605, at a Chartreuse monastery in Vauvert, Paris, the monks were given an ancient manuscript entitled *An Elixir of Long Life* by the marshal of artillery for King Henri IV. The monastery's apothecary, Frère Jerome Maubec, was put in charge of a study of the manuscript in 1737, which resulted in the preparation of the first Chartreuse Elixir.

The 'Elixir Vegetal de la Grande-Chartreuse' is still made only by Chartreuse monks following the original recipe, but because it was often drunk as a beverage rather than as a medicine the monks developed the less potent (55 per cent alcohol) drink that is sold today as Green Chartreuse. After the French Revolution, which resulted in the flight of the monks from France, the recipe was smuggled to a monk who was still in hiding near Chartreuse and from him it was taken to a Grenoble pharmacist and then, after his death, it went back to the monastery in 1816. A sweeter, milder form of the original recipe was developed in 1838 and became known as Yellow Chartreuse.

Chartreuse trademark number 743.

On 14 January 1876 the Revd Gabriel Grézier applied for British trademarks (numbers 742–5) on behalf of the Monastery of La Grande Chartreuse and number 744 was still registered until 1988. In June 1876 a further series of trademarks that had already been in use for forty years were registered, including 6,723–4 for 'a liquid for cure of toothache' and 6,725 for a 'steel or mineral ball of medicinal nature'. Trademark number 6,721, 'GDE. CHARTREUSE, DOUZE FRANCS', for a 'liqueur or liquid for medicinal use known as elixir vegetal de la Grande-Chartreuse', also remained in force until it expired in 1988.

The French government nationalised the distillery in 1903 and the monks fled to Spain, taking the manuscript with them. In due course they built a new distillery in Tarragona. The trademark Chartreuse was sold to a firm that called itself 'Compagnie Fermiere de la Grande Chartreuse' and then, after the firm went bankrupt in 1929, was given back to the monks. The monks returned to Chartreuse and resumed production of true Chartreuse liqueurs not far from the monastery. After the distillery was destroyed by an avalanche in 1935 a new distillery was built nearby in Voiron, where it still operates today.

The selection and mixing of the secret herbs and plants used in producing the liqueurs is done in the monastery by three monks who are entrusted with the secret recipe. The process is said to involve soaking 130 herbs, plants, roots, leaves and other natural vegetation in alcohol, then distilling it and mixing the product with distilled honey and sugar syrup. The liqueur is put into oak casks for maturation in the world's longest liqueur cellar.

CINZANO VERMOUTH

Cinzano is a vermouth aperitif created by infusing white wine with herbs and spices to a secret recipe. The name vermouth is derived from the herb wormwood, with which vermouth was originally flavoured.

Cinzano can trace its history back to before 1757, the year in which Carlo Stefano Cinzano and his brother Giovanni Giacomo were admitted to the University of Confectioners and Spirit Manufacturers in the Italian city of Turin. In the same year the Cinzano brothers opened their wine shop on fashionable Via Dora

Opposite, top: Cinzano trademark number 15,323.

Opposite, far right: There are many similarities between the Cinzano mark and this 1893 Martini vermouth trademark (number 174,730), although they were presumably considered to be distinctive when registered.

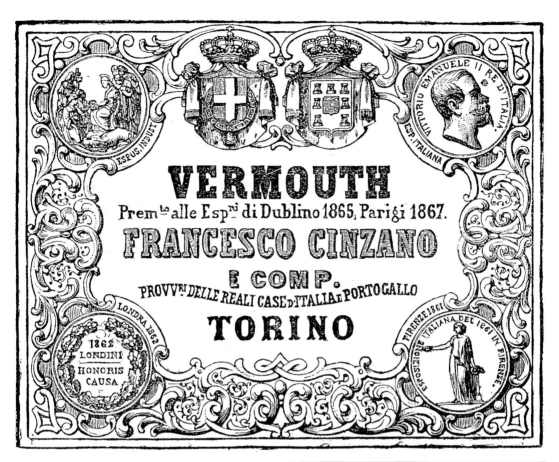

VERMOUTH

Prem.^{to} alle Esp.ⁿⁱ di Dublino 1865, Parigi 1867.

FRANCESCO CINZANO

E COMP.

PROVV.ⁿⁱ DELLE REALI CASE D'ITALIA E PORTOGALLO

TORINO

Grossa. In 1863 the Cinzano firm rented property at Santa Vittorio d'Alba from King Carlo Alberto of Savoy and opened cellars at San Stefano Belbo. After ten years the firm bought the property, which is still used for the production of Cinzano. The cellars acquired fame through the 1969 film *The Secret of Santa Vittoria*, adapted from a Robert Crichton novel. The story is based on an event that occurred during the German occupation of the town in 1943, when citizens hid over a million bottles of wine in caves beneath the Cinzano cellars and the town drunkard, elected mayor, tried to thwart the search for the wine.

From the middle of the nineteenth century Cinzano was exported widely. In 1878 Francisco Cinzano e Cia applied for a British trademark (number 15,323), which shows that the drink was supplied to the royal houses of Italy and Portugal as it bears depictions of the coats of arms of both countries. The mark has been used in Britain since 1863 and is still registered today. In 1999 Cinzano's big rival, the Campari Group, acquired the firm.

CLAYMORE WHISKY

In 1879 James Greenlees, a merchant from Basinghall Street in London, registered a trademark (number 20,194) for the Claymore brand of Highland malt whisky. The mark shows that Bruce Wallace & Co. was then the sole proprietor of this brand and the firm registered other marks at the same time for different Scotch and Irish whisky brands. In 1890 a further trademark for Claymore (number 151,505) was registered and this is still active today. The Claymore, *claidheamh-more* in Gaelic, was a two-handed broadsword used by the Scottish Highlanders against the English and rival clans in the sixteenth century. Today's bottles of Claymore blended whisky show crossed swords on a shield.

Claymore trademark number 20,194.

The Claymore brand later became one of the Whyte & Mackay whiskys. Charles Mackay was the manager of a bonding business who joined with James Whyte to set up as whisky merchants. The partners created their own blended whisky, Whyte & Mackay Special Reserve, and marketed it in Glasgow and the west of Scotland. The group now owns and operates five malt distilleries, a grain distillery and various bottling and packaging facilities in Scotland, and sells 9 million cases of spirits a year.

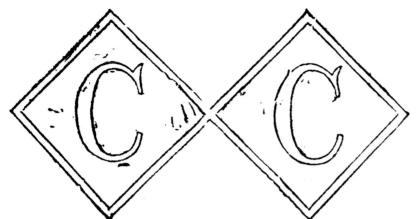

Cockburn's simple trademark (number 15,004).

COCKBURN'S PORT

Robert Cockburn, a Scot, founded the company of Cockburns at the mouth of the River Douro in Portugal in 1815. In the early days Britain took most of the firm's exports of port wine, so Robert Cockburn sent his two sons, Archibald and Alexander, to open an office in London in 1830. The Smithes family joined Cockburn to manage the Portuguese company in 1854, forming Cockburn Smithes, and the Smithes family connection continued until 1970. The Cobb family joined the business in 1863 and after four generations a Cobb is still a director of the firm in Portugal.

The company applied for a series of British trademarks in 1878 (numbers 15,003–7) and of these number 15,005, for Cockburns, is still in force. The Cockburn family crest, a cockerel on a coronet, was used by the company as a logo in some of its later trademarks (for example number 932,683 from 1968). In 1961 the Anglo-Spanish firm Allied Domecq acquired Cockburns, as well as the sherry firm Harveys of Bristol.

A present-day port bottle bearing the Cockburn crest moulded into the glass.

F.COURVOISIER &'CURLIER FRERES

Fournisseurs brevetés de S.M.l'Empereur,

COGNAC

COURVOISIER BRANDY

The start of the Courvoisier rise to fame dates from 1811, when Napoleon visited the warehouses that stored the Courvoisier family's cognac. When Napoleon was sent into exile on St Helena, it is said that English officers on the ship also took along several barrels of cognac which they named the Brandy of Napoleon. In 1835 Felix Courvoisier set up in Jarnac in the Cognac region of western France and in 1843 established the Courvoisier company in partnership with Jules Gallois.

F. Courvoisier & Curlier Freres applied for a British trademark (number 6,036) in 1876 when it was claimed the brand had been in use for nineteen years in the UK (from about the time when the firm became the official supplier to the court of Napoleon III). Felix Courvoisier died without issue in 1886 and the firm was run by his nephews, the Curlier brothers, until it was bought out by the Simon family from England in 1909. The brand, featuring the silhouette of Napoleon and the Josephine bottle, began to be developed during the twentieth century. The firm was acquired by the Canadian group Hiram Walker in 1964 and then was taken over by Allied Lyons, which evolved into Allied Domecq. When Allied Domecq was acquired in 2005 by Pernod Ricard, the Courvoisier brand was sold to Fortune Brands.

DOMECQ SHERRY

The Domecq bodegas were founded in Jerez in Spain in 1730 by the Domecq family, who originated in the Pyrenees. Pedro Domecq Lembeye changed the name of the company to Pedro Domecq & Co. in 1822 and ran the sherry business until his death in 1839. His brother Juan Pedro Domecq then ran the firm until 1869, when it passed to his adopted son Juan Pedro de Aladro, who worked alongside his cousin Pedro Domecq Loustau.

Pedro Domecq Loustau expanded the business by producing the first Spanish

Right: Domecq's trademark number 15,816 was based on the Spanish royal coat of arms.
Below: Domecq's 1907 trademark for brandy (number 289,558).

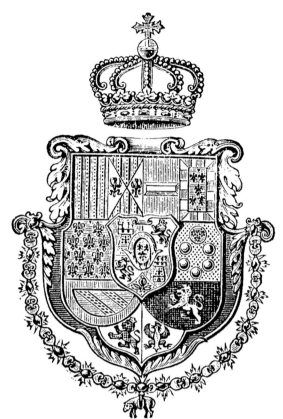

Domecq's Brandy "Monopole"

Pedro Domecq

Jerez de la Frontera

brandy and by developing markets abroad, including in Latin America. His son, Pedro Domecq Núñez de Villavicencio, who continued the business, was visited by King Alfonso XIII in 1904 and was granted the title of Marquess of Domecq D'Usquain in 1920. The Domecq family continued to run the business until it was taken over in 1994 by Allied Lyons, which later became the drinks group Allied Domecq, which in turn was acquired by Pernod Ricard in 2005. Domecq applied in 1878 for a series of trademarks (numbers 15,810–24), some of which feature the royal coat of arms of Spain. Many of these were kept in force until 1991.

ELDRIDGE POPE BEER

In 1837 Charles and Sarah Eldridge established the Green Dragon Brewery in Dorchester, and by 1880 the brewery had moved to its present site and Edwin and Alfred Pope had purchased shares. It is said that Alfred Pope was a friend of the author Thomas Hardy, who was born near Dorchester in 1840 and was inspired to write by the strong beer produced by the brewery.

Eldridge Pope's trademark number 25,219.

In November 1880 Eldridge Pope applied for a trademark (number 25,219) for the firm's beer, malt liquor, wines and spirits.

From 1921 the firm used a jovial huntsman as its main logo. Interestingly this was shared with Tetleys, which used it in the Midlands and north of England while Eldridge Pope used it in the south. Eldridge Pope became well known for its strong, dark, Thomas Hardy ale that was first brewed in 1968 for a festival commemorating the author.

The brewery was run by the Pope family until 1997 when there was a management buyout. Eldridge Pope plc then sold the brewery to concentrate on pub ownership but the brewery was closed down in 2003. Trademark number 25,219 is no longer registered but other Eldridge Pope marks are still held by Eldridge Pope plc.

FLOWER'S BEER

The Flower's brewery was set up in Stratford-on-Avon in around 1831–3 by Edward Fordham Flower. The Flower family soon became one of the largest employers in the town and had sales worth over £100,000 by 1866. They bought up land along the River Avon, and one of the family, Charles Flower, subsequently donated land and £1,000 to launch a fund to build the Shakespeare Memorial Theatre, which was opened in 1879.

In April 1876 the company applied for two trademarks for Flower & Sons India Pale Ale (numbers 5,244 and 5,255) featuring an image of William Shakespeare, which they stated had then been in use for twenty years. In 1954 the business was taken over by J.W. Green Ltd of Luton, though the Flowers brand was retained. This firm was taken over in turn by Whitbread in 1961, the Stratford upon Avon brewery being closed in 1968. Trademark number 5,244 is still registered today by Interbrew.

Flower's trademark number 5,244 is a portrait of William Shakespeare.

GAYMER'S CIDER

One of the first trademarks to be registered in 1876 was that of cider and perry maker William Gaymer & Sons of Banham

Gaymer's apple orchard trademark, number 4,951.

A modern Gaymer's bottle label, indicating that the firm was established in 1770.

in Norfolk. Trademark number 4,951, showing an orchard, had been in use for twenty years before the trademark application was made in April 1876 and is still registered today.

The earliest member of the Gaymer family known to make cider was Robert Gaymer (1738–1821), who farmed near Attleborough in Norfolk. Robert was succeeded by his son John (1770–1843), known as Long John because of his height of 6ft 10½in, and in turn by his son William (1805–1884). The second William Gaymer (1842–1936) started cider manufacture on a commercial basis, introducing the first hydraulic press in 1870 and building a new factory at Attleborough in 1896.

After the incorporation of the business in 1906 the Gaymer family ran the firm until it was sold to Showerings in 1961, and they continued to be involved for some years. In 1968

A 1930s show card for Gaymer's cider on a nationalistic theme. (*The Robert Opie Collection*)

Showerings merged with Allied Breweries. Matthew Clark plc (now Constellation Europe), which also owns the Stones Ginger Wine trademarks, purchased the Gaymer business and brand in 1994 and moved production from Norfolk to the West Country.

CASTLE TRADE MARK

Gilbey's castle trade-mark, number 1,149.

Gilbey's 1905 trademark for gin includes a small castle logo (number 276,666).

GILBEY'S GIN

Brothers Walter and Albert Gilbey worked as clerks for the Army pay department during the Crimean War and on their return to England in 1856 borrowed money from their elder brother Henry to import South African wines. A shop was opened at 372 Oxford Street, London, to bring wine to the masses and within months they had more than 20,000 customers. Agents were appointed throughout the country to sell their wines to grocers' shops, and larger premises had to be found in Oxford Street.

In January 1876 they applied for trademarks for wines, spirits and liqueurs (numbers 1,149–1,151), claiming use since 1859. In 1895 the firm began distilling gin and soon Gilbey's Gin became a well-known brand. Similarly in 1912 an advertising campaign for Gilbey's Invalid Port made it a best-

seller and a household name. In 1914 Walter's eldest son Walter Henry inherited the baronetcy given to his father and he later became chairman of W. & A. Gilbey Ltd. The company merged with United Wine Traders in 1962 to become International Distillers and Vintners, which was taken over by brewers Watney Mann in 1972, only to be absorbed by Grand Metropolitan later in the same year. The brands are now owned by drinks group Diageo, which was formed by the merger of Guinness and Grand Metropolitan.

GONZALEZ BYASS SHERRY

In 1835 Manuel Maria Gonzalez Angel acquired a small bodega in Jerez de La Frontera in the sherry-making area of Spain and began exporting his own wine. His life-long friend Juan Dubosc was sent to find agents for the business abroad and appointed Robert Blake Byass as his English representative. In 1855 Byass went into partnership with Gonzalez and as Gonzalez Byass the business soon became famous, especially for its fino sherry, Tio Pepe, and its Soberano and Lepanto brandies.

In May 1876 the company applied for a series of trademarks (numbers 5,427–71), which had already been in use since 1835. Trademark number 5,428, showing the Spanish royal coat of arms, is still registered today in the name of Gonzalez, Byass & Co. Ltd. Rival sherry-maker Domecq also used this coat of arms in its early trademarks.

Top, right: The Gonzalez Byass heraldic trademark, number 5,462.

Right: A 1907 trademark shows Gonzalez Byass was then selling port (number 293,000).

Greene's trademark number 26,636 for beer.

GREENE KING BEER

In 1799 Benjamin Greene completed his apprenticeship with brewer Samuel Whitbread in London and moved to Bury St Edmunds in Suffolk to set up Buck and Greene's Brewery. Greene later acquired an outspoken Tory newspaper and opposed the abolition of slavery. The brewing business prospered, in part through brewing 'stale' ale that could be sold to other brewers for blending with their own brews, and in 1831 produced 5,000 barrels of beer. Benjamin's third son Edward became sole owner in 1836 and had increased output to 40,000 barrels by the 1870s.

In 1881 E. Greene & Son, as the firm was then known, applied for a trademark (number 26,636) for beer featuring the Great Gate of Bury St Edmunds' Benedictine Abbey. In 1887 Edward merged the firm with his rival in the same town Fred King and the Greene King company was formed. More recent trademarks have featured variations on an Abbot logo for Abbot Ale and a king design.

Greene King's current labelling of Abbot Ale.

The brewery that was founded on Westgate Street, Bury St Edmunds, still operates today and the annual turnover of Greene King plc, including pubs, is now £733 million. Benjamin Greene's other legacy is literary: his great-great-grandson Christopher Isherwood and great-great-nephew Graham Greene are well-known writers.

A panoramic view of Greene King's Westgate Brewery in the early 1880s. (*Greene King plc*)

GUINNESS STOUT

In 1755 Arthur Guinness used his inheritance of £100 from his godfather, the Archbishop of Cashel, to set up a small brewery in Leixlip, County Kildare, Ireland. Four years later he bought a 9,000-year lease on a run-down brewery in St James's Gate, Dublin. From this simple beginning the business grew and by 2001 the Guinness brand was estimated to be worth £950 million in the Interbrand survey of global brands. The Guinness family controlled the expanding business for 227 years, Arthur himself helping the dynasty by fathering twenty-one children. First the Guinness firm brewed porter, a dark, sweet ale made from black malt, and then, in the middle of the nineteenth century, it concentrated on brewing stout, the dark, stronger beer which soon became synonymous with the name Guinness.

Guinness trademark number 209.

A few days after the Trademark Registry opened its doors in London on 1 January 1876, the merchants John Swire & Sons applied to register 'Guinness's, bottled expressly for Australia'

A 1894 German trademark featuring the Guinness harp.

Nr. 980. G. 80. Guinneß Son & Co. Ld., James Gate, Dublin, Irland. Anmeldung vom 1. 10. 94. Eintragung am 8. 12. 94.

Geschäftsbetrieb: Herstellung und Vertrieb von Bier.

Waarenverzeichniß: Bier.

Der Anmeldung ist eine Beschreibung beigefügt.

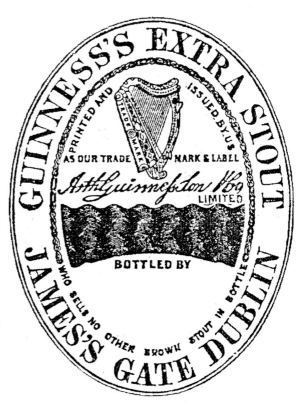

A 1902 British trademark for stout destined for export (number 247,908).

(number 209) and then in April the Guinness firm registered two marks (numbers 4,473–4) for the Guinness harp logo and for 'Guinness Extra Stout – Arthur Guinness', both of which are still registered. A number of Guinness bottlers also applied for trademarks: Dawkes and Co. (number 6,213), Molne & Co. (number 1,798) and Charles Arrowsmith & Co. (number 8,109 for 'Guinness's Stout'). More recently the Guinness brand has been supported by its famous advertising campaigns which include the slogans 'Guinness for strength', 'Guinness is good for

The current branding for Guinness.

you', 'My Goodness – My Guinness', 'Lovely day for a Guinness' (featuring a toucan), and 'Guinness – pure genius'.

In 1986 Guinness acquired the Distillers Company, owner of famous brands such as Johnnie Walker Scotch Whisky, and then in 1997 Guinness plc combined with the food and drinks group Grand Metropolitan to form Diageo, in what was at the time the UK's largest ever merger.

HEERING'S CHERRY LIQUEUR

In about 1818 Peter Heering, a Copenhagen grocer, started selling his Cherry Liqueur, a dark crimson drink made from Danish black cherries and flavoured by the bitter cherry stones. Heering was soon exporting the drink in characteristic red bottles.

Heering's trademark number 11,975.

Heering's 1903 trademark with medals and royal appointments (number 253,924).

73

In May 1877 he applied for British trademarks (numbers 11,975–8) for Cherry Brandy, Cherry Cordial and P F Heering, claiming the latter name had been in use since 1818. A trademark showing the many medals and royal appointments acquired for Heering's cherry brandy was registered in 1903. Though these particular trademarks are no longer active, the name Peter Heering has been registered again more recently. In 1990 Heering was acquired by Danish Distillers, later renamed Danisco. In turn Danisco was taken over in 1999 by the Swedish drinks group V&S, which owns brands such as Absolut.

HEIDSIECK'S CHAMPAGNE

Heidsieck's trade-mark number 4,275.

One of a series of French Heidsieck trademarks from 1887.

In 1785 Florens-Louis Heidsieck, the son of a Lutheran minister from Westphalia in Germany, set up the Heidsieck champagne house in Reims, France. He had started to work in Reims as a cloth merchant but soon started producing wines. When he died in 1828 the business was taken over by his nephews, the eldest of whom, Henri-Louis Heidsieck, later took control. A cousin of these nephews, Henri Piper, became a partner and the firm became Piper-Heidsieck. In 1860 they registered Monopole as a French trademark and in 1923 this was integrated into the company name, becoming 'Champagne Heidsieck & Co. Monopole, founded in 1785'.

1571. — M. p. être apposée sur des bouteilles de vin de Champagne, déposée le 3 juin 1887, à 11 h., au greffe du tribunal de commerce de Reims, par la *Société veuve Heidsieck et Cⁱᵉ*, négociants à Reims.

Cette marque a 0.066 de haut sur 0.107 de large. Le fond est blanc glacé; l'encadrement et les mots *Grand Vin Royal Heidsieck & Co. Reims* sont imprimés en or; l'autre inscription est en lettres noires. L'aigle est noir; il porte une couronne d'or et tient dans ses serres un globe et un sceptre de même couleur.

The first British trademarks (numbers 4,275–86 and 7,752–7) were applied for in 1876, having been in use for twenty-five years. None of the original British marks is still registered, though other newer marks for Heidsieck and Monopole are. In 1996 Heidsieck & Co. Monopole was acquired by the Vranken Champagne Group.

HENNESSY'S COGNAC

Irishman Richard Hennessy set up a business in Cognac, France, to produce 'eaux de vie' (brandy) in 1765 and the firm took its present name, Jas Hennessy & Co., in 1813 from his son James, who ran the firm. Eight generations of Hennessys have run the business and since Jean Fillioux became master blender in 1800 many generations of the Filloux family have also been involved in producing the cognac.

The first recorded use by Hennessy of the battle-axe 'Bras Armé' logo, still in use on its labels, was in 1856 and in 1864 the firm registered its first trademarks in France. In Britain the firm registered several trademarks (numbers 1,286–96) within a

Hennessy's trade-mark number 1,286 from 1876.

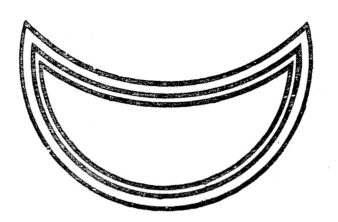

month of the Trademark Registry opening its doors in January 1876. Numbers 1,294 and 1,296 are still registered. In 1971 the firm became part of the Moët-Hennessy Group and in 1987 Moët Hennessy Louis Vuitton (MHLV) was formed. Hennessy now sells 42 million bottles of cognac each year and the brand is worth $3.2 billion.

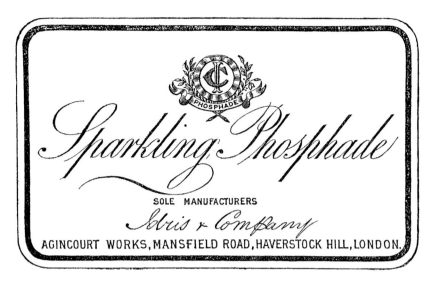

Idris's Sparkling Phosphade trademark number 22,771.

IDRIS BEVERAGES

Thomas Howell Williams founded Idris & Company in 1873 to manufacture mineral and aerated water. The name Idris particularly appealed to him because of its association with the Welsh mountains and he actually later changed his own name to Idris by deed poll.

In 1880 the company started to produce flavoured drinks and applied for the trademark Sparkling Phosphade for beverages, food and fermented liquors and spirits (number 22,771). At this time Robert Rowe and Thomas Adpar Jones were also partners in the company, which was based in Haverstock Hill in London. By 1893 the company had assets of £215,000. The company (including an Idris trademark (number 46,692) from 1885) is now owned by Britvic Soft Drinks Ltd, which also owns R. Whites. The current branding is very different.

IND COOPE BEER

The Ind Coope brand began in 1845 when Octavius and George Coope joined Edward Ind in the latter's brewery business in Romford, Essex. Ind himself had bought the brewery, originally founded in 1708 as the Star Brewery, in 1799. In 1856 Ind Coope opened its second brewery in Burton on Trent.

Ind Coope's Double Diamond trademark (number 3,283).

In March 1876 Ind Coope registered a series of trademarks for pale ale (numbers 3,282–9), of which number 3,282, depicting Britannia, has found its way into the ownership of the brewing concern Interbrew. Number 3,283, the Double Diamond symbol, is the most famous of Ind Coope's marks, and is still registered. The other trademarks, including a single diamond logo, have been allowed to lapse over the intervening years, along with numbers 7,862–7 registered in July 1876.

A framed show card for Ind Coope featuring the trademarked Britannia logo, c. 1880. (*The Robert Opie Collection*)

Ind Coope merged with Allsopp's Brewery in 1934 and then in 1961 with Ansells and with Tetley-Walker to form the Allied Brewers Group. Allied expanded into pubs, food, wine and spirits and by 1992 had a turnover of £5.4 billion. Ironically, Allied pulled out of brewing in about 1990, putting these interests into Carlsberg Tetley, later totally owned by the Danish brewer Carlsberg. The Burton brewery was sold to Bass and the original Romford brewery closed. So the Double Diamond trademark has ended up with Carlsberg.

MACKESON'S STOUT

Mackeson's trademark number 27,516.

In 1801 Henry and William Mackeson inherited a brewery at Hythe in Kent in 1801 that had been in existence since the 1600s. Two centuries ago the business thrived, particularly because military activity in the area – constructing the Royal Military Canal and other fortifications against the threat of invasion by Napoleon – meant that troops and supporting civilian workers quaffed Mackesons in large amounts.

Sweet stouts first became popular in London in the early 1900s. By 1936 Mackeson's Milk Stout, produced using lactose (milk

A 1905 Mackeson trademark (number 275,336).

sugar) at the brewery in Kent, was available nationally. In 1960 half the sales of Whitbread, which had taken over the business, were of Mackeson's sweet stout.

In 1880 Henry Mackeson applied for a trademark for Mackeson Champagne Ale (number 22,737) and in 1882 for marks 27,515–16 for Anglo-Lager Ale. These older trademarks are no longer registered but the business still maintains more recent marks for Mackeson, Mackeson Stout and Mackeson's Milk Stout. Mackeson's was acquired by H. & G. Simmons Ltd of Reading in 1920 and then by the Kent brewer Jude Hanbury & Co. in 1929. In turn, Hanbury's was bought out by Whitbread. More recently the Mackeson trademarks became an Interbrew brand.

Martell's trademark number 1,260.

A 1906 registration by Edouard Martell for a martel and swift design (number 284,583).

One of a series of French marks from J. & F. Martell in the form of bottle neck labels. This one is for VSOP (Very Special Old Pale).

MARTELL'S COGNAC

At the age of 20 Jean Martell moved from Jersey in the Channel Islands to Cognac in western France where, in 1715, he set up a brandy export business. When he died in 1753 his sons Jean and Frédéric continued the business as J. & F. Martell, selling the cognac to Britain and the rest of northern Europe. Following the devastation of the French vineyards caused by the spread of *phylloxera* from North America after 1863, many Britons changed to drinking Scotch whisky but Martell managed to retain its market for cognac in Britain.

In January 1876 the firm applied for two British trademarks (numbers 1,259–60), the first of which, for J. & F. Martell Cognac ML, is still on the trademark register. Some of these early labels

1048. — M. p. être apposée sur des bouteilles contenant de l'eau-de-vie, déposée le 31 janvier 1887, à 4 h., au greffe du tribunal de commerce de Cognac, par les sieurs *Martell et Cie*, négociants à Cognac.

Cette marque a 0.024 de haut sur 0.057 de large. Le fond est bleu et porte, en lettres blanches, le nom *J. & F. Martell* répété sur toute sa surface; la bordure est argent avec filet intérieur blanc; les initiales V. S. O. P. sont imprimées en blanc entouré de bleu

depicted the martel (hammer) and the swift and these emblems have also been retained by the firm. In 1912 another family member, Edouard Martell, created Cordon Bleu Cognac. The company, now part of the Pernod-Ricard Group, sells 1.2 million cases in 140 countries each year.

McEWAN'S BEER

William McEwan was born in Scotland in 1827 and became apprenticed to his uncles John and David Jeffrey, who were Edinburgh brewers. In 1856 he set up his own business from scratch, the Fountain Brewery, in Edinburgh. He was one of the first to introduce new technology such as Steel's patent mashing machine in 1857. McEwan soon established a large market and in the 1860s was successfully exporting to the colonies.

This McEwan's trademark from 1880 (number 22,818) is still registered.

When William McEwan entered politics in 1886, his nephew became the firm's manager. McEwan & Co. applied for trademarks in August 1888 and two, both for McEwan's, Edinburgh, are still registered. Number 22,772 had, according to the firm, been in use already for fifteen years and another, number 22,818, for nine years. William McEwan & Co. Ltd was valued at £408,000 at the time of registration as a limited company in 1889.

Nr. **3201.** C. 128. William Mc Ewan & Co. Limited, Edinburgh, Schottland; Vertr.: Friedrich Emil Bärwinkel, Justizrath, Leipzig. Anmeldung vom 6. 10. 94/ 22. 1. 81. Eintragung am 22. 2. 95.

Geschäftsbetrieb: Bierbrauerei.

Waarenverzeichniß: Bier.

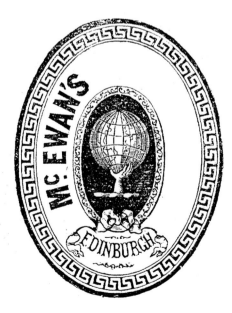

McEwan's German mark from 1895 is similar to the earlier British trademark but without the flags.

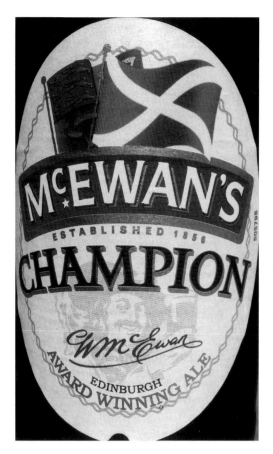

One of the latest McEwan's bottle labels for Champion beer shows more flags: the Royal Standard and Scottish Saltire.

The company acquired the Boroughloch Brewery in Edinburgh from Alexander Melvin & Co. in 1907. It merged with William Younger & Co. Ltd in 1931 to become Scottish Brewers Ltd and with Newcastle Breweries in 1960 to become Scottish & Newcastle plc, the largest brewer in the UK. The Fountain Brewery was closed in 2004.

MOËT & CHANDON CHAMPAGNE

In about 1700 Dom Pérignon discovered a sparkling wine while working as the cellarmaster of the Saint-Pierre Abbey at Hautvillers in France. Supposedly, he went on to develop the 'méthode champenoise'

Moët trademark number 6,798.

82

768. — M. p. désigner du vin de Champagne, déposée le 25 mars 1887, à 2 h., au greffe du tribunal de commerce d'Epernay, par les sieurs *Chandon et Cie*, négociants à Epernay.

Cette marque consiste en une empreinte de 0.022 de diamètre. Elle s'applique sur le bouchon des bouteilles contenant le produit.

for making champagne. In 1743 Moët & Chandon was founded by Claude Moët in Champagne, France, and shortly afterwards it acquired the Benedictine abbey and the 'Dom Pérignon' name.

In 1876 the firm applied for twenty-eight British trademarks (numbers 6,790–6,817). Trademark number 6,792 was on the register until 1988 but the oldest mark continuously registered by the firm dates from 1888 and is for Dry Imperial Moët & Chandon Finest extra quality (number 73,970). 'Dom Pérignon' is still a trademark of Moët & Chandon. The firm is now part of the MHLV group (see Hennessy, p. 76) and is the largest champagne house, producing 24 million bottles a year. Interbrand value the Moët & Chandon brand at $3 billion.

A trademark for bottle corks was among a series for Moët & Chandon registered in France in 1887.

MUMM'S CHAMPAGNE

Brothers Jacobus, Gottlieb and Philipp Mumm were from a family of rich German wine merchants who owned vineyards in the Rhine valley. In 1827 they went to Reims in France where they set

Jules Mumm's bird and bell trademark (number 7,915).

83

G.H. Mumm's bird
trademark number
4,172.

up the firm P.A. Mumm et Cie, named after their father Peter
Arnold Mumm, and quickly established themselves as champagne
producers. In 1853 the partners split up and part of the company
was taken over by Georges Hermann Mumm, a son of one of the
brothers, and this became G.H. Mumm et Cie, which is its name
today.

In 1876 the firm applied for ten British trademarks (numbers
4,172–81), one of which, number 4,174, is still registered. At the
time of application Alexandre de Bary, from another German
champagne family, was a partner and the name G. de Bary appears
on all the marks. Among the logos used was the Cordon Rouge
(red ribbon) which had been introduced in 1875. The other part
of the original business became Jules Mumm & Co.; this was run
by a son of Jacobus and was wound up in 1910. Jacob Bernhard
Mumm von Schwarzenstein applied for a series of British
trademarks on behalf of this firm in 1876 (numbers 7,914–17).

NOILLY PRAT VERMOUTH

Joseph Noilly of Lyon in France and Claudius Prat started to produce dry vermouth in 1813. Noilly had developed the recipe after noticing that wine transported by sea in barrels changed colour and increased in body. In the Noilly process Blancs de Blancs wine is mixed with Muscat (grape juice and alcohol), fruit, spirits, herbs and spices and stored for a year in oak barrels exposed to the air to produce the Noilly Prat vermouth.

Louis Prat applied for two British trademarks in 1876 (numbers 6,692–3), the first of which had been in use since 1855 for Vermouth Noilly Prat & Cie. This earliest mark was also registered in France in 1887, and is still registered and used by the same company. Bottle labels today are hardly changed from those of a century and a half ago. The second British trademark in 1876 was for 'Extrait d'Absinthe', while another French trademark for the firm in 1887 was for Bitter.

Noilly Prat's label trademark number 6,692.

An 1887 Noilly Prat French trademark for Bitter.

1705. — M. p. être apposée sur des bouteilles contenant du bitter, déposée le 11 novembre 1887, à 5 h., au greffe du tribunal de commerce de Marseille, par les sieurs *Noilly Prat et C*ie, négociants à Marseille.

Cette marque a 0.079 de haut sur 0.106 de large. Le fond est rouge verni et le dessin formant l'encadrement blanc; les mots *Bitter... Noilly Prat et C*ie sont en lettres blanches bordées de noir; les autres inscriptions sont imprimées en noir.

PERNOD'S ABSINTHE

In 1797 Major Dubied of Couvet, Switzerland, obtained a secret recipe for the drink absinthe, which he started to produce there. He soon set up shop with his son Marcellin and son-in-law Henri-Louis Pernod, and in 1805 they started production at Pontarlier in France in order to avoid paying excise duty. The absinthe plant (wormwood) was grown around Pontarlier and distilled with seeds of green aniseed to produce the drink. Dubied himself went back to Couvet and the firm Dubied Père et Fils later passed to a cousin, Fritz Duval, and thence into rival hands.

The younger of Pernod's two sons, Louis, ran the Pernod Fils business in Pontarlier and increased the factory's output dramatically, exporting some of the product. In 1876 the firm applied for a British trademark for Pernod Fils Couvet Suisse & Pontarlier Doubs (number 4,561), which is maintained to this day. By 1901 Pernod Fils was producing 30,000 litres per annum but in that year the factory was hit by fire and to reduce the risk of explosion much of the

Pernod's 1876 Absinthe trademark (number 4,561).

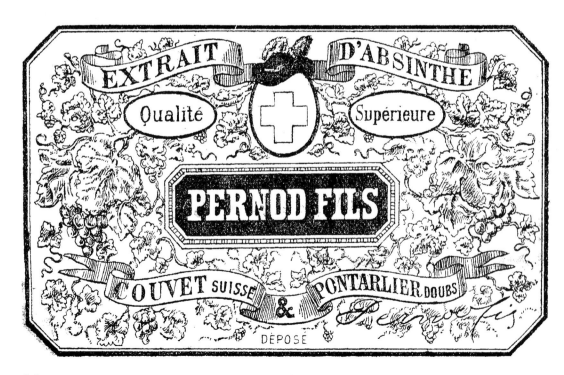

Today's Pernod bottles have a very similar ivyleaf design to that on the 1876 trademark.

absinthe on site was drained into the River Doubs which flowed past the premises. It is said that the day was long remembered as the occasion when townsfolk were able to enjoy a free drink just by dipping their glasses into the river.

In 1915 absinthe, which was thought to cause hallucinations, was banned in France and though the formulations were changed the business slumped. Around this time Pernod Fils merged with distilleries owned by other members of the Pernod family. Today the firm is the major drinks conglomerate Pernod Ricard.

ROSE'S LIME CORDIAL

The Rose family were shipbuilders at Leith in Scotland when in 1865 Lauchlan Rose set himself up as a ship's chandler supplying ships with provisions including lime juice. After it was found that limes prevented scurvy, which was common among sailors, the Merchant Shipping Act of 1867 was passed to make it compulsory for ocean-going ships to carry lime juice rations. Consequently demand for the product soared. Rose's sales to ships increased and he also introduced sweetened lime-juice cordial for general consumption.

Rose's Lime Juice Cordial trademark, number 2,931.

In 1876 Lauchlan applied for two trademarks that had already been in use for nine years (numbers 2,931–2) on behalf of L. Rose & Co. and both are still registered today. The following year he applied for a trademark (number 11,733) for Rose's Citronade, an aerated beverage. The company purchased estates in Dominica in 1891 and adapted an old sugar factory to the processing of limes. In the 1940s the firm also became well known for its lime marmalade.

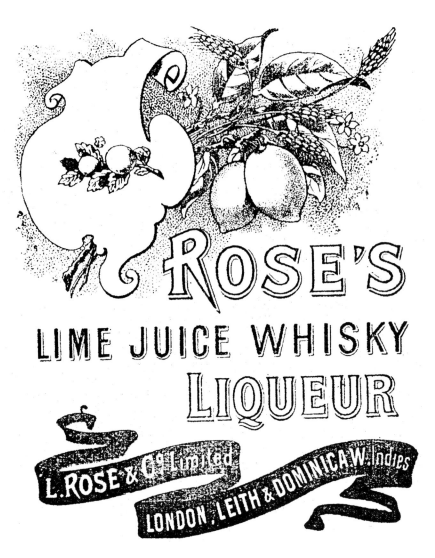

Rose's 1900 trademark for lime juice liqueur (number 230,070).

In 1957 the company was bought out by Schweppes and the trademarks were recently acquired by Atlantic Industries, a Coca-Cola company. Rose's marmalade is now produced by Premier Foods.

SCHWEPPES CARBONATED DRINKS

Jacob Schweppes was born in Witzenhausen, Germany, in 1740. After working for a travelling tinker and then a jeweller he went to Geneva, where, in partnership with Jean Dunant, he built a successful jewellery business. Later he gave up jewellery to concentrate on producing artificial mineral water in Geneva and in 1790 he set up a partnership with a rival, Nicolas Paul, and a

Schweppes's trademark for Malvern water, with the fountain logo (number 4,744).

pharmacist, Henry Gosse. Then in 1792 Jacob was dispatched to set up production in Drury Lane in London. Business was not immediately good and the partners squabbled so that in 1793 it was agreed that Jacob would keep the London business while the others would share the Geneva interests. The enterprise in London grew gradually but by 1798 Jacob had sold three-quarters of the firm to three Jerseymen. In 1969 the Schweppes company merged with chocolate manufacturer Cadbury to form Cadbury Schweppes plc.

Back in the 1830s the firm was producing a range of carbonated beverages, including lemonade, and in 1837 it received a royal warrant from Queen Victoria. The range was extended again in 1870 with the introduction of Indian Tonic Water and American Ginger Ale. Sales of tonic water grew rapidly in India as it contains quinine, which is used to prevent malaria. On 7 April 1876 the then partners in the firm, Henry Evill and John Welch, applied to register a series of trademarks (numbers

A modern can of soda water shows a variation on the original fountain logo.

89

EXCLUSIVELY SUPPLIED AT THE BARS OF THE ROYAL OPERA HOUSE

An advertisement for
Schweppes's Table
Waters, *c.* 1900.
(*The Robert Opie
Collection*)

4,742–5) featuring the fountain logo that is still used today. Trademark number 4,744 shows Holywell, a well situated above the village of Malvern Wells, where Schweppes bottled water from the 1850s onwards. Trademark number 4,742 was recently transferred to drink concentrates manufacturer Atlantic Industries.

STONE'S GINGER WINE

Joseph Stone was the thirteenth child of John Stone, a grocer in High Holborn, London. In about 1826 he went into employment with the firm of Bishop and Harrington, at their Finsbury Distillery. The Bishop family had been distilling since at least the seventeenth century and set up at Finsbury in London in 1740. In 1848 Stone set up on his own as a wine and spirit merchant not far from Bishop's distillery. At this time, or shortly after, the Finsbury Distillery was supplying Stone with wines and cordials labelled as Stone's while also selling products, especially spirits and liqueurs, under the Bishop's brand.

The wine trade flourished, particularly the importing of French wine, after the Chancellor of the Exchequer, William Gladstone, revised the excise system of duty on wine in 1860. In 1861 George and James Bishop, then owners of the firm of Bishop & Sons, signed an agreement with Joseph Stone: he would act as salesman for the Bishops for a fee of £200 per annum and commission, while they would have the exclusive right to Stone's brands.

In 1876 Bishop & Sons took out a series of trademarks, notably for Bishop & Sons Finsbury Distillery (number 2,094), Stone's Original Green Ginger Wine (number 2,095) and several others

Stone's trademark number 2,095.

A 1905 trademark for Stone's Lime Juice Cordial (number 267,776).

for Stone's wines such as port and sherry. None of these marks is registered today but two further marks filed with the Trade Mark Registry in 1886 for Stone's Original Green Ginger Wine (number 56,712) and Stone's Jamaica Ginger Wine (number 58,697) both survive on the register, along with one for Stone's Original Green Ginger Wine registered in 1893 (number 174,828).

In the early 1960s Bishop & Sons, still a private company, held discussions with several cider and perry manufacturers, including Gaymers and Showerings, about mergers but nothing came of them. Today these brands are owned, along with other well-known brands including Gaymer's, V.P. and Babycham, by Constellation Europe Ltd.

A 1907 trademark for gin from Stone's Finsbury Distillery features the City of London coat of arms (number 291,676).

TENNENT'S LAGER

According to some sources, Hugh and Robert Tennent founded a brewery business in 1740 in Glasgow, while others suggest that the family established its first brewery there as early as 1556. Certainly by 1769 Hugh Tennent's sons John and Robert were running the family business, under the name J. & R. Tennent, and they expanded in the 1790s to incorporate the adjacent brewhouse of William McLehose at Drygate, where the brewery was renamed Wellpark.

Hugh Tennent, the great-great-grandson of the co-founder Hugh, assumed control in 1884. In 1881 he had been to Germany, and on his return created Tennent's Lager, which was reported to be the first lager brewed in Scotland. It was soon being exported to over a hundred countries. In another, later, innovation the company was one of the first businesses in the United Kingdom to sell beer in cans.

On 8 March 1876 the company applied for five trademarks (numbers 3,691–5), the first of which is still registered for Pale Ale. Number 3,694 for the letter T is also still registered but the others have been allowed to lapse. Tennent's beer is still strongly associated with a red T.

The company was taken over by the English brewer Charrington United Breweries Ltd in 1963 and ended up as part of the Belgian Interbrew group. To this day about half of all the lager drunk in Scotland is brewed by Tennent's.

A Tennent's trademark from 1907 for the letter T but limited to the colour red (number 292,296).

Tennent's Pale Ale trademark, number 3,691.

Tetley's trademark number 1,124.

TETLEY'S BEER

The Tetley brewery was set up in 1822 in Leeds by Joshua Tetley, who came from a family of maltsters. Tetley paid £400 for the brewery and within a year he was in debt to the tune of £2,700. Despite this, the business grew fast and in 1834 he was able to incorporate the malting business which he had inherited from his father. After Joshua's death in 1859, the business passed to his son Francis. By 1874 Tetley was selling over 160,000 barrels a year and had to open a new office to cope with the growth. In January 1876 Tetley was one of the many brewers applying to register trademarks. Two, showing a coat of arms in a star and crest that had already been in use for ten years, were registered (numbers 1,124–5), and the first of these is still used today.

Tetley's Huntsman logo on a label from the 1970s was also used by Eldridge Pope for its beer. (*The Robert Opie Collection*)

A recent can design for Tetley bitter bearing Joshua Tetley's signature.

In 1911 Joshua Tetley & Son challenged the famous escapologist Harry Houdini to escape from a padlocked metal cask full of Tetley's beer. On the night set for the escape, Houdini's assistant Franz Kokol became alarmed by the silence behind the curtain and looked into the cabinet to find Houdini only semi-conscious. Kokol quickly pulled him out of the cask and saved his life.

From 1890 onwards Tetley was buying public houses and by the mid-1950s owned a thousand or so pubs. In 1961 Tetley joined with Ind Coope and Ansells to form Allied Breweries. Today the brand is owned by Danish brewer Carlsberg.

THWAITES' BEER

In 1806 excise officer Daniel Thwaites, along with George Clayton and Edward Duckworth, found spring water in Blackburn, Lancashire, which they knew would be suitable for making beer. The following year they leased some ground from the vicar of Blackburn and established the Eanam Brewery (later to become the Star Brewery). In 1808 Daniel married Edward Duckworth's daughter Betty, who inherited her father's share in the business after his death in 1822. When Daniel died in 1843 three sons, Daniel Jr, John and Thomas inherited their father's share of the business. In 1858, five years after the death of his mother, Daniel Jr became the sole owner of the brewery and went on to become the richest man in England.

In 1882 Thwaites & Co. applied for a trademark

Thwaites' trademark number 29,703.

95

A present-day bottle of Thwaites 'Lancaster Bomber' showing the firm's horses' heads logo.

(number 29,703) for East Lancashire Pale Ale but this is no longer registered. A trademark featuring the same heraldic design used on the earlier mark was registered in January 1898 (number 210,819) and this is still used by the firm.

Both the Star Brewery and the Thwaites firm, now Daniel Thwaites plc, are still in existence and the company is ranked among the top six UK brewers. It is still run by the Thwaites family and the chairman of the company, Ann Yerburgh, is a direct descendant of the original Daniel.

WHITBREAD'S BEER

Samuel Whitbread was born in 1720 and on reaching the age of 14 was sent from his home in Bedfordshire to London to be a brewery apprentice. By age 22 Whitbread had invested £2,600 in the two breweries in London owned by the Shewell family, becoming a partner with Thomas Shewell. The Goat Brewhouse in the City of London made porter and the Brick Lane brewery in London's East End produced paler beers. Whitbread found that porter could be made in very large containers, so helping him to keep up with the growing demand. Business was good and in 1750 he built a new brewery at Chiswell Street in the City, which was operational until 1975. In about 1761 Whitbread bought out his partner for £30,000, by which time the firm was one of the largest brewers of porter in England. When Samuel Whitbread died on 11 June 1796 the *Gentleman's Magazine* claimed he was worth over £1,000,000.

Whitbread's first trademark
(number 10,098).

A 1908 trademark
showing the
Whitbread deer's
head.

Whitbread's Brewery
in 1820 (from an
engraving from a
painting by
D. Wolstenholme Jr).

In December 1876 Whitbread & Co. applied for a trademark (number 10,098), claiming six years of prior use, bearing the name of the sole agent for bottles of Whitbread's beer, R. Baker. The deer's head used in the trademark has continued in use as a Whitbread logo to the present day.

Whitbread plc sold its brewing interests, including the production and marketing of pale ale, bitter beers and stout, to Interbrew in 2000 for £400 million while retaining its interests in pubs and its licence to brew Heineken beer.

R. WHITE'S LEMONADE AND GINGER BEER

Robert and Mary White started to produce R. White's lemonade and other carbonated drinks in Camberwell, London, in 1845. In 1885 the firm of R. White & Sons applied for three trademarks (numbers 48,853–5) for their ginger beer which, along with other drinks, had become very popular. Other trademarks followed, including the currently used mark (number 69,780) for R. White, which has been on the trademark register since 1888. More recently, R. White bottles have often featured striped labels.

The firm merged in 1891 with H.D. Rawlings, another carbonated beverage manufacturer that supplied soda water in siphons. The combined business was taken over by the brewers Whitbread in 1969 and then became part of Britvic Soft Drinks Ltd, which was floated off in 2005 by its then majority owner, InterContinental Hotels Group. Production of R. White's lemonade continues.

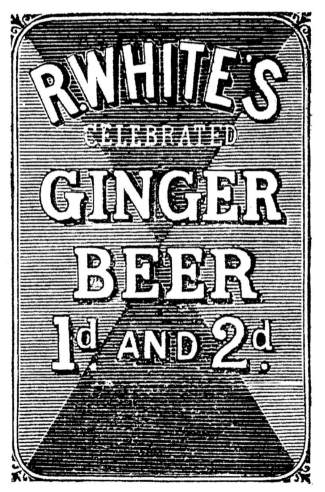

R. White's Ginger Beer trademark, number 48,853.

Delicious! Wholesome!! Refreshing !!!
LIME JUICE CORDIAL
from the Finest Selected
WEST INDIAN LIMES

R. White also sold Lime Juice Cordial, but not under the R. White's name, for which the company registered this trademark in 1905 (number 270,550).

WORTHINGTON'S BEER

William Worthington, who was born in Leicestershire, moved to Burton on Trent in Staffordshire in 1744 to work as a cooper. Some time after 1760 he established a brewery in Burton. In this respect he was some years ahead of William Bass, another Leicestershire man, who set up a brewery in the town in 1777, but it was Bass & Co. that was much later to buy out

99

Worthington's trademark number 3,665 showing the original white shield.

A 1900 version of the white shield trademark used on mineral water (number 233,249).

The Worthington white shield used on a modern bottle.

Worthington's brewery business. When Worthington died in 1800 he was succeeded by his sons, one of whom, also named William, married the daughter of another Burton brewer, Henry Evans. This marriage meant that the Evans brewery was eventually subsumed by Worthington. Worthington & Co. grew further by buying out other breweries in Burton in 1790 and 1879.

Worthington was one of the early applicants for trademarks, applying in March 1876 for 'Worthington & Co., Burton on Trent. Strong Burton Ale, Brewers by appointment to HRH The Prince of Wales' (number 3,665) and similar marks for Mild Burton Ale and India Pale Ale (numbers 3,666–7). At the same time the firm applied separately to register just the dagger in shield logo (number 3,664) which is used within the other marks. This shield mark has been continuously used since 1863, although the current white shield is somewhat different. Worthington amalgamated with Bass in 1927. The trademarks are now owned by the American brewer Coors, having been briefly held by Interbrew, which bought Bass.

WILLIAM YOUNGER'S BEER

After the death of the first William Younger, an exciseman and brewer, in 1770, his widow Grizel Syme continued to run and expand the brewery business. In the 1780s she married Alexander Anderson, who had been brewing in Kirkgate, Leith, Scotland, since at least 1758. The William Younger & Co. business was further developed by Grizel until her retirement in 1794, and she was helped by her sons, including William Younger Jr. One of the sons, Archibald Younger, set up on his own in business in 1778, establishing a brewery at Holyrood Abbey, Edinburgh, and then later other breweries in Edinburgh and London.

William Younger's first trademark (number 3,800).

The second William Younger opened his own brewhouse at Holyrood Abbey in 1796 and acquired another in Holyrood in 1803. In 1806 he started brewing porter with his brother Archibald, and soon took his brother-in-law Robert Hunter into the business, which then became known as Younger and Hunter. After Hunter's death in 1818 William took Alexander Smith, the brewery superintendent, into partnership and the firm became William Younger & Co.

In 1876 William Younger & Co. registered a series of trademarks for fermented liquors (numbers 3,800 and 3,804 for India Pale Ale; 3,801 for Edinburgh Ale; 3,802 for Extra Stout and 3,803 for Sparkling Ale). All except number 3,804 are still registered. Around this time the firm hired its first chemist, who visited Pasteur's laboratory in a quest to improve the quality of the fermentation but in 1878 financial trouble with Scottish banks brought anxious months to the firm. Though Tennent claims to be the oldest Scottish brewer of lager, Younger had registered a trademark (number 27,671) for Lager beer by 1882.

Younger's Lager beer trademark of 1882, still showing a view of Holyrood (number 27,671).

The business continued to be run by the families of Younger and Smith, becoming a limited company in 1889. By 1891 the company was producing 400,000 barrels of beer each year and brewed a quarter of all the ale produced in Scotland. In January 1931 the company merged with William McEwan & Co. to become Scottish Brewers Ltd, which later became part of Scottish and Newcastle plc.

4

FOOD

From Sugar and Confectionery to Mustard and Vinegar

Many of the companies that provide us with food today still employ the trademarks of the pioneers in the business from the nineteenth century and earlier. The stories behind brands that survive often show how the businesses grew out of innovations, some important and some seeming almost trivial. These innovations include Liebig's food preservation and processing (which generated Fray Bentos tinned meat, Bovril drink, Brand's essence of beef and other trademarks), McDougall's self-raising flour, Quaker's packaging of oats into convenient quantities, improved marmalades from Keiller and Robertson, and Spratt's dog food in biscuit form.

Improvements in transport meant that firms could expand by shipping their products widely and biscuit-bakers like Carr, Jacob, Huntley & Palmer and Peek Frean became known throughout Britain and then grew into worldwide brands.

Many firms that registered trademarks for food products did not survive and little detail is known about most of them. Interestingly, the firm of Brown & Polson, started by John Polson and William Brown, went on to meet with great success with their cornflour but the cornflour manufacturer William Polson &

Co. disappeared with little trace. It seems likely that there was some Polson family connection between these two Paisley firms.

In the eighteenth century chocolate was an extremely expensive luxury and only a few rich people could afford to take it as a drink. In the nineteenth century the increased supply of cocoa beans and innovations in their processing meant that not only did the drinking of chocolate become popular but bars of solid chocolate could be produced. Soon confectionery as we know it today was being made by companies like Fry, Cadbury, Suchard and Van Houten.

William Polson's trademark (number 28,984), not to be confused with Brown & Polson.

ALLINSON'S FLOUR

Thomas Allinson was born in 1858. He worked as an assistant to a chemist on leaving school and then went on to train as a doctor in Edinburgh. As a vegetarian and non-smoker, he was interested in the health benefits of a diet that included wholewheat flour. He set up in general practice in London in 1885 and in the following year he published a book, *A System of Hygienic Medicine, or the only rational way of treating disease*, which was subsequently republished many times. He also toured the country lecturing on the virtues of bread containing whole grain and eventually his crusade led to his name being removed from the Medical Register in 1895, about which he demonstrated much pride.

Allinson's 1891 trademark number 157,268.

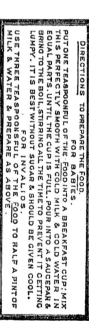

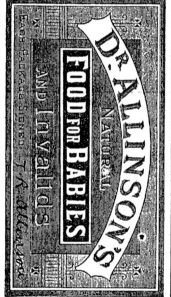

He bought a flour mill in Bethnal Green, London, and in 1891 applied, as the Natural Food Company, for two trademarks (numbers 157,268 and 158,255) for his food for babies. Another trademark (number 183,546) was registered in 1894 showing his photograph and signature followed by the initials LRCP (Licentiate of the Royal College of Physicians); this is still on the trademark register today despite his being struck off the medical register! From 1915 several variations of windmill logos were registered and they have been used ever since on Allinson's flour.

In 1918 Allinson died and his eldest son took over, followed by his youngest son in 1946. The demand for the company's flour increased and mills were bought in Newport, Monmouthshire, and

Trademark number 183,546 showing Allinson's portrait.

in Castleford, Yorkshire. The Castleford Mill was expanded and is today the largest stone-grinding flour mill in the world. The company became Allinson Ltd in 1946 and was taken over by Booker McConnell plc, but it is now a part of Associated British Foods.

ATORA SUET

Frenchman Gabriel Hugon lived in Manchester and ran an engraving business. One day he saw his wife chopping up suet by hand and realised there would be a market for ready-shredded suet. In 1893 he sold his engraving business and set up Hugon & Co. to make suet at a factory in Openshaw, Manchester.

TRADE MARK

His first trademark (number 177,089), registered in 1893, for beef suet and lard was a winged hourglass to represent the time-saving nature of his product. The name Atora, derived from the Spanish word for bull, *toro*, was registered in 1895 (number 184,774) and is still registered today. For many years publicity was generated by transporting the product around the country in colourfully painted Atora wagons pulled by six pairs of Hereford bullocks. The business was bought by Rank Hovis McDougall (formerly McDougall Brothers) in 1963 and in 1974 suet production was moved to Hartlepool, Cleveland.

Bird's ship and globe trademark, number 725.

BIRD'S CUSTARD POWDER

Alfred Bird was born in Birmingham in 1811 and set up a chemist's shop in Digbeth, Birmingham, in 1837. His wife Elizabeth was allergic to eggs and yeast, which prompted Alfred to cook meals without these ingredients. He produced custard powder from cornflour instead of eggs, and baking powder so that bread could be made without yeast.

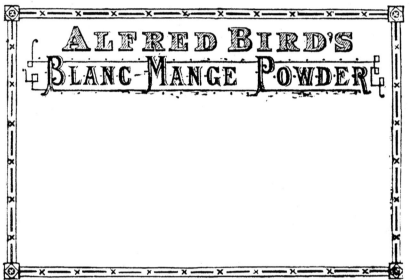

Bird's 1878 trademark for blancmange powder (number 14,395).

These products were apparently served to his dinner guests at home and when they met with their approval Alfred started the firm of Alfred Bird & Sons Ltd in 1843 to make them in large quantities. By the next year Bird's Custard Powder was being sold internationally. Alfred's son developed the company and introduced new products, including blancmange powder, which was one of the first Bird's products to have a registered trademark.

In 1876 the company registered the ship and globe trademark (number 725) for medicinal preparations, vegetable acids, water filters, violet powder for use as a cosmetic, and custard powder, and this registration remained in force until 2002. In 1878, the year of Alfred's death, two trademarks were registered: a weathervane logo (number

Bird's 1906 trademark, still using the weathervane logo (number 279,323).

14,205) for patent medicines, filters, confectionery, perfumery, games and chemical substances used in philosophical research, and number 14,395 for blancmange. The three birds logo was first used in 1929 in a large advertising campaign and was registered for baking powder in 1936.

In 1947 Bird's was taken over by the General Foods Company which merged with tobacco company Philip Morris in 1985. Three years later, when Philip Morris acquired Kraft, Bird's became part of the Kraft General Foods business but the brand was sold off to Premier Foods at the end of 2004. Apparently, one in three of us in Britain today has Bird's Custard in our cupboards.

BORWICK'S BAKING POWDER

George Borwick was a Lancashire schoolmaster who married Jane Hudson in 1831. George's father-in-law, so the story goes, offered them a formula for baking powder which the couple experimented with in an attic for eleven years before selling the product at a penny an ounce. In about 1853 George was joined in the business by his son and in 1864 the firm had set up a factory in London to meet the increasing demand.

George Borwick & Sons applied for trademarks for baking powder in July 1878. The firm also established the mark for custard, egg and pastry powder as well as trademarks for polish. A whole series of marks (12,721–41) was registered for Borwick's, Model Baking Powder and Penny Custard. Trademark 12,738, showing medals obtained for the baking powder in 1868 and 1869, is still registered.

THE MODEL
BAKING POWDER,
For making Bread without Yeast,
PUDDINGS WITHOUT EGGS,
And Pastry with half the usual quantity of Butter.

DIRECTIONS FOR USE.

For Bread.—Mix thoroughly a teaspoonful of the powder heaped up, and the usual quantity of salt, with each pound of flour in a *dry* state—then pour on gradually, about half a pint of *cold* water or milk (a little more if the flour be either the finest or brown), mixing quickly into a dough *of the same consistence as when using yeast,* put it into a tin previously warmed, and then into a *quick* oven. It should be put into the oven with as little delay as possible. It seldom does well in a baker's oven, on account of the lowness of the temperature. It is recommended that parties should not try large loaves till they have first accustomed themselves to small ones or tea-cakes. If the bread is required to be kept moist long, the addition of about one tablespoonful of rice, thoroughly swollen, to about one pound of flour, is a great improvement; but as there is more in weight, so also will a little more powder be required.

Tea Cakes.—Prepared as bread, with milk, are very short and delicious, but with the addition of an egg they are very superior.

Pastry, Pie-Crusts, &c.—Mix about half a teaspoonful of the powder with a pound of flour, then work in about half the usual quantity of butter, dripping or lard.

Plum, Suet, and other Puddings.—A teaspoonful to a pound of flour, makes them both light and digestible, and effects a great saving in eggs and butter—in fact they may be entirely dispensed with.

Norfolk Dumplings.—Prepare as for bread, put into the boiling water immediately, and boil same as common Yeast Dumplings.

Sweet Biscuits, Pound Cakes, School Cakes, Sponge Cakes, Bath Buns, &c.—Put a teaspoonful and a half of powder to every pound of flour, and half the quantity of butter, &c., recommended in most receipt books, will be found sufficient.

George Borwick & Sons were selling their products during those early days in Walthamstow, now part of greater London but then only a small town. At one time, probably after the establishment of a market in about 1885, they were selling from a stall, and the baking powder continued to be sold in Walthamstow from a shop in the High Street in the 1920s and 1930s. By the 1890s *Borwick's Cookery Book* was already in its eighth edition and selling for sixpence. Later Borwick's issued illustrated recipe cards for dishes such as 'Christmas pudding – and excellent plum pudding', extolling the cook to 'Try this recipe, and you will be delighted with the result, but be sure and use BORWICK'S BAKING POWDER'.

Borwick's baking powder is still sold but it is now manufactured by the giant Irish food manufacturing company, Kerry Group.

Borwick's trademark number 12,724 does not mention the Borwick name!

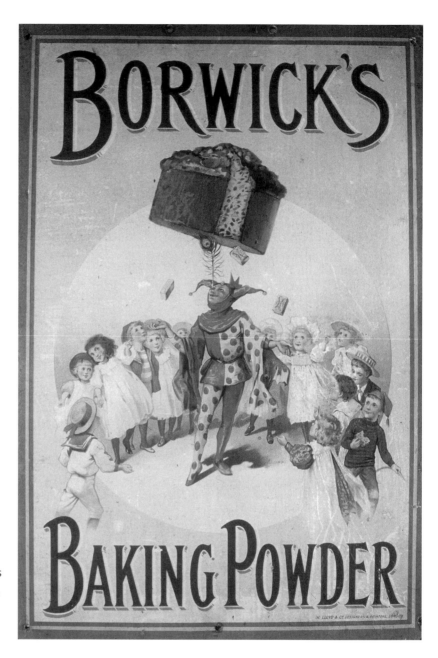

An advertisement from about 1900 showing the lightness of cakes made using Borwick's Baking Powder! (*The Robert Opie Collection*)

BOVRIL BEEF DRINK

At the age of 35 Scotsman John Lawson Johnston won a contract to supply a million tins of beef to the French army in 1873. He opened a factory to produce the meat in Quebec in Canada while at the same time developing Johnston's Fluid Beef, which was later to become Bovril. In Montreal, to where he moved

production in 1879, he sold the hot beef drink to people during the winter carnival.

Johnston moved back to London in 1884 and set up a factory to produce the drink, taking out a trademark for Johnston's Fluid Beef in 1886 (number 58,404) and others for Bovril (numbers 58,405, 60,501, 76,550 and 76,860) and Bové (number 75,218) in 1887–8. By this time more than three thousand public houses and bars were serving hot Bovril to their customers. The name Bovril came from the Latin for beef (*bos, bovis*) and 'vril', the mysterious life-force in the 1871 book *The Coming Race* by Sir Edward Bulwer-Lytton.

The Bovril Company was formed in 1889 with a capital of £150,000 but soon after a drought in Australia brought a crisis to the supply of beef. Johnston died in 1900 and his son George took over the company. In 1908 the firm bought half a million acres of land in Argentina on which to

Above: Bovril trademark number 76,860.

Below: A 1904 Bovril trademark not for the drink but for paper bags and other paper items (number 260,791).

THE GLORY OF A MAN IS HIS STRENGTH

A 1905 Bovril trademark for food products (number 270,031).

rear its own Shorthorn cattle. Early advertising did not simply promote the name but was designed to give an impression of warmth, goodness and cheerfulness. In 2004 Unilever Bestfoods, which now owns the brand, decided to remove beef altogether from Bovril so as to allay fears about BSE ('mad cow disease') and to make it acceptable to vegetarians.

An advertisement from 1900 showing the cavalry drinking Bovril. (*Illustrated London News*)

BRAND'S ESSENCE OF BEEF

In the 1820s King George IV's chef, Mr H.W. Brand, developed an essence of chicken as a health food for the king and on his retirement in 1835 he started to sell Brand's Essence of Chicken as a food for convalescents and invalids. In 1873 his widow passed the business to John James Mason, who was joined in partnership by Thomas Dence. The two partners applied for trademarks on behalf of Brand & Co. in 1876 for all manner of preserved provisions, including essence of beef and essence of chicken (numbers 200–3). Trademark number 201 is still registered and owned by the firm of Cerebos.

Thomas Dence, a Kentish man, built a new factory for the firm in 1887 in Lambeth, London, to dry meat. The drying plant was based on the principle of a Kentish oasthouse used for hop-drying. Cubes of meat were dried above a wood fire in a brick kiln and a good draught was created by a conical roof.

Brand & Company was bought by table salt manufacturer Cerebos Pacific Ltd in 1959 and this firm was in turn acquired by Rank Hovis McDougall plc (RHM) in 1968. In 1990 the Japanese company Suntory purchased RHM's share in Cerebos Pacific Ltd. In the Far East and Australasia Brand's products have a huge market, with 100 million bottles sold in 2003. Brand's museums have been opened in Thailand and Taiwan. In 2001 a container labelled Brand & Co.'s Essence of Beef was discovered on Mount Everest – where it had been left by the 1933 British Everest Expedition.

Brand's trademark number 201.

BRAND & CO.'S ESSENCE OF BEEF.

This Essence consists solely of the juice of the finest beef, extracted by a gentle heat, without the addition of water or of any other substance whatever, by a process first discovered by ourselves, in conjunction with a celebrated physician.

DIRECTIONS.—It is best taken cold. In cases of extreme exhaustion or urgent danger, one teaspoonful may be administered as often as the patient can take it; in less urgent cases one may be taken three times daily, with a small piece of bread and a little wine. *It should be kept, previous to use, in a cool place, if possible* ON ICE. If in bottle, should be kept uncorked; cases should be opened at the smooth top, and, when once opened, the essence allowed to remain exposed to the air. The essence in bottle (and in case, when once opened) will only keep good about two days.

CAUTION.—BEWARE OF IMITATIONS.

Each article bears the firm's signature and address as under, without which **NONE** *are genuine.*

Brand Compy.

No. 11, LITTLE STANHOPE STREET, HERTFORD STREET, MAYFAIR, W.

(TOP OF DOWN STREET, PICCADILLY.)

Brand's mock turtle soup from about 1920 still retains the trademark signature. (*The Robert Opie Collection*)

BROOKE BOND TEA

Arthur Brooke, the founder of the firm Brooke Bond, was born in 1845 and by 1869 he had opened his first shop in Manchester. He called the business Brooke Bond & Co. because it seemed to him 'to sound so well', and not because anyone named Bond was involved. He began blending teas to obtain a consistent quality, which was appreciated by his customers, and encouraged by this success he opened shops in Liverpool, Leeds, Bradford and, later, London and Scotland. In the 1870s the business suffered from the depression and, apparently, from poor business decisions made by Brooke's brother-in-law Arthur Bushell.

In February 1876 Brooke applied for a trademark for the company's tea, spices and coffee (number 2,086) which, he

Brooke Bond's trademark number 2,086.

stated, had then been in use for three years. This trademark is no longer registered though others are still active.

In 1892 Brooke started to sell wholesale and turned the business into a limited company. After his death in 1918 he was succeeded in the business by his eldest son Gerald. During the early part of the twentieth century the firm expanded abroad and purchased tea plantations, and in 1956 started a series of long-running TV advertisements featuring 'talking' chimpanzees. The company was taken over in 1984 by the Anglo-Dutch giant Unilever, which by then also owned the Lipton tea business.

A 1905 trademark tells how to make Brooke Bond tea (number 276,097).

BROWN & POLSON'S CORNFLOUR

The Brown & Polson trademark is synonymous in Britain today with cornflour. It was John Polson who, in 1854, invented a process for making very pure starch from maize (British patent number 668) and he continued to invent, later taking out another six patents connected with the preparation of starch.

Together with William Brown, Polson set up a business in Paisley, Scotland, to make starch for the local shawl industry but it was edible starch that made their business a success. In 1936 Corn Products Co. Ltd (CPC), an affiliate of the American Corn Products Refining Company, acquired Brown & Polson. CPC became Bestfoods and was taken over by Unilever in 2001 but the Brown & Polson name was sold to Premier Ambient Products (UK) Ltd at the end of 2003.

Brown & Polson's triangle trademark (number 1,300).

Brown & Polson's 1905 trademark is an adaptation of the original triangle (number 269,614).

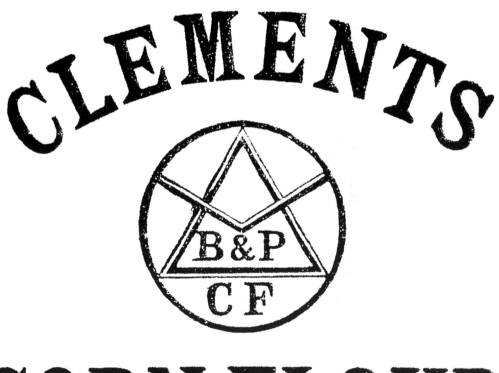

The company's products had been widely counterfeited in the nineteenth century so the firm was quick to register its first trademark (number 1,300) in 1876 – a triangle logo for starch and patent cornflour, which was claimed to have been used for about twenty years previously. Confusingly, in 1882 trademark number 28,984 (see page 103) was registered for cornflour to a company named William Polson & Co., also from Paisley, having been in use for five years.

BURGESS'S ANCHOVY PASTE

In 1760 John Burgess began selling imported luxury foods such as reindeer tongues, Dutch herrings and anchovies caught by fishing boats off Leghorn, and in 1788 the Burgess products were advertised in the first issue of the London *Times*. John established his first premises at 101 Strand, London, but this was soon outgrown and the business was moved to 107 Strand, where it stayed for 122 years.

Burgess's trademark number 7,993 displaying the royal coat of arms.

A show card from about 1890 includes the Burgess trademark. (*The Robert Opie Collection*)

In 1818 Lord Byron made reference to Burgess's anchovy sauce in his poem *Beppo*:

> And therefore humbly I would recommend
> 'The curious in fish-sauce,' before they cross
> The sea, to bid their cook, or wife, or friend,
> Walk or ride to the Strand, and buy in gross
> (Or if set out beforehand, these may send
> By any means least liable to loss).
> Ketchup, Soy, Chili-vinegar, and Harvey,
> Or by the Lord! a Lent will well nigh starve ye.

In 1850 and 1858 John Burgess & Co. took out injunctions against individuals who had copied the firm's labels and on 8 July 1876 the company applied for two trademarks (numbers 7,992–3). Number 7,993 is still registered for 'BURGESS'S Genuine Anchovy Paste' by John Burgess & Son Ltd of Edmonton, London.

At the turn of the twentieth century the company was sold to family relatives, the Brookes, and in 1954 Rayners, themselves old-established manufacturers of flavourings and essences, bought out the firm. In 1990 the business became part of the Hero group and then in 1997 a management buy-out resulted in the formation of the Rayner Food Group, comprising Rayner & Co. Ltd, Rayner Essence, Rayner Burgess, and Cauldron Foods.

Over the years the Burgess products have been taken far and wide: it was reported that Admiral Lord Nelson took some to the Battle of the Nile in 1798 and that in 1910 Captain Scott took some on his ill-fated Antarctic expedition.

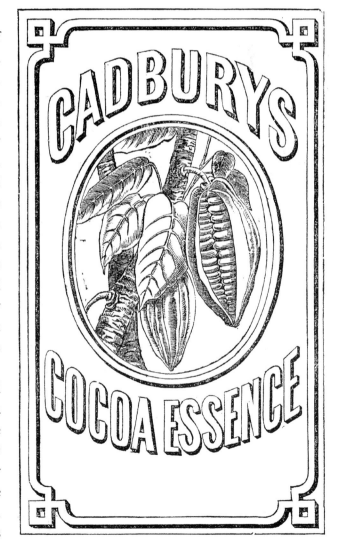

Cadbury's trademark number 1,682 showing cocoa growing.

CADBURY'S CHOCOLATE

In 1824 John Cadbury, the son of a prominent Quaker, opened a shop in Bull Street, Birmingham, to sell coffee, tea, hops, mustard, cocoa and drinking chocolate. In 1847 John took his brother Benjamin into partnership, forming Cadbury Brothers, and set up a new factory in the centre of Birmingham. Through the first half of the nineteenth century the price of cocoa beans fell slowly but the duty remained very high until it was reduced by Gladstone in 1853, after which chocolate sales rose and Cadbury's business flourished.

John's sons George and Richard took over the cocoa factory in 1861. To escape the pollution of the town, in 1879 George rebuilt the cocoa factory on a greenfield site outside Birmingham at Bournville, where the firm still produces

119

This modern-looking Cadbury's trademark from 1902 is still registered (number 245,779).

CADBURY Brothers, Limited.

A 1903 trademark for Cadbury's tea (number 247,971).

"*The essential particular of the Trade Mark is the combination of devices, and the applicants disclaim any right to the exclusive use of the added matter, except in so far as it consists of their own names*"

247,971. Tea. CADBURY BROTHERS, LIMITED, Bournville, near Birmingham ; Manufacturers. —7th August 1902.

An 1884 advertisement for Cadbury's cocoa. (*Illustrated London News*)

chocolate. George soon began to build high quality, affordable housing for the Cadbury workers. In 1919 Cadbury Brothers merged with J.S. Fry and the company became British Cocoa & Chocolate with a capital of £2.5 million. Until the merger with Schweppes plc in 1969, the Cadbury family held the majority of shares in the firm.

On 3 January 1876 the firm applied for two trademarks (numbers 1,681–2) for cocoa essence. Neither of these is still registered but the Cadbury and Cadbury Brothers trademarks from 1886, along with many other Cadbury marks, still are. Cadbury is now the world's biggest confectionery brand.

CALLARD & BOWSER'S BUTTERSCOTCH

Above: Callard & Bowser's first trademark (number 80).
Below: An 1878 trademark for Callard & Bowser showing the thistle logo (number 15,275).

One of the first firms to apply for a trademark when the British Trademark Registry opened its doors in January 1876 was Callard & Bowser. Daniel James Callard applied on 3 January for a Thistle trademark (number 80), which had been in use by the London wholesale confectioner for nine years for his company's butterscotch. The business had been established in 1837 and became well known for its butterscotch, toffee and other confectionery. At some time in the nineteenth century the firm took over Smith & Co., makers of Altoid mints, which are still widely sold in the United States and are advertised as the 'Original Celebrated Curiously Strong Peppermints'.

In the twentieth century the Callard & Bowser brand changed hands many times. Its owners included Arthur Guinness, Beatrice Foods, Terry's of York, Kraft and now, in the twenty-first

century, Wrigley. Ironically Callard & Bowser sweets are now very difficult to find in Britain but British trademark numbers 80 and the Callard & Bowser name (number 81,266) from 1888 are still maintained on the register.

A different style of Callard & Bowser trademark from 1880 (number 21,252).

CAMP COFFEE

Robert Campbell Patterson was a Glasgow merchant who sold provisions to households in the middle of the nineteenth century. In 1868 his son Campbell joined what was then R. Patterson & Sons and the firm started to produce sauces and fruit wines. In 1874, after Robert's death, the company was asked by the Gordon Highlanders to make a coffee drink that could be quickly prepared by the army in the field in India. Patterson's produced an essence of coffee-beans, chicory and sugar, and this first 'instant' coffee met with almost instant success.

Early advertisements and trademarks for the product showed British officers in their foreign field camps being

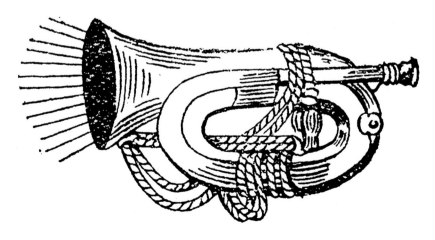

Camp coffee trademark number 279,880 is still registered.

A Camp coffee essence bottle label trademark from 1902 (number 244,990).

A Camp trademark from 1902 for coffee (number 245,120).

served coffee by servants, but it was not until 1906 that the word Camp was registered for coffee extracts, essences and mixtures thereof (number 284,174). This mark is still registered, as is the firm's other 1906 trademark (number 279,880) showing the image of a bugle. The coffee is now produced in Paisley, Scotland, and the trademarks are held by McCormick (UK), the American-owned spice, condiment and flavouring company.

CHICORY & COFFEE
ESSENCE
WITH ADDED SUGAR

A modern label for Camp coffee essence. The design is still very similar.

CARR'S CRACKERS

Jonathan Dodgson Carr was born into a Quaker family in Kendall, Westmoreland, in 1776. His father ran a grocery business but Jonathan became apprenticed to a baker and then set up a bakery on his own. In 1831 he moved to Carlisle with the idea of building a factory to produce bread. It took him six years to build his factory but the business of baking bread and also biscuits did well, especially after the coming of the railway to the town. In 1841 he was the first biscuit manufacturer to gain a royal warrant.

Jonathan's brothers worked in the business for a time and then his sons joined but they later fell out with each other in the difficult times following a succession of poor harvests in the

MILK CRACKER

1870s. After Jonathan's death, following a stroke, in 1884 the
milling and biscuit-baking businesses were run almost as separate
concerns by different branches of the family. The following year a
number of trademarks were taken out for biscuits, including
Costume, Menagerie, Hominy, CC, Kennel, Scotch Oaten and

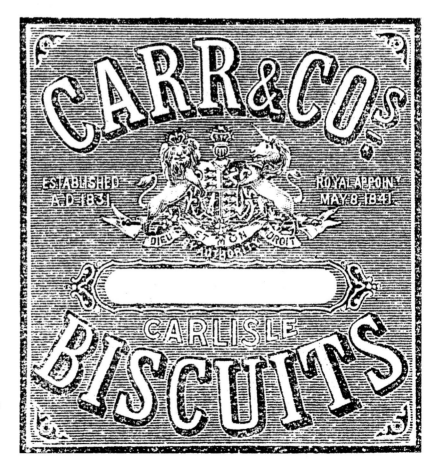

126

A 1901 British trademark for wafer biscuits destined for France (number 241,617).

Milk Cracker (number 45,517). At this time the firm was making 128 varieties of biscuit, producing 950 tons a year and employing a thousand workers.

The biscuit-making business was bought by Cavenhams in 1964 and became part of United Biscuits in 1972. Still the Carr family held some shares in the business and Ian Carr, a grandson of the founder, was chairman until 1997.

COLMAN'S MUSTARD

In 1804 Jeremiah Colman moved from the village of Bawburgh in Norfolk to the town of Norwich and bought a flour mill. Ten years later he was evidently making mustard because on 7 May 1814 this advertisement appeared in the *Norfolk Chronicle*: 'Jeremiah Colman, having taken the stock and trade lately carried on by Mr Edward Ames, respectfully informs his customers and the public

Colman's trademark
number 90.

in general that he will continue the manufacturing of mustard.'
From then the business grew to supply the whole of Britain with
this condiiment. When Jeremiah died, the business was taken over
by his great-nephew, also Jeremiah Colman, and in 1856 it was
moved to Carrow in Norwich where mustard is still made today.

The well-known Bull's Head logo appeared on the company's
English Mustard (presumably from the association of mustard
with beef) in about 1855 and was registered as the firm's
trademark in 1876 (numbers 90 and 91) for mustard, starch,
indigo and ultramarine blues. These trademarks have recently
expired but other similar marks have replaced them.

In 1866, the company was granted a royal warrant as
manufacturers to Queen Victoria. Rival mustard manufacturer
Keen, by then known as Keen, Robinson & Company, was bought
out in 1903. In 1938 the firm merged with Reckitt and the resulting
company, Reckitt & Colman, was bought out by Unilever in 1995.

28,787. MUSTARD AND TABLE-MUSTARD. J. & J. Colman, London, England. Filed July 20, 1896.

Essential feature.—The words "Colman's Durham Mustard," a bull's head, and a holly wreath. Used since 1862.

One of Colman's American trademarks registered in 1896.

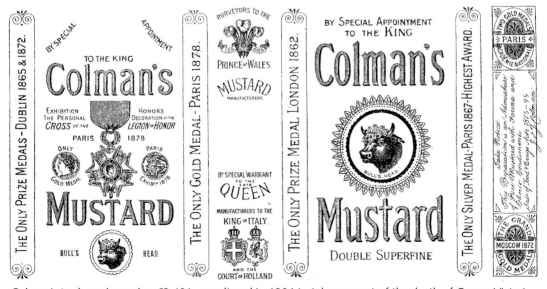

Colman's trademark number 63,401 was altered in 1904 to take account of the death of Queen Victoria.

Colman's 1900 trademark for Fairy Glaze starch (number 229,501).

CROSSE & BLACKWELL'S PICKLES

Two of the earliest trademarks to be registered in 1876 were those of Crosse & Blackwell, a name that is still familiar today. The original trademarks for 'pickles, sauces, jams, preserved fruits and provisions and the like' (numbers 301–2) are no longer in force, though others for the firm from 1925 and later still are. The company had its origins in the condiment business of West & Wyatt set up in London in 1706 but its name came from Edmund Crosse and Thomas Blackwell, who

"READY TO SERVE"

founded their company in 1830 and bought the Wyatt & West concern.

The firm became famous for its Branston pickle, itself registered in 1929. The name Branston was used because the recipe came from a Mrs Caroline Graham, who lived with her husband and daughters at Branston Lodge in Burton upon Trent in Staffordshire.

The firm of Crosse & Blackwell was bought in 1960 by Nestlé, which then sold the UK business to Premier International Foods in 2002, which owns other well-known food brands like Sarsons and Brown & Polson.

Above, left: Crosse & Blackwell's trademark number 302 showing the royal appointment.

Above: A 1920s show card for Crosse & Blackwell's soups. (*The Robert Opie Collection*)

EPICURE FOOD

Epicure, a brand known today for specialist foods, is owned by Petty Wood & Company. The original company was set up in Threadneedle Street, London, by Matthew Wood, who in 1816 started to import delicacies directly from abroad. Soon his friend

An Epicure Brand trademark from 1891 (number 158,797).

Mr Petty became a partner but later left the company and Matthew was joined by two cousins, William Wood and Henry Wood. William developed the firm and constructed offices and warehouses in Southward Bridge Road in London in 1879.

The Epicure name was first registered as a trademark in 1891 (number 158,797) and means someone who cultivates a refined taste for eating. This trademark only expired in 2003 but other Epicure trademarks are still registered by the company. The London warehouse was closed in 1974 and a new facility opened in Andover, Hampshire. The Wood family continued to run the business until 1992. Petty Wood had a turnover of £30 million in 2003 from its food distribution business selling Epicure pickles, condiments, vegetables, Turkish delight and other branded foods.

EXPRESS DAIRY

George Barham set up the Express Country Milk Supply in 1864 to bring fresh milk into London by train. The firm became the Express Dairy Company Ltd in 1882 and two years later applied for a trademark for a preparation of milk used as food (number

Express Dairy's
trademark number
38,712.

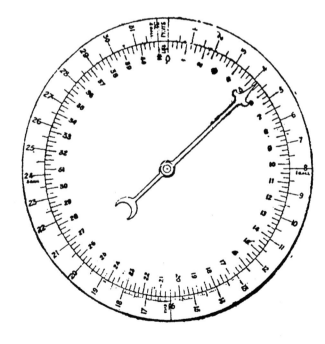

Spring balances chiefly applicable for milk. The dial is graduated for pints as well as lbs., so that the capacity of the fluid for which the balance is intended is shown as well as its weight.

The 1888 patent for milk scales invented by George Barham of the Express Dairy (GB 1,468).

133

38,712). George Barham has a number of British patents for inventions to his name, including a lactometer to detect adulteration of milk (GB 603 of 1880) and a scale for measuring and weighing milk (GB 1,468 of 1888). He is reported to be the inventor of the milk churn and set up a separate company to supply equipment to dairies. Express Dairy grew, purchasing an experimental dairy farm in Finchley, London, in 1890 and running Express tea-shops.

In 1969 the company was bought by Grand Metropolitan and sold on in 1992 to Northern Foods. After a de-merger Express Dairies merged again in 2003 with Arla Foods UK plc, a subsidiary of a Scandinavian company. Express was taken over by Dairy Crest in August 2006.

FRAY BENTOS CORNED BEEF

Fray Bentos trademark number 25,798 from 1881.

The Fray Bentos name became almost synonymous with corned beef in the UK until 1964, when an outbreak of typhoid in Aberdeen, Scotland, causing more than five hundred cases and

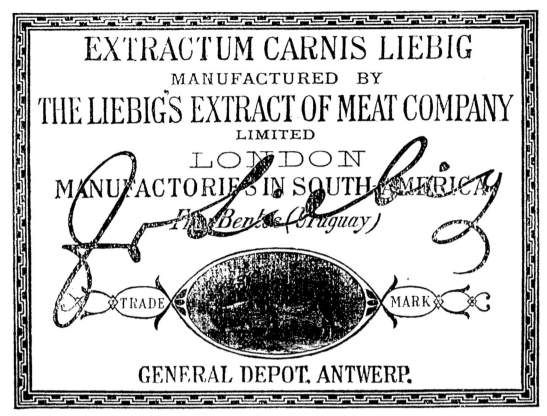

Liebig's first trademark (number 185).

three deaths, was linked to a tin of the meat. Sales of corned beef then fell dramatically as the Fray Bentos product was rejected by consumers.

The Fray Bentos trademark (number 25,798) was first registered for glue and extracts of meat in 1881 by the Liebig Extract of Meat Co., which had been created in 1865. Justus Liebig was a very influential chemist and teacher who, through his research and books, revolutionised food production in the nineteenth century. The company was set up to exploit Liebig's work on meat extraction in Fray Bentos, a small town in Uruguay, and successfully expanded until Liebig's death in 1873. At its peak the Fray Bentos factory employed four thousand people to slaughter six thousand cattle a day but the

Liebig's 1905 trademark for OXO (number 278,153).

135

enterprise closed in 1971 and was recently turned into an industrial museum.

The Liebig Extract of Meat Co. itself had earlier registered several trademarks, including number 185, in 1876 for meat extract. The company first registered the OXO trademark, derived from the word ox, for fluid beef in 1899 (number 221,355) and followed it by other OXO trademarks for chemicals, fermented liquors, spirits, aerated water and ginger beer, candles and many other products. Many OXO trademarks are now registered by Campbell Soup UK Ltd for its well-known gravy flavouring and other products. The company merged in 1968 with tea business Brooke Bond & Co.

FRY'S CHOCOLATE

The forerunner of Fry's business was started by Walter Churchman, an apothecary from Bristol, who was granted a patent in 1730 (GB 514) for an 'Engine for making chocolate'. The business passed to Walter's son Charles, and after his death in 1761 it was taken over by Dr Joseph Fry. Born in 1728 into a Quaker family, Fry was apprenticed to an apothecary in Basingstoke and then set up in business for himself in Bristol. As well as chocolate, Fry had interests in many other businesses. On

Fry's trademark number 46,802.

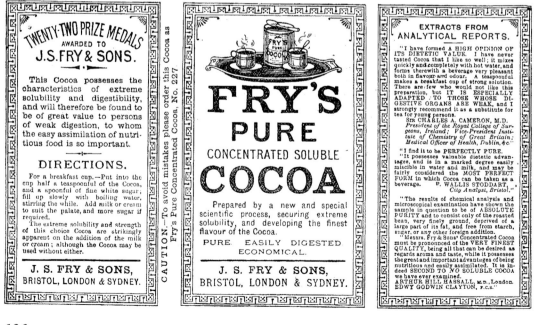

FRY'S MILK CHOCOLATE

One of Fry's Five Boys trademarks from 1903 (number 250,904).

A Fry's Five Boys cocoa trademark from 1903 (number 253,952).

his death in 1787, the chocolate business passed to his wife Anna and son Joseph Storrs Fry.

After Anna's death in 1803, her son went into partnership with Dr Hunt and the business became Fry & Hunt, but after Hunt's retirement Joseph Storrs' three sons Joseph, Francis and Richard became partners and it became J.S. Fry & Sons. In 1847 the firm discovered a way to mix cocoa butter back into pressed cocoa creating a paste that could be moulded into a chocolate bar. By 1886 the Fry's Chocolate Cream bar was in production and this remained a hugely popular product for years to come.

In 1885 the firm applied for a trademark for Fry's Pure Concentrated Soluble Cocoa (number 46,802), which remained on the register until 1998. J.S. Fry & Sons Ltd merged with Cadbury in 1919. In the 1930s production was moved to a new factory built at Somerdale, between Bristol and Bath, where chocolate now leaves the door at the rate of 50,000 tonnes per year. Present-day trademarks, which are owned by Cadbury, include J.S. Fry & Sons, Fry's Five Boys and Fry's Turkish Delight.

HEINZ FOOD

Henry John Heinz was born in 1844 near Pittsburgh, Pennsylvania, and by the age of 8 he was working in his father's brickyard. He also started growing his own vegetables and at the age of 12 was selling them to local shopkeepers. In 1869 Heinz and Clarence Noble began the firm of Heinz & Noble selling grated horseradish bottled in clear glass to show its quality. The business did well and registered two American trademarks in 1873 but in the banking panic of 1875 it was forced into bankruptcy.

Heinz started up again, this time with brother John and cousin Frederick, and was soon producing tomato ketchup and other sauces and pickles. In 1886 Heinz travelled to London, where he went to Fortnum & Mason – which accepted all the seven varieties of product he offered. Ten years later a London office was opened. At this time Heinz adopted the 57 Varieties mark and in 1899 H.J. Heinz & Co., as it was then known, applied to register a British trademark (number 222,302).

In the first part of the twentieth century factories were opened in Peckham and Harlesden in London. Henry Heinz died of pneumonia in 1919 and the business was taken over by his son Howard, followed in 1946 by his grandson H.J. 'Jack' Heinz II, who was chairman of the company until his death in 1987. Today the H.J. Heinz Company sells five thousand varieties of food products in two hundred countries and the Heinz brand is valued at almost $7 billion.

Heinz trademark number 222,302 of 1899.

33,551. CERTAIN NAMED FOOD PRODUCTS. HENRY J. HEINZ, Pittsburg, Pa. Filed Mar. 11, 1899.

Essential feature.—The representation of a cluster of fruit and a cucumber isolated therefrom. Used since March, 1898.

A Heinz American trademark from 1898.

HORLICK'S MALTED MILK

James Horlick was born in 1844 in Ruardean in Gloucestershire and qualified as a pharmacist in 1869. He formulated a milk food for infants and in 1873 joined his brother William in America, where they formed a partnership to produce the food in Chicago. Production was moved to Wisconsin in 1875.

In 1883 William obtained a patent (US 278,967) for a granulated food for infants and invalids prepared from barley malt, cereal and milk. James returned to England in 1890 to import this food and later set up a factory to make it at Slough in Berkshire. The following year a British trademark was registered (number 156,036) and this remains in force today.

In 1921, after James's death, the firm split into two: one covering the Americas, run by William, and the other Britain and the rest of the world, run by James's sons. In 1945 the British

Horlick's trademark number 156,036.

140

A leaflet for Horlicks from about 1900 includes the 1891 trademark. (*The Robert Opie Collection*)

firm, Horlicks Malted Milk Co., acquired the American branch and in 1969 it was bought out by Beecham's, now Glaxo SmithKline. Though Horlicks is no longer so popular in the USA or Britain, it is widely drunk in many parts of Asia.

W.H. & F.J. Horniman & Co.

Horniman's original
trademark number
1,123.

HORNIMAN'S TEA

John Horniman set up as a tea merchant in London in 1826. He was possibly the first merchant to sell tea in packets, which helped to protect his product from adulteration and his brand from counterfeiting.

His son Frederick John carried on the business and at the age of 60 began collecting, inspired by his interest in natural history, archaeology, anthropology and musical instruments. While many of the other tea traders of the time collected while travelling on business, it seems that most of Horniman's collection was purchased through auction houses. When the collection outgrew his house in Forest Hill he commissioned architect Charles Townsend to design a new museum in south London, which he gave to the people of London in 1901. It is still open today. By the turn of the twentieth century Horniman was the largest supplier of tea in the world.

A trademark bearing the name W.H. & F.J. Horniman was taken out in 1876 (number 1,123) and kept in force until 2002. W.H. Horniman may have been another of John's sons but he does not feature in their annals. Other trademarks still protect Horniman tea. Horniman's was sold to Lyons in 1918 and then, as part of the Tetley tea group, was acquired by the Indian company Tata in 2000.

HP SAUCE

Edwin Samson Moore had worked for a pickle manufacturer in Portsmouth, Hampshire, and for the Cambrian Vinegar Co., but he wanted to set up his own business. After persuading his cousin Edward Eastwood to provide some capital, he bought the Birmingham branch of Cambrian Vinegar and established the Midland Vinegar Company at Tower Road, Aston Cross, Birmingham, in 1875.

The original Horniman trademark appears on the tea chest but is not prominent in this trade card from about 1895. (*The Robert Opie Collection*)

HP trademark
number 254,988.

Moore sold his vinegar to grocer's shops, including that of Mr F.G. Garton in Nottingham, who used it to produce Garton's HP Sauce. Garton claimed that a bottle of his sauce had been seen in a restaurant at the Houses of Parliament and hence he adopted the abbreviation HP. On a visit to Garton's shop Moore cancelled the outstanding debt owed by the grocer and instead paid him £150 for the recipe and name. Demand for the sauce was high and there was a problem in keeping up the production, so an adjoining property was acquired to enable expansion.

In 1903 the Midland Vinegar Co. and F.G. Garton applied jointly for a trademark that depicted the Houses of Parliament

Certificate of Analysis.

Dear Sirs,

I beg to report that I have Analysed the sample of Garton's Sauce received from you on the 18th inst., and find it to be made from the best materials.

The well-known MIDLAND VINEGAR COMPANY'S Vinegar, than which, in my opinion, there is no better in the market, is used in its preparation. It is of a pleasant and piquant flavour, and is in every respect a thoroughly Good Sauce.

Yours faithfully,

A. Bostock Hill

County Analyst

M.D., D.P.H., F.I.C.

MIDLAND VINEGAR C°
BIRMINGHAM
ENGLAND

HOUSES OF PARLIAMENT

IS a combination of the choicest **ORIENTAL FRUITS SPICES AND PURE MALT VINEGAR** blended with the utmost care to ensure a **DIGESTIVE RELISH** even for the most fickle appetite; this object having been attained by years of practical experience in the Sauce Trade.

MANUFACTURED BY

MIDLAND VINEGAR C°
BIRMINGHAM
ENGLAND

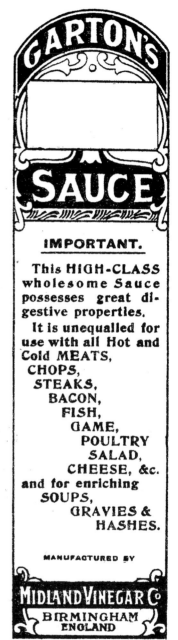

IMPORTANT.

This HIGH-CLASS wholesome Sauce possesses great digestive properties.

It is unequalled for use with all Hot and Cold MEATS, CHOPS, STEAKS, BACON, FISH, GAME, POULTRY SALAD, CHEESE, &c. and for enriching SOUPS, GRAVIES & HASHES.

MANUFACTURED BY

MIDLAND VINEGAR C°
BIRMINGHAM
ENGLAND

(number 254,988). In the previous year the two companies had applied for a trademark for Garton's Dominica Lime Juice Cordial (number 244,061) but presumably sales of this product did not match those of HP Sauce. Soon HP Sauce was exported worldwide as salesmen were sent round the British Empire.

Garton's HP Sauce trademark from 1905 (number 275,689).

GARTON'S "DOMINICA" LIME JUICE CORDIAL

This Lime Juice is made from the Finest West Indian Limes, and makes a very refreshing beverage with Spirits, Soda, Potash, and all Aerated Waters.
MANUFACTURED BY F. G. GARTON & Co.,
ASTON MANOR, ENGLAND.

A Garton's Lime Juice Cordial trademark from 1902 (number 244,061), demonstrating that the firm made other products besides HP Sauce.

Edwin Samson Moore retired in 1921 and died seven years later. In 1924 the business was floated by the British Shareholders Trust with issued capital of £560,000 and in 1930 it merged with Lea & Perrin. The trademarks are now owned by HP Foods Ltd, part of Heinz, which recently announced transfer of production from Aston to Holland.

HUNTLEY & PALMER'S BISCUITS

Huntley and Palmer, known worldwide for its biscuits and its biscuit tins, was among the first companies to register its

Huntley & Palmer's
first trademark
(number 2,713).

trademarks when the Trade Mark Registry opened its doors in 1876. Two trademarks were registered (numbers 2,713–14), the first of which is still registered today.

Joseph Huntley was born in 1775 into a Quaker family. His father was a headmaster while his mother, by all accounts, baked biscuits in the school oven and sold them outside the school gates. Joseph became a schoolmaster but after being widowed he opened a bakery in Reading, Berkshire, in 1822. His son Thomas, who had completed a two-year apprenticeship at a bakery, made the biscuits while Joseph ran the business. By 1829 the firm was known as Huntley & Son but in 1841, three years after his father's retirement, Thomas went into partnership with fellow Quaker George Palmer. At this time the firm had a mere eight employees.

George Palmer was born in 1818 and as soon as he was 14 he was apprenticed to his uncle, a confectioner and miller in Taunton. At 22 George moved to Reading and in 1841 he paid £550 for a half-share of the Huntley business, which then became Huntley & Palmer. George Palmer brought business acumen to the firm and later became Member of Parliament for Reading. Within two years of joining with Huntley he had set up the first continuous machinery for making fancy biscuits. By the turn of the century the firm was the largest biscuit manufacturer in the world and employed five thousand people. Distinctive biscuit tins bearing the famous Huntley & Palmer trademarks were made for the firm by Huntley, Boorne and Stevens, a company founded by another member of the Huntley family.

In the twentieth century Huntley & Palmer, together with two other famous biscuit manufacturers that had originated in the nineteenth century, Peek Frean and W. & R. Jacobs, became part of Associated Biscuit Manufacturers. In 1982 the firm was bought by the American manufacturer Nabisco (originally the National Biscuit Company). Since 1994 it has been part of the French group Danone. The Huntley & Palmer name still lives on through many actively used trademarks.

W. & R. JACOB'S BISCUITS

The biscuit-making firm W. & R. Jacob was set up by Quaker brothers William and Robert Jacob in Waterford, Ireland, in 1851 and moved to Dublin shortly afterwards. The company grew to be the second-largest employer in Dublin after

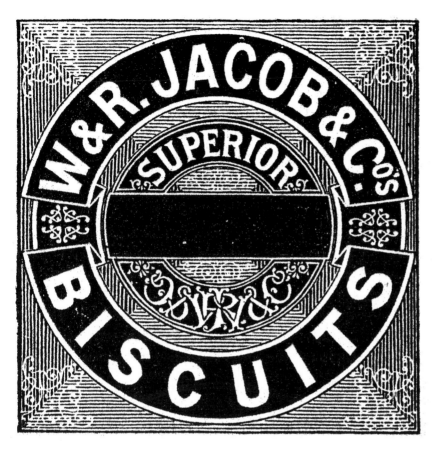

Jacob's trademark
number 27,424 from
1882.

Guinness, and in Quaker tradition the workers were well looked after and provided with facilities such as a canteen, a doctor and even a roof garden. Despite this, Jacob's workers joined the Great Strike and Lock-Out in 1913 and were the last to return to work.

Jacob's biscuits became famous across the British Isles and across the world. In 1882 the firm took out a British trademark (number 27,424) for 'substances used as food or ingredients in food, namely biscuits'. The oldest trademarks still registered by the firm are numbers 65,822 for W. & R. Jacob & Co. and 65,823 for Jacob & Co.'s Biscuits, both dating from 1887. Nowadays the firm is particularly known for its fig rolls and its cream crackers, but it is owned by French food giant Danone.

This leaflet from about 1890 for Jacob's Cream Crackers shows a modification of the circular trademark on the box. (*The Robert Opie Collection*)

There is a change of style on this modern Jacob's biscuit packet.

KEEN'S MUSTARD

The firm's 1878 trademark (number 13,591) states that mustard itself was being used before William Shakespeare's day, by using a quotation from *The Taming of the Shrew*, and also states that Keen's mustard had been made since 1742. The expression 'keen as mustard' first appeared in the seventeenth century, according to the *Oxford English Dictionary*, and so, though probably not as early as Shakespeare, pre-dates Keen's mustard. The saying was certainly a useful advertisement for the firm, even if it wasn't its own tagline. The firm's first trademarks (numbers 6,591–3) registered in 1876 featured shell logos, and these continued to be used within later trademarks.

The company which produced the mustard was Keen, Robinson, Belville & Co., a famous producer of barley water in Victorian times. It had also applied for another mark for Keen's Mustard in 1887 (number 61,861), which is still registered today. At that time the firm was described as a 'mustard manufacturer, patent barley and patent groat manufacturer, indigo and ultramarine blue manufacturer, chicory and spice

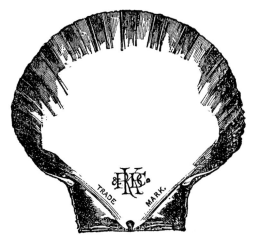

grinder &c'. In 1903 Keen, Robinson & Co. was taken over by rival starch and mustard manufacturer J. & J. Colman, later to become Reckitt & Colman, which in turn became part of Unilever. Today Keen's mustard is much less well known than Robinson's Barley Water drink, which is often associated in people's minds with the Wimbledon tennis championships.

One of Keen's shell trademarks (number 6,592).

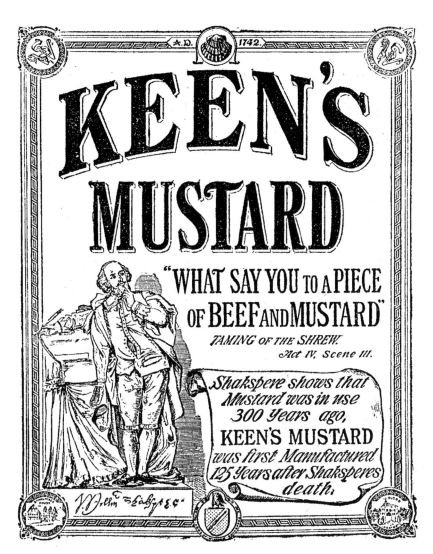

Keen's 1878 trademark (number 13,591) contains a shell logo at the top.

KEILLER'S MARMALADE

Legend has it that James Keiller – or rather his wife Janet – invented marmalade. In the 1770s James heard that a vessel carrying a cargo of Seville oranges was seeking refuge from a storm in the River Tay near Dundee, and he purchased the lot to pass on to Janet to sell. Instead of selling the bitter oranges Janet cooked the fruit and produced Dundee marmalade. In fact, marmalade has been known since at least the sixteenth century, long before this alleged incident. What the Keillers did was to produce and popularise marmalade containing the bitter peel. In 1797 James Keiller set up his firm, which became James Keiller & Son in 1828 when he was joined in the business by James Jr. James Sr died in 1839 and it seems that the business was then run for over twenty years by his second wife Margaret.

In 1864 Wedderspoon Keiller, who later died at the age of 33 at the firm's outpost in the Channel Islands, obtained a patent for his

Keiller's trademark
number 2,820.

153

process of preparing marmalade using machinery for pulping the fruit. Despite several family feuds along the way, the firm's marmalade increased in popularity and in 1876 the firm was granted trademark number 2,820 for James Keiller & Son's Dundee Marmalade. This mark shows the City of Dundee coat of arms and the medals won for the product. It is no longer in force but the name James Keiller & Son Est. 1797 Dundee is still registered.

The current marks are owned by Centura Foods Ltd, part of the RHM food manufacturing group. Centura also own marks for another well-known marmalade brand, Robertson's.

The Keiller's jar label on this 1930s display shows a few similarities with the original version. (*The Robert Opie Collection*)

LEA & PERRINS' SAUCE

Lea & Perrins' trademark number 4.

Few trademark signatures are as famous throughout the world as those on Lea and Perrins' sauce bottles. A series of marks for the Worcestershire sauce bearing the signatures were deposited at the British Trade Mark Registry on the day it opened its doors on 1 January 1876 and numbers 4–9 were assigned to it.

In 1842 sales amounted to 636 bottles but by 1855 some 30,000 bottles were being sold. Currently approximately 25 million bottles a year roll off the production lines in Worcestershire – but it could all have been very different. The legend is that it was first produced at Lea & Perrins' chemists in 1835 from a sauce known in India, where Lord Sandys, Governor of Bengal, obtained the recipe. Back home, Sandys passed the formula to Lea and Perrins, who tried to replicate it. But the combination of vinegar, sugar, molasses, salt, anchovies, onions, garlic, tamarinds and spices apparently tasted so dire that they put it in a stoneware crock in their basement and forgot about it. Eventually, when it was rediscovered, the blend had fermented into the hot sauce known today. Certainly Lord Sandys had his seat in Ombersley, about 10 kilometres from Worcester, but the assertion that he was Governor of Bengal is dubious.

John Wheeley Lea was born in 1791 and William Henry Perrins two years later, both into farming families of seven children. Both young men started to train as chemists, Lea in Worcester and Perrins in nearby Evesham. In 1822 they set up in business together, opening their first shop in 1823.

In 1930 Lea and Perrins merged with its distributor, the manufacturer of HP Sauce. Although the trademarks are still registered to Lea and Perrins Ltd, the firm is now owned by Heinz.

Top, right: A tin label for Lea & Perrins from about 1870. (*The Robert Opie Collection*)
Right: After 130 years bottle labels still display the Lea & Perrins signature.

MACONOCHIE'S PRESERVED FOOD

The firm of Maconochie Brothers was set up by Archibald and James Maconochie to can fish at Lowestoft, Suffolk, in 1873. In 1877 the firm applied for the first of many trademarks for its food products (number 13,862) and the following year others for Yarmouth Sardines, Sardine Mackerel and English Sardines (numbers 15,870–2). Soon they were producing other 'preserved provisions' including bottled fruit (such as shown in trademark 46,406).

The company became well known during the First World War when it supplied rations for the troops. 'Maconochie' became a

Maconochie's trademark for bottled fruit (number 46,406).

156

synonym for tinned meat and vegetable stew. The soldiers either loved it or hated it – mostly the latter. Maconochie had food-processing plants on the Isle of Dogs in London, in Hull, Yorkshire, and elsewhere.

One of its most famous brands was Pan Yan pickle, the name being chosen as a result of a competition among its London workers and registered in 1903. The Pan Yan mark is now owned by Premier Ambient Products and the only remaining Maconochie mark – for Maconochie's Herrings in Tomato – is now owned by International Fish Canners (Scotland) Ltd of Fraserburgh, Aberdeenshire.

MARMITE YEAST EXTRACT

The Marmite Food Extract Company Ltd was formed in 1902 to exploit a process developed in Dresden, Germany, to make a spread from spent yeast. The company rented a disused malt-house in Burton upon Trent, one of the major centres of brewing

Marmite trademark number 249,997.

A present-day
Marmite jar showing
a slightly changed
logo.

in Britain. British brewer's yeast was different from the continental type and changes in the manufacturing process had to be made before a yeast extract product was ready to be put on sale.

On 15 November 1902 the company applied to register its first trademark (number 249,997) for 'a concentrated preparation, being an article of food'. Marmite was sold in small earthenware pots, of a type that was illustrated in the trademark and also appears on the glass jars used since the 1920s. The origin of the word Marmite is the cooking pot of the same name used in France.

The popularity of Marmite increased and in 1907 a new factory was opened at Camberwell Green in London. In the 1930s the Marmite company was acquired by Bovril, which was bought in 1971 by Cavenham. The brand eventually ended up with Unilever, which now holds many Marmite trademarks, including number 321,670 from 1910, which shows the identical pot of spread used in the first trademark but with the omission of the original company name. Sales of Marmite are now about £23 million every year.

McDOUGALL'S FLOUR

Today, McDougall's is a well-known brand of self-raising flour. (This is flour that contains baking soda and, usually, an acidic phosphate to enable dough and baked products to rise without yeast.) In 1879 McDougall Brothers applied for a trademark (number 20,826) for their self-raising flour, claiming the brand had been in use since before 1867. The brothers Alexander, Isaac, James Thomas, John and Arthur had all worked in the family business, a chemical works, since they were old enough to help, although the two eldest, Alexander and Isaac, had tried to run away to America to escape their kindly but autocratic father. This episode obliged their father to retire from the business and accept the sale of the firm to the sons for a sum of £36,000 over twelve years, later increased to £40,000 when they were late paying some of the instalments!

The father, also called Alexander, was born in 1809 in Coldstream, on the Scottish border, and later became a teacher in Carlisle. He had a strong interest in science. In 1833 he married and set up home in Manchester, where he continued to teach until about 1846. His interest in things scientific continued and in 1845 he was granted a patent (the first of many) for 'Certain improvements in the method of working atmospheric Railways, which improvements are also applicable to Canals and Rivers'. In 1846 his interest in science prevailed and he set up a chemical works in Manchester, where, helped by his sons, he set up a process to recover grease from the water used in washing wool and cotton. The grease was then to be used to make soap for washing fibres. He also manufactured potash and soda, obtained various products from bones and later prepared insecticides for use on sheep. Other experiments led to substitutes for yeast in baking.

McDougall's flour trademark (number 20,826).

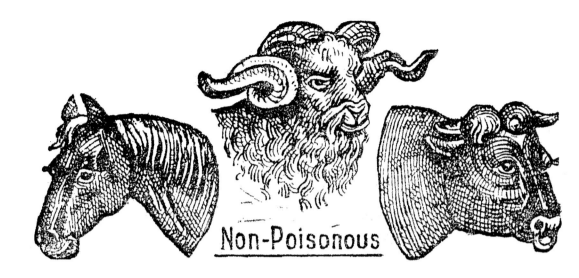

Non-Poisonous

Arthur, the seventh of the thirteen children, is credited with the invention of self-raising flour, though this invention was never patented. In 1862 one of the younger siblings noted that brother Arthur was still at college every day except Sunday but that he was 'very anxious about some gun-powder he has made'. In 1865 an aunt wrote from New York, 'We are pleased to hear of Arthur's success at college and hope that McDougall's Phosphatic Yeast Substitute will be a profitable success.' Around this time one part of the family business was in flour milling and it is said that this business was set up when the family was unable to sell their baking powder to local millers. Milling became a key part of the business and by 1869 the family had set up the Wheatsheaf Mill in the East End of London.

The eldest of the brothers, Alexander, continued in the business but spent much of his time trying to improve the lot of the poor. He was a Manchester City Alderman and Justice of the Peace until his death in 1909. One of the later McDougalls, Sir Robert, continued the educational work of the family through the McDougall Trust.

In 1961 McDougall became part of Rank Hovis McDougall (RHM), one of the largest bakers and food producers in the UK. The McDougall brand for flour is still owned by the RHM group and is used to this day.

NESTLÉ'S MILK FOOD

The company Nestlé was founded in Switzerland and is known throughout the world for its food and drink products. Its trademark, a bird feeding its young in the nest, is almost as well known. The trademark was originally the coat of arms of the firm's founder Henri Nestlé, because in Swiss German the word Nestlé means 'little nest'. He

was born in Frankfurt in 1814, and moved to Vevey in Switzerland in his 20s, becoming a pharmacist and inventor.

Nestlé's trademark for baby milk (number 1,200).

Henri experimented with combinations of cow's milk, flour and sugar as an alternative source of nutrition for infants whose mothers were unable to breastfeed, producing a formula in 1867 that he called 'Farine Lactée Henri Nestlé'. It is said that the first customer was a premature baby boy who had been given up for lost by doctors because he could not tolerate either his mother's milk or any of the available substitutes. Astonishingly, the boy survived on Henri's new formula

A Nestlé trademark for condensed milk from 1903 did not include the company name (number 255,011).

and demand rocketed. In 1868 Henri set up an office in London and was soon exporting outside Europe. Nestlé was one of the first trademarks to be registered in Britain in January 1876 (number 1,200 for milk food) and in 1884 the nest logo itself was registered.

The Nestlé Company was purchased by Jules Monnerat in 1875. At about this time it started to produce condensed milk to compete with the Anglo-Swiss Condensed Milk Company, which had started to produce infant foods in competition with Nestlé. The two rivals merged in 1905 under the name 'Nestlé & Anglo-Swiss Milk Company'. The firm expanded into chocolate and coffee and later into other products, more recently acquiring cosmetics company L'Oréal in 1974 and British confectioner Rowntree in 1991.

PEEK FREAN'S BISCUITS
In 1857 James Peek and George Hender Frean set up the company Peek Frean & Co. in the Bermondsey area of London to

Peek Frean's first trademark, number 3,996.

manufacture biscuits. By 1861 they were exporting biscuits to Australia, soon afterwards to South America and India and in the 1870s to Canada.

In 1876 the company registered its first British trademark for biscuits (number 3,996), which had then been in use for fifteen years. By then James Peek had left the firm and been replaced by other partners. Many more trademarks followed, of which number 182,469 for 'Peek Frean & Co. Limited' from 1894 is the earliest still registered.

In 1921 Peek Frean joined Huntley & Palmer in becoming a subsidiary of Associated Biscuit Manufacturers Ltd, which was purchased by Nabisco in 1982. In 1994 it became part of the French group Danone. Mrs Peek's Christmas pudding, currently a best-selling brand in the UK, was first made by James's wife in Bermondsey over a century ago.

AIGRETTE

A 1901 trademark for Peek Frean's biscuits, cakes and other food products (number 236,129).

QUAKER OATS

Henry D. Seymour and William Heston started the Quaker Mill Company in Ravenna, Ohio, in 1877. It is said that Seymour had been searching for a name for his business and was impressed by the qualities of purity and honesty associated with the Quakers and so chose Quaker as the product name. The Society of Friends objected to the use of the name for a business and petitioned Congress to stop its use but was unsuccessful.

The Quaker
packaging trademark
(number 182,569)
from 1894.

The firm was soon being run by Henry Crowell, who quickly gained sales by advertising and by packaging the oats in one or two pound paper packages with cooking instructions, as shown in British trademark number 182,569. In the late 1880s the firm merged with other American cereal mills run by Robert Stuart from Iowa and Chicago and Ferdinand Schumacher from Akron, Ohio. The American Cereal Company, as it became, applied for three British trademarks in 1894: one for the Quaker name, showing an image of a Quaker man holding a scroll bearing the inscription 'pure', and two for the Quaker packaging (numbers 180,403–4 and 182,569). In 1901 the firm became the Quaker Oats Company and was run by Robert Stuart and succeeding generations of the Stuart family until 1979. In August 2001 Quaker, with worldwide sales of over $5 billion, merged with PepsiCo Inc. The three British trademarks from 1894 are still registered to Quaker Oats Ltd.

The illustration of the Quaker has changed in this 1904 trademark for oat biscuits (number 268,374).

164

ROBERTSON'S MARMALADE

James Robertson first worked in a thread mill but soon became apprenticed to a grocer in Paisley, Scotland. In 1859, after three years' apprenticeship, he set up his own grocery business in Causide Street. The story is told that James took pity on a struggling salesman and bought a barrel of bitter oranges. He decided, along with his wife Marion, to produce marmalade to sell in the shop and this was a great success. The recipe, which was gradually perfected, managed to reduce the bitterness while retaining the tanginess of the fruit.

The business grew and the marmalade was sent to England and then to other parts of the world. In November 1882 James Robertson took out his first trademark for Queens Golden Shred marmalade (number 29,708), Golden Shred and Silver Shred becoming the firm's main trademarks.

James Robertson & Sons Ltd moved to its present jam works in Droylsden, Manchester, in 1890. It was in 1910 that the firm adopted the Golliwog black doll logo (see colour plate 6) after it had been popularised by Bertha and Florence Upton in their books for children written between 1895 and 1909. In 1928 Robertson's introduced the Golly brooch collector scheme, which

Robertson's trademark for Queen's Golden Shred (number 29,708).

A Victorian jar of Golden Shred marmalade. (The Robert Opie Collection)

became the longest-running collector-scheme in history, only coming to an end in 2001 – by which time the symbol had become politically incorrect and, according to some, racist.

The current marks are owned by Centura Foods Ltd, part of the RHM food manufacturing group. Centura also owns marks for other famous marmalade brands including James Keiller.

SARSON'S VINEGAR

Thomas Sarson started the Sarson's Vinegar business in London in 1794. Thomas's son Henry James took over from his father in 1850 when he was 25.

In 1884 Henry Sarson & Co. at the vinegar works in the City Road, London, registered the trademark Sarson's Virgin Vinegar

Sarson's trademark of 1884 (number 37,223).

166

A show card for Sarson's vinegar, *c.* 1915. (*The Robert Opie Collection*)

(number 37,223), which was apparently inspired by the parable of the wise and foolish virgins, though why the wise virgins would put vinegar in their lamps is a mystery! This trademark was dropped in the 1950s, though other Sarson's trademarks remain on the register.

Sarson's Virgin Vinegar was initially sold mainly through greengrocers alongside vegetables either as a dressing or for pickling, and sales were good. Henry's sons Henry Logsdail and Percival Stanley continued to run Sarson's as a family business. In 1932 Sarson's amalgamated with other vinegar manufacturers to form British Vinegars Ltd, but the Sarson's brand continued in use. Today the firm sells over 7 million gallons of vinegar every year but is owned by Premier Ambient Products (UK) Ltd.

SPRATT'S DOG FOOD

James Spratt was an American electrician from Cincinnati who set off for England to sell lightning conductors some time in the middle of the nineteenth century. In 1860 he was granted a British patent for lightning conductors. He was

Spratt's trademark for dog cakes (number 70).

evidently something of an inventor, already having filed a provisional patent for strengthening paper by adding threads to the pulp. Later more patents were to be granted to Spratt.

The story goes that on his arrival at the quayside in England Spratt saw stray dogs feeding off hard tack biscuits that had been discarded from ships along the docks. From this he was inspired to produce the first biscuits especially for dogs. Spratt's dog cake was made by mixing wheat-meal with rendered meat and vegetables, and then baking the mixture. James Spratt patented his dog food in 1861 and later received patents for a machine for cutting hay (1865), feed for horses (and humans) containing dates (1868), packages of coffee and tea (1870) and for cat food (1872).

On 1 January 1876 the trademarks numbers 69–76 were registered for dog biscuits, dog soap and preparations for feeding dogs, cats, poultry and other animals by Spratt's Patent Ltd at Spratt's Patent Biscuit Works in London. Spratt's Patent Meat Fibrine Dog Cakes were sold as a superior way to feed pets. Fresh beef, Spratt claimed, could 'overheat the dog's blood' and even the most wholesome 'table scraps will break down his digestive powers [making] him prematurely old and fat'.

Top, right: Spratt's trademark for game and poultry meal (number 71).

Right: By 1903 Spratt's was packaging Poplar brand beans for human consumption (number 251,236).

After leaving college in 1876, Charles Cruft became an employee of James Spratt, selling dog cakes for Spratt in Holborn, London, and was soon promoted to travelling salesman. By 1891 Cruft had set up the eponymous dog show in London.

In the early twentieth century Spratts dog cakes and puppy biscuits were being sold throughout Europe and the USA. Spratts was later taken over by Spillers, which was itself acquired by the milling and food concern Dalgety in 1979. Dalgety then sold its petfood business for £715 million to Nestlé in 1988. Spratt's branded dog food has since been discontinued, though its trademarks are still registered.

SUCHARD'S CHOCOLATE

Suchard's trademark number 14,181.

Philippe Suchard was born in 1797 in Boudry, Switzerland, and in 1815 he started work as an apprentice confectioner with his

Suchard's 1907 trademark featuring a Swiss scene with a St Bernard dog (number 288,176).

elder brother Frédéric in Berne. In 1824 he left to sell Swiss products in the United States but he met with little success and at the end of the year returned to Switzerland to open a confectioner's business in Neuchâtel. He produced between 25 and 30 kilograms of chocolate bars each day with the help of a single assistant.

In 1878 Philippe Suchard applied for his first British trademark for Chocolat Suisse (number 14,181). He opened the first foreign branch in Lorrach, Germany, in 1880 but just four years later he died. Milk chocolate was introduced by

Suchard in the 1890s and in 1901 the trademark Milka (derived from Milch and Kakao) was registered in Britain (number 239,542).

The Suchard company and Swiss chocolate maker Tobler merged in 1970 and in 1992 the firm merged again with coffee-maker Jacobs. The resulting Jacobs Suchard company was acquired by Kraft General Foods International for $4.1 billion in 1993.

SWINBORNE'S GELATINE

Swinborne's gelatine is not a product that is used now but in its day it was well known. George Swinborne was born in 1822 in Coggeshall, Essex, but by 1847 he was living in Pimlico, Middlesex (now London), and took out an English patent (GB 11,975) for the 'Manufacture of gelatinous substances; apparatus to be used therein', and in 1848 obtained a similar patent in Scotland for 'Certain improvements in the manufacture of gelatinous substances'. George Swinborne claimed that his process of producing gelatine was far simpler than existing

Swinborne's grandiose lion and unicorn trademark, number 12,852.

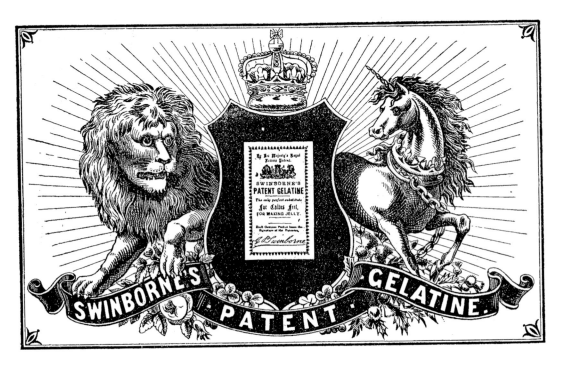

methods and that the resulting product was of the best quality, suitable for culinary purposes. He reduced pieces of hide to thin shavings which were first soaked in cold water then in hot. The resulting gelatine was strained through linen fabric then run into thin films, dried on nets and cut into narrow strips for use.

Soon after taking out the patents he returned to Coggeshall to put his process to work commercially and in 1848 took in a partner, Richard Archer Wallington of Leamington, and the firm became Swinborne, Wallington & Co. The trademarks for Swinborne's Patent Gelatine and Isinglass (numbers 12,850–2) were registered in 1878 to G.P. Swinborne & Co. George Swinborne died in 1883 but the factory continued producing isinglass (a pure form of gelatine) in Coggeshall until 1999.

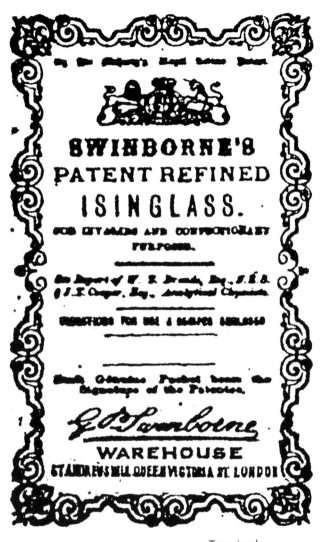

Two simple trademarks were registered by Swinborne for isinglass (number 12,851) and for gelatine.

TATE & LYLE SUGAR

Henry Tate was born in Chorley, Lancashire, in 1819, the seventh son of a clergyman. At 13 he became apprenticed to a grocer and then worked on his own and by 1855 he had a chain of six shops. In 1859 he became a partner of John Wright, the owner of a sugar refinery in Manesty Lane, Liverpool. Three years later he sold his shops and opened his own refinery in Earle Street.

By 1869 the partnership had dissolved and Henry took his two sons Alfred and Edwin into the business, which then became Henry Tate & Sons. A new refinery was built in Love Lane in 1872 and within ten years it was processing over 1,100 tons of

Lyle's original lion trademark, number 40,178.

sugar a year. Meanwhile Tate had also set up a refinery in London which produced 214 tons in the first year. Henry Tate was very successful in the refinery business and was made a baronet. He later provided many endowments, including to the Tate Gallery in London.

Abram Lyle worked briefly in a lawyer's office, then went into his father's cooperage and later became a very successful ship-owner. Lyle went into partnership with John Kerr in the 1850s and from then on the two were inseparable. In 1865 they took over the Glebe sugar refinery but after Kerr's death in 1872 it was sold, as were the shipping interests. Lyle built two sugar refineries in London just upstream from Tate's refinery in 1881. Despite the bottom falling out of the sugar market just as the refinery was being completed, the plant was soon producing sugar and Lyle's Golden Syrup.

Lyle, a deeply religious man, registered a trademark in 1884 showing a swarm of bees coming from a hive in a lion's carcass with the caption 'Out of the Strong Came Forth Sweetness', which comes from a riddle posed by Samson in the Bible (Judges 14:14). This mark is still registered today (number 40,178) and is used on tins of Lyle's Golden Syrup, although there have been

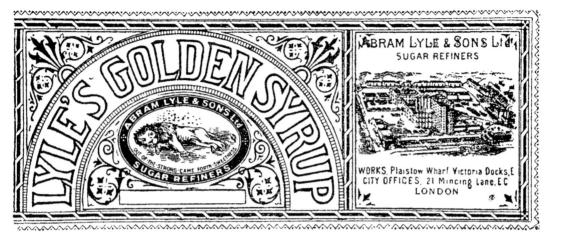

minor changes to the illustration down the years. Tate applied in the same year for a trademark depicting six letter Ts in diamonds which the firm had used since 1873. Both Lyle's Sugar and Tate have been continuously registered since 1887.

In 1918 Ernest Tate suggested the amalgamation of Tate's and Lyle's refineries to two of Abram's sons, Charles and Robert, but it took until 1921 for the firms to merge. The resulting company was very successful and exists today as Tate & Lyle plc.

A 1904 trademark for Lyle's Golden Syrup with an altered lion logo (number 267,446).

TEBBUTT'S PORK PIES

Melton Mowbray in Leicestershire has been a centre for English pork pie manufacture since about the 1820s and for Stilton cheese-making since long before that. In 1885 Tebbutt & Co. of Melton Mowbray registered a trademark showing a view of the town (number 41,500) for their pies. At about that time the firm was also known to be selling cheese. Subsequently Tebbutt merged with Tuxford's creamery and the company Tuxford & Tebbutt was formed. Cheese-making and pork pie manufacture continued at the firm's Melton Mowbray factory until 1966, when it concentrated on cheese.

The firm now employs eighty staff and is one of only six creameries able to produce Stilton cheese. 'Tuxford and Tebbutt' trademarks are still used and are owned by the Cheese Company Ltd, which is part of Glanbia, an international dairy, consumer foods and nutritional products concern.

TERRY'S CONFECTIONERY

Joseph Terry, who was born in 1793, married into the Bayldon family which owned the York firm of Bayldon and Berry, makers of lozenges and candied peel since 1767. Joseph developed the confectionery side of the business and on his death in 1850 his three sons took over the firm. One of his sons, also Joseph, built a chocolate factory in Clementhorpe, York, in 1862.

In 1876 Joseph Terry and Sons applied for its first trademarks for confectionery (numbers 536 and 7,867–8). The company was proud of its connection with York and their first trademark shows medieval York, while trademark number 7,867 depicts York Minster, the largest Gothic church in England, and number 7,868 the city's coat of arms.

Terry's first trademark described as 'York Castle in a diamond' (number 536).

By 1923 the business was in the hands of Frank and Noel Terry and they launched new brands such as Terry's All Gold and Chocolate Orange. The Terry family continued to run the business until 1963. In 1975 Terry's of York was acquired by United Biscuits, which sold it on to Kraft General Foods in 1993; the latter amalgamated it with Jacobs Suchard to create Terry's Suchard. The last York factory closed in 2005.

Terry's trademark (number 7,867) showing York Minster.

VAN DEN BERGH AND JURGENS MARGARINE

Margarine was invented and patented in 1869 (GB 2,157) by the French chemist Hippolyte Mège-Mouriès. In 1871 the butter wholesaler Jurgens of Osch in Holland obtained rights to the patent and began margarine production. Soon the firm of Van den

Bergh, another butter wholesaler from the same village, started margarine manufacture as well. Most of the margarine produced by the two firms was exported, especially to Britain.

In 1885 the Van den Bergh brothers applied for a British trademark (number 44,464) for their 'butterine', as margarine was sometimes known. The earliest margarine brands introduced in the late 1890s were Jurgens' Solo and Van den Bergh's Vitello, and then in 1901 Jurgens registered the Stork trademark (number 232,441) for margarine and butter. In fact, in 1885 Timothy O'Neil, a provisions agent from London, had taken out the almost identical Stork trademark for margarine which Jurgens adopted sixteen years later. In 1906 Jurgens took out the trademark Superbum for food but this evidently proved less popular than Stork!

After the First World War there was intense competition in the British market between the Dutch firms and Lever Brothers. Then

STORK

BRAND

Jurgens's 1901 trademark for Stork margarine before the firm merged with Van den Bergh (number 232,441).

in 1927 Jurgens and Van den Bergh merged to form Margarine Unie, which merged two years with Lever Brothers to create the giant company Unilever.

VAN HOUTEN'S CHOCOLATE

In the history of chocolate the Dutchman Conrad Van Houten is an important figure. His principal claim to fame is his invention of the cocoa press and the 'Dutching process' in 1828. The press squeezed out some of the cocoa butter from the beans and the product was treated with potassium or sodium carbonate ('Dutching') to produce a smoother and cheaper chocolate drink.

179

Above, left: Van Houten's trademark number 11,407.

Above, right: Packaging from about 1900 reflects Van Houten's earlier trademark. (*The Robert Opie Collection*)

In 1877 C.J. van Houten and Zoon, of Weesp, Holland, applied for a British trademark (number 11,407), which was registered for Van Houten's Pure Soluble Cocoa until 1989. The company Van Houten GmbH still owns a number of British trademarks, including Chocolate Challenge and Van Houten Heaven.

1. A poster advertising Humber bicycles, from the late nineteenth or early twentieth century, shows the original trademark illustrated on page 7. (*Motoring Picture Library*)

2. A show card for Singer Cycles from about 1900 promotes cycling as a leisure activity. Earlier Singer trademarks showed a simpler or more technical style. (*The Robert Opie Collection*)

3. A 1905 advertisement for Christy's hats using the heraldic British trademark. (*The National Archives*)

4. Edouard Manet's painting of *A Bar at the Folies-Bergère* showing Bass ale bearing the red triangle logo. (*Samuel Courtauld Trust/Courtauld Institute of Art Gallery/The Bridgeman Art Library*)

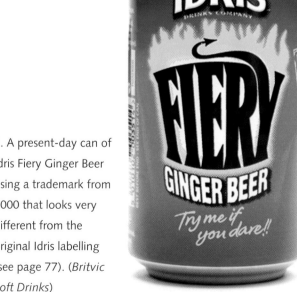

5. A present-day can of Idris Fiery Ginger Beer using a trademark from 2000 that looks very different from the original Idris labelling (see page 77). (*Britvic Soft Drinks*)

6. A 1950s Robertson's Silver Shred display card featuring the Golly logo. (*The Robert Opie Collection*)

7. A late 1890s leaflet for Goddard's plate powder. (*The Robert Opie Collection*)

8. This 1924 Eno's advertisement in *Punch Almanack* uses a derivation of the sun logo from the 1876 trademark illustrated on page 290. (*Mary Evans Picture Library*)

9. Webb's seed catalogue, *c.* 1884. (*British Library*)

10. *Bubbles* by Sir John Everett Millais was used in Pears' advertising for its soap. (*Elida Gibbs Collection, London, UK/The Bridgeman Art Library*)

11. The contemporary style used in this 1950s advertisement for Pond's creams was very different from that of the original trademark illustrated on page 306. (*The Robert Opie Collection*)

12. An advertisement for Victor gramophones from *The Theatre*, c. 1910, after Francis Barraud. Victor licensed the mark for use in the United States from HMV. (*Private Collection/Archives Charmet/The Bridgeman Art Library*)

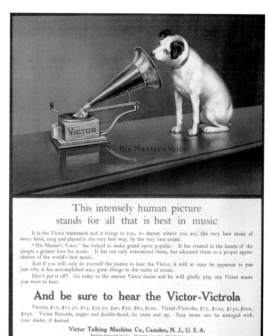

13. Slazenger made Truflite golf balls, as well as tennis rackets, as shown on this 1890s trade card. (*The Robert Opie Collection*)

14. A 1933 advertisement for Reeves & Sons' colours shows the Greyhound trademark.
(© *ColArt Fine Art & Graphics Ltd*)

15. A label from Stephens' 'Violette Noire' ink, *c.* 1900, based on trademark number 241,444
shown on page 347. (*The Stephens Collection, Finchley, London*)

5

HOUSEHOLD GOODS

From Candles to Electric Lamps, Crockery to Silver Plate

It is not surprising that potters were early in the queue to register trademarks when the new law took effect in 1876. Chinese pottery dating from 2700 BC and later Roman pottery bearing marks indicating the name of the maker had begun the tradition of pottery marks. The British firms Crown Derby, Doulton, Minton, Wedgwood and Royal Worcester all registered trademarks in 1876.

Cutlery marks were also known before the trademark registration system was introduced and cutlery had a special place of registration. Under the 1875 Act of Parliament that brought in trademark registration the Cutlers' Company (more formally the Master, Warden, Searchers, Assistants and Commonalty of the Company of Cutlers in Hallamshire in the County of York) was allowed to be a registering authority for trademarks for metal goods from the Sheffield area.

Other household essentials like candles and matches were also subject to trademark activity. Price's patent candles and Bryant & May matches became very well known and their trademarks were essential to maintain sales of the products. Ultimately matches and

Price's lavishly illustrated trademark for candles from 1904 (number 258,165).

candles fell out of favour as the electric light began to replace them. Electric light pioneers Edison and Swan both registered marks for their lamps.

Retailers, like Whiteley in London, could not register the shop itself but could register trademarks for the products they sold. Whiteley took advantage of this, as did the Co-operative Society. The Salvation Army, which was soon trading in all manner of goods, was also able to register.

AVERY'S SCALES

William and Thomas Avery manufactured stilliards, or scales, in Digbeth, Birmingham, continuing in the business which was known to have been carried out there since 1731. From the original owner, James Ford, the business passed to William Barton, then to Thomas Beach and Joseph Balden, husband of Mary Avery. In 1813 the business passed to William and Thomas Avery.

The business expanded in 1854 with the building of a new factory and iron foundry at the Atlas Works in West Bromwich, where rival scale-maker Salter also set up. The company W. & T. Avery applied in 1885 for a trademark (number 48,166) for weighing machines, which had already been in use from 1870. In 1897 the company moved to the Soho Foundry in Handsworth, made famous by Matthew Boulton, James Watt and William Murdock during the industrial revolution.

Avery's trademark, number 48,166, for weighing machines.

The company remained a family concern until 1894, when it became a public company with a capital of £200,000. The last family member to be involved died in 1918, by which time the firm employed three thousand staff. In the early 1970s Avery used a circle of As as its principal trademark and company logo. In 1979 the company was acquired by the GEC Group as weighing equipment became increasingly electronic but in 2000 it was sold by GEC to Weigh-Tronix Inc. of America.

BERGER'S PAINT

In 1760 Louis Steigenberger came from Frankfurt to London to sell Prussian Blue made using his secret formula. He was accompanied by his brother John, but he soon returned to Germany. Within six years Louis had established a company with Frederick Smith. He soon changed his name to Lewis Berger and married Elizabeth Alger, setting up home and business in East London at Homerton. The colours were sold through a shop in Cheapside, London.

Berger died in 1814 and was succeeded in the firm by his sons John and Samuel. John's sons Lewis Curwood and Capel Berrow Berger, then another of Lewis's sons, Arthur, subsequently ran the business. Arthur was an innovator and started to make new products including coach paints. In 1877 Lewis Berger & Sons registered two trademarks for their paint, varnish and oils (numbers 11,715–16), the first of which shows Mercury, a long-lived theme of the firm.

Berger's Mercury trademark (number 11,715).

Berger's Mercury

First published
September, 1914·

—under the title of
"Good Business News"

A monthly magazine of interest to makers,
sellers and users of Berger's Products.

No. 10. Vol. III.   HOMERTON, E.9.   MAY, 1917.

'Mr Berger made
Fine Colours in
London in 1760.

TWO GENTLEMEN OF CREDIT AND RENOWN WHO MAY BE DEPENDED ON
TO RECEIVE OUR NEW TITLE DESIGN WITH WARM APPROVAL.

A 1917 cover of Berger's *Mercury* magazine showing 'Mr Berger' and Mercury.

At the beginning of the twentieth century control of the firm left the Berger family when it was bought by American company Sherwin Williams, but the business prospered with the establishment of factories around the British Empire and the development of colours for printing and synthetic enamels and varnishes. The firm became Berger, Jenson & Nicholson Ltd through a merger and was then taken over by Hoechst AG, which sold it to Williams Holdings. It was sold on to Crown Paints and eventually became part of the Dutch Akzo Nobel company.

BRYANT & MAY'S MATCHES

William Bryant was born in 1804 in Tiverton, Devon. In 1835 he went into partnership as a general merchant with Edward James. The business grew and soon they set up a soap factory. In 1836 Bryant invented and patented the 'Manufacture of liquid and paste blacking, by introducing India rubber, oil, and other articles and things'. Francis May was born in 1803 and was apprenticed to a grocer in Epping, Essex, in 1822, after which he started his own

Bryant & May's Noah's Ark trademark, number 690.

PROTECTION FROM FIRE.

SECURITY

BRYANT & MAY'S

SPECIAL PATENT SAFETY MATCH

IGNITES ONLY ON THE BOX

1862 LONDINI HONORIS CAUSA

PRIZE

MEDAL

An 1878 trademark for Cigar Lights (number 14,807).

tea and grocery business in Bishopsgate, London. By 1843 Bryant and May had met and set themselves up as provision merchants in Tooley Street and Philpot Lane in London.

In 1850 Carl Lundström went to London to get orders for his Swedish firm's matches and met Bryant and May, who soon placed orders. By the following year they were almost the only agents for the factory in Jönköping in Sweden and in 1860 they sold almost 28 million boxes. To increase the supply from Sweden, Bryant & May put money into the Swedish business. In 1852 Lundström invented the safety match, which was patented in Britain in 1855 and the patent sold to Bryant & May for £100. The Swedish factory could not keep up with the demand for safety matches and in 1861 Bryant & May started production at the Fairfield Works, Bow, in London. The well-known Swan Vestas smoker's matches were first manufactured in the same year.

In 1876 the firm applied for a series of trademarks (numbers 690–704). The first two featured the still familiar Noah's Ark design, which had been in use since 1862. Bryant & May became a public limited company in 1884 with a capital of £300,000.

In 1888 there was a three-week strike of Bryant & May match-girls in protest at the sacking of three of their colleagues. The firm had accused them of telling lies about working conditions to

a radical journalist, Annie Besant. The strike became a national issue that was only settled by the firm offering concessions. By 1902 Bryant & May was the biggest match-maker in Britain. The firm merged with J. John Masters & Co. and the UK interests of the Swedish Match Company in 1926 to become the British Match Corporation. As match sales steadily declined from around 1955 to 1971 the company diversified and in 1973 it merged with Wilkinson Sword. There was a reversal of ownership in 1987 when the Wilkinson Sword Group became a wholly owned subsidiary of Swedish Match.

Bryant & May's 1908 Swan Vesta trademark (number 304,212).

CHUBB'S LOCKS

Charles Chubb was born in Fordingbridge, Hampshire, in 1779 and after being apprenticed as a blacksmith he started a business as a ship's ironmonger, first in Winchester and then in 1804 in Portsmouth. His brother Jeremiah, who was born in 1793, later joined Charles in the business. In 1818 Jeremiah patented the Detector lock that indicated if an attempt had been made to pick it (patent number GB 4,219) and in 1824 Charles patented a further improvement (patent number GB 4,972).

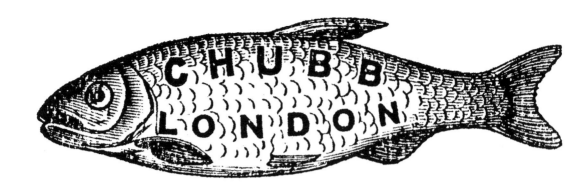

It is said that one of the firm's Detector locks was given to a convict, who was himself a locksmith and who was at that time in a prison ship at Portsmouth, to see if he could pick it. Despite a £100 reward and the offer of a pardon if he could undo the lock, he had still not succeeded after three months. Whether from the publicity gained from this stunt, or from Chubb receiving a government award for making a lock that could not be opened by any other than its own key, or from the story which spread in which the Prince Regent sat on a Chubb lock and key, the firm flourished. Chubb soon moved the firm to Wolverhampton and started to produce safes and other security products. By the mid-1840s Chubb had become a household word, appearing in playbills and popular verses of the time. Charles was succeeded in the business by his son John and later two of John's sons took over.

In February 1876 Chubb & Son applied to register its first trademark (number 1,817 for iron doors, iron and tin boxes, locks and keys, portmanteaus and strong-rooms). The trademark was split into two in 1985 and the registration for strong-rooms has been maintained, although it was renumbered 1,818 by the Trademark Registry. The logo used by the firm is a fish, presumably derived from the freshwater chub. Since the 1980s the principal Chubb trademark and logo has consisted of a letter C formed to resemble a keyhole.

By the second half of the twentieth century Chubb had expanded its operations to many aspects of security work in the UK and abroad. The Racal Electronics Group purchased Chubb in 1984 but sold it in 1997 to Williams plc. In August 2000 Chubb was acquired by Assa Abloy, a Swedish lock manufacturer.

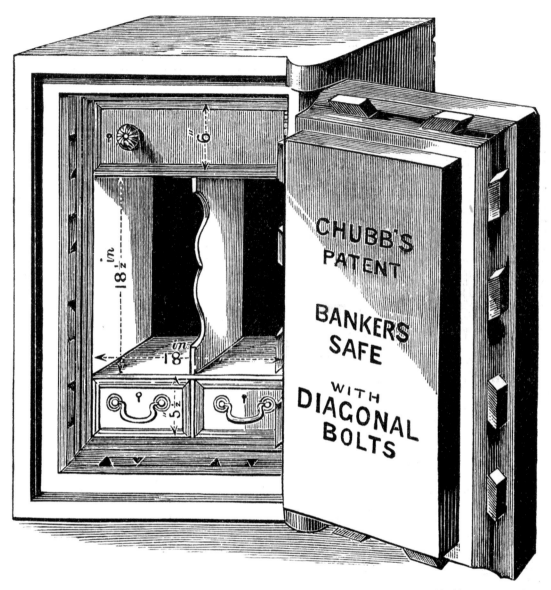

Chubb's patent safe, *c.* 1900. (*Unnamed artist in* Das Buch der Erfindungen *vol. 6 p. 543/Mary Evans Picture Library*)

CODD'S BOTTLE STOPPER

Codd is no longer a household name but in the last quarter of the nineteenth century and the first quarter of the twentieth it certainly was. In 1870 Hiram Codd registered his invention for a bottle with a marble stopper with the British Patent Office (patent number GB 3,070). The invention used a glass ball seated against a rubber gasket in the mouth of the bottle to seal in carbonated beverages. To pour the drink the stopper was

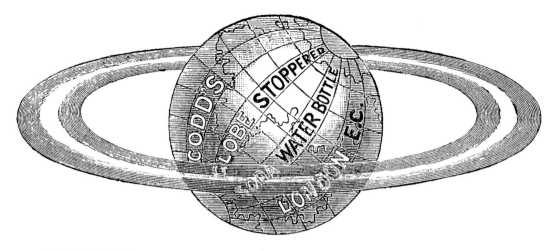

A.D. 1871. Aug. 22. N.º 2212.
CODD'S SPECIFICATION

FIG. I.

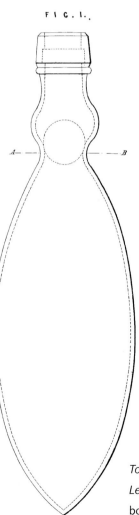

pushed into the bottle. In later improvements (GB 2,212 of 1871 and 2,621 of 1872) the neck of the bottle was constructed so as to prevent the ball from falling into the liquid or back into the mouth when emptying the contents. His bottle, the 'Codd', soon became a standard in Europe and the British Empire. Codd also took out patents in America.

In March 1883 Codd applied for a British trademark (number 31,687) for his stopper. The trademark shows a globe labelled 'Codd's Globe Stoppered Soda Water Bottle'. Hiram Codd died in 1887 and was buried in Brompton Cemetery in London.

It is suggested that the slang word codswallop, meaning nonsense or drivel, derives from the gassy drink that came out of Codd's bottles but the *Oxford English Dictionary* gives the earliest reference to the word in a 1963 issue of the *Radio Times*, so the connection to Codd is unproven.

Top: Codd's trademark number 31,687.

Left: Codd's patent for bottle stoppers shows a glass ball in the neck of the bottle.

CO-OPERATIVE SOCIETY

The co-operative movement started with the Rochdale Pioneers in 1844. The idea was for each branch to run a shop selling local produce with members of the co-operative holding shares in the shop. The manufacturing of goods for sale would also provide employment for the co-operative's members.

The North of England Co-operative Wholesale Society Ltd was created in 1864 to buy and manufacture goods for all the individual co-operatives. In 1872 the words North of England were dropped from the title and the Co-operative Wholesale Society, based in Manchester, was formed.

By 1877 the Society had applied for its first trademark depicting a wheatsheaf (number 11,908) for candles, hats, boots, fruit and all manner of other goods. Although the wheatsheaf logo has

The Co-operative Society's wheatsheaf trademark, number 42,334.

"PIONEER"

EXTRA PATENT.

One of the many later Co-operative Wholesale Society trademarks – in this case a mark for flour from 1901 (number 42,334).

been used by the CWS in different forms ever since, the original trademark, along with many others registered over the years, is still on the trademark register and is owned by the Co-operative Group (CWS) Ltd. Today, following the merger of several wholesale and retail societies, the group is a major UK operator of convenience stores and financial services, not to mention undertakers! It has recently announced a revamp of its branding at an estimated cost of £100 million.

ROYAL DELFT POTTERY

The Koninklijke Porceleyne Fles is the only one remaining of the thirty-two earthenware factories that were established in Delft in Holland in the seventeenth century. About that time white Chinese porcelain decorated in blue began to be imported into Holland and Dutch potters started to imitate it using local clay. De Porceleyne Fles (The Porcelain Jar) was founded in 1653 by David Anthonisz v.d. Pieth in Delft. After two years the factory passed into the hands of Wouter van Eenhoorn and Quirinus van Kleijnoven. In 1663 van Eenhoorn sold his share of the company to van Kleijnoven, who died in 1695. After two years of running the business, his widow sold it to Johannes Knotter, who was the first to use a jar logo as a trademark.

Royal Delft trademark number 43,316.

In the eighteenth century porcelain clay and, later, white baking clay were discovered in Europe and Delft pottery declined. The firm had changed hands many times before 1876 when Joost Thooft, a Delft engineer, bought the factory and together with an associate produced strong hand-painted Delft Blue using a new mixture of clay. Joost Thooft added the word Delft and his monogram JT to the trademark. Delft pottery became world famous and in 1885 the company applied for a British trademark (number 43,316). The Porceleyne Fles received the designation Koninklijke (Royal) in 1919.

ROYAL CROWN DERBY CHINA

Huguenot Andrew Planche established the first china works in Derby before 1750 and then joined with William Duesbury in 1756 in a very successful partnership manufacturing high-quality china. King George III granted the factory the privilege of incorporating a crown into the backstamp in 1775. William Duesbury died in 1786, leaving his son and subsequently his grandson to carry on the business. Robert Bloor took control of the factory in 1811 and began to build a team of very fine painters. When he died in 1845 the factory was run by Thomas Clarke until 1848.

Samson Hancock's trademark (number 11,435) became the property of Royal Crown Derby.

Some of the factory's craftsmen opened a small works in King Street, Derby, and one of them, Samson Hancock, was finally left to carry on the Derby tradition. In 1876 Samson Hancock applied for a trademark (number 11,435). In the same year the Derby Crown Porcelain Co. was formed and by 1878 it had registered its own trademark (number 14,156) for porcelain, terracotta and earthenware. Both trademarks are still registered today by Crown Derby.

In 1890 the company was allowed by Queen Victoria to add the designation Royal to the company name ahead of the crown given by King George III. In the early 1960s Royal Crown Derby was acquired by the Pearson family company and then merged with Royal Doulton but it was bought out by its management in 2000 and is independent again. The firm operates today from a factory opened at Osmaston Road, Derby, in 1877.

Royal Crown Derby trademark number 14,156 showing a kiln.

DOULTON'S POTTERY

In 1815 John Doulton went into partnership with widow Martha Jones, who had inherited her late husband's pottery in Lambeth, London. John Watts, the former factory foreman, was taken into partnership and the firm became Jones, Watts & Doulton. The company assumed the Doulton name in 1853 and John Doulton with his son Henry established the firm as makers of fine stoneware. In 1876 James Duneau Doulton registered the firm's first trademarks (numbers 1,818–19) for faience pottery and in 1879 the trademark Doulton Impasto (number 20,334) was registered for potteryware. None of these is still registered but

Doulton's trademark (number 1,819) containing a Four D design.

A 1900 Doulton lion trademark for earthenware sanitary articles (number 228,776).

the trademarks Doulton and Doulton & Co. (numbers 55,418–19) from 1886 are still active.

In 1877 Doulton bought a small china factory in Burslem, Staffordshire, in the heart of The Potteries, and soon this was producing bone china. The factory was granted a royal warrant in 1901 by King Edward VII, who also permitted the company to adopt the name Royal Doulton. Today the company produces fine bone china, fine china and Royal Doulton Lambethware but all production in the UK ceased in 2004 after the company had been losing money and staff for some years. Most is now made in Indonesia.

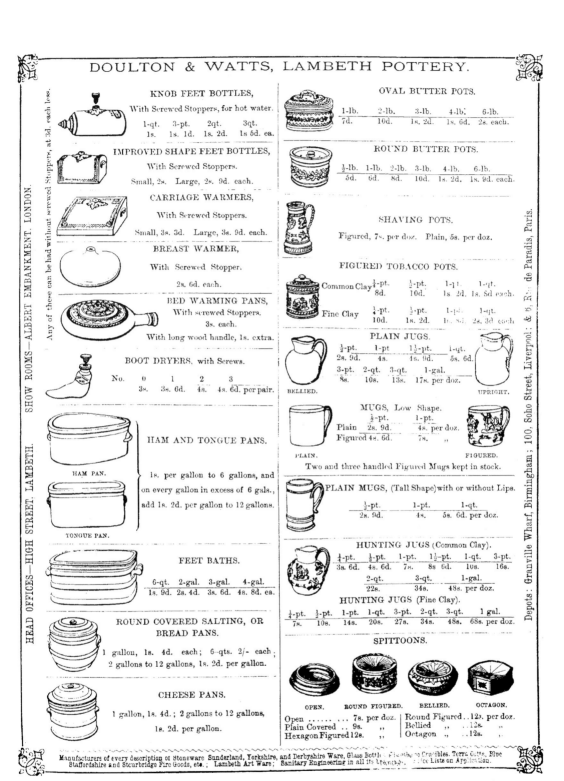

DOULTON & WATTS, LAMBETH POTTERY.

SHOW ROOMS—ALBERT EMBANKMENT. LONDON.

HEAD OFFICES—HIGH STREET. LAMBETH.

Depots: Granville Wharf, Birmingham; 100, Soho Street, Liverpool; & 6, Rue de Paradis, Paris.

Any of these can be had without screwed Stoppers, at 3d. each less.

KNOB FEET BOTTLES,

With Screwed Stoppers, for hot water.

1-qt.	3-pt.	2qt.	3qt.
1s.	1s. 1d.	1s. 2d.	1s 5d. ea.

IMPROVED SHAPE FEET BOTTLES,

With Screwed Stoppers.

Small, 2s.   Large, 2s. 9d. each.

CARRIAGE WARMERS,

With Screwed Stoppers.

Small, 3s. 3d.   Large, 3s. 9d. each.

BREAST WARMER,

With Screwed Stopper.

2s. 6d. each.

BED WARMING PANS,

With screwed Stoppers.

3s. each.

With long wood handle, 1s. extra.

BOOT DRYERS, with Screws.

No.	0	1	2	3
	3s.	3s. 6d.	4s.	4s. 6d. per pair.

HAM AND TONGUE PANS.

HAM PAN.

TONGUE PAN.

1s. per gallon to 6 gallons, and on every gallon in excess of 6 gals., add 1s. 2d. per gallon to 12 gallons.

FEET BATHS.

6-qt.	2-gal.	3-gal.	4-gal.
1s. 9d.	2s. 4d.	3s. 6d.	4s. 8d. ea.

ROUND COVERED SALTING, OR BREAD PANS.

1 gallon, 1s. 4d. each; 6-qts. 2/- each; 2 gallons to 12 gallons, 1s. 2d. per gallon.

CHEESE PANS.

1 gallon, 1s. 4d.; 2 gallons to 12 gallons, 1s. 2d. per gallon.

OVAL BUTTER POTS.

1-lb.	2-lb.	3-lb.	4-lb.	6-lb.
7d.	10d.	1s. 2d.	1s. 6d.	2s. each.

ROUND BUTTER POTS.

½-lb.	1-lb.	2-lb.	3-lb.	4-lb.	6-lb.
5d.	6d.	8d.	10d.	1s. 2d.	1s. 9d. each.

SHAVING POTS.

Figured, 7s. per doz.   Plain, 5s. per doz.

FIGURED TOBACCO POTS.

	¼-pt.	½-pt.	1-pt.	1-qt.
Common Clay	8d.	10d.	1s. 2d.	1s. 8d. each.
Fine Clay	10d.	1s. 2d.	1s. 8d.	2s. 3d. each

PLAIN JUGS.

BELLIED.   UPRIGHT.

½-pt.	1-pt.	1½-pt.	1-qt.
2s. 9d.	4s.	4s. 9d.	5s. 6d.
3-pt.	2-qt.	3-qt.	1-gal.
8s.	10s.	13s.	17s. per doz.

MUGS, Low Shape.

PLAIN.   FIGURED.

	½-pt.	1-pt.
Plain	2s. 9d.	4s. per doz.
Figured	4s. 6d.	7s. „

Two and three handled Figured Mugs kept in stock.

PLAIN MUGS, (Tall Shape) with or without Lips.

½-pt.	1-pt.	1-qt.
2s. 9d.	4s.	5s. 6d. per doz.

HUNTING JUGS (Common Clay).

¼-pt.	½-pt.	1-pt.	1½-pt.	1-qt.	3-pt.
3s. 6d.	4s. 6d.	7s.	8s. 6d.	10s.	16s.
		2-qt.	3-qt.	1-gal.	
		22s.	34s.	48s. per doz.	

HUNTING JUGS (Fine Clay).

¼-pt.	½-pt.	1-pt.	1-qt.	3-pt.	2-qt.	3-qt.	1 gal.
7s.	10s.	14s.	20s.	27s.	34s.	48s.	68s. per doz.

SPITTOONS.

OPEN.   ROUND FIGURED.   BELLIED.   OCTAGON.

Open	7s. per doz.	Round Figured	12s. per doz.
Plain Covered	9s. „	Bellied	12s. „
Hexagon Figured	12s. „	Octagon	12s. „

Manufacturers of every description of Stoneware Sunderland, Yorkshire, and Derbyshire Ware, Glass Bottles, Fire Clay Crucibles. Terra Cotta, Blue Staffordshire and Stourbridge Fire Goods, etc.; Lambeth Art Ware; Sanitary Engineering in all its branches. Price Lists on Application.

An early Doulton & Watts catalogue showing the range of products.

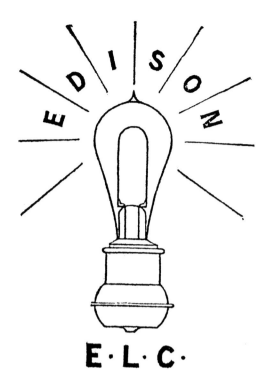

E·L·C·

Edison's trademark
number 29,111.

EDISON'S ELECTRIC LIGHT

American Thomas Alva Edison and English-man Joseph Swan are famous as independent inventors of the incandescent electric light. Swan was perhaps the first to perfect the carbon filament but Edison perfected the lamp and was the first to patent widely.

In March 1882 the Edison Electric Light Company Ltd was set up in London as a subsidiary of the US company to control Edison's British patents for his inventions connected with lighting. By 14 September of that year the company had applied for a British trademark for electric lamps (number

A 1908 trademark
for the Edison &
Swan United Electric
Light Company
(number 297,406).

198

T. A. EDISON.
Electric-Lamp.

No. 223,898.　　　　　　**Patented Jan. 27, 1880.**

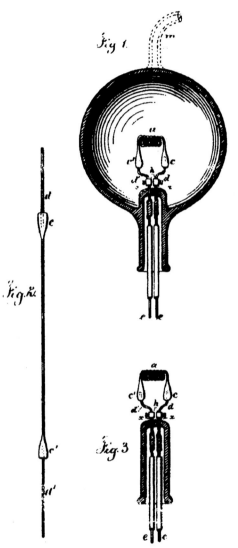

Edison's American 1880 patent for the electric lamp.

29,111). Swan had already applied for trademarks for his own electric lamps.

By October 1883 the Edison & Swan United Electric Light Company Ltd was set up in the UK to merge Edison's interests with the Swan United Electric Light Company Ltd. In 1892 this firm was merged into the General Electric Company.

SAMUEL FOX'S UMBRELLAS

One of the very first applicants for a trademark in January 1876 was Samuel Fox, who in 1852 had taken out a patent (GB 14,055) for the Paragon umbrella frame – a steel rib and stretcher with a U section formed from flattened wire. The frame had been invented by Joseph Hayward, an employee, and the story goes that another worker told Fox that Hayward was asleep at work, whereupon Fox replied, 'Thee go and mind thy work, he's worth more to me asleep than thou art wakken.'

Samuel Fox was born on 17 June 1815 at Bradwell, Derbyshire, and was later apprenticed to a firm of wire-drawers that specialised in needle-wire. He went to Stocksbridge in 1842 and leased an old cotton mill to start his own wire-drawing business. From about 1848 he started selling umbrella frames but it was the strong and light Paragon frame that brought prosperity. Fox continued to innovate and had many patents to his name. In 1854 he started to cold-roll strips of wire to supply crinoline manufacturers and in about 1860 he started to manufacture steel, particularly for the expanding railway network.

Fox's Paragon trademark (number 1,656).

A 1905 trademark for Fox's umbrellas (number 273,484).

A 1905 trademark for Fox's umbrella ribs and stretchers (number 276,934).

William Hoyland approached Fox in 1876 with a new design for an umbrella frame but in the end started a new business at Eckland Bridge Works in co-operation with him. Samuel Fox died on 25 February 1887 and for a short time the business, now with over two thousand employees, was run by his son William Henry.

The first trademark for Paragon (number 1,656) is still registered by Hoyland Fox Ltd, currently the largest supplier of umbrella frames in Europe. The company has used many trademarks featuring images of foxes in various forms over the intervening years.

GODDARD'S SILVER POLISH

Joseph Goddard was born in Market Harborough, Leicestershire, in 1813 and became a chemist in Leicester. In 1839 he produced and sold a treatment for foot-rot in sheep called Halt Remedy and a 'Non-Mercurial Plate Powder' for cleaning silverware. At this time the newly discovered process of electroplating was being widely used to produce silver-plated cutlery, which had to be cleaned more gently than solid silver. Goddard's powder became very popular and he soon sold it through other retailers. Goddard's polish was awarded six gold medals in the late 1800s at international trade exhibitions around the world.

Goddard's son, also Joseph, joined the business before Joseph Sr died in 1877. Goddard's grandsons and a great-grandson followed in the family business, expanding it to produce a range of other polishes.

Goddard had registered a trademark in 1876 (number 188) for plate powder, furniture cream, silvering solution, polishing paste and rouge and another in 1879 (number 20,967) for Goddard's non-mercurial plate powder, for which use was claimed for thirty-five years. The latter mark was registered until 1991. Newer trademarks continue in existence but were transferred to the American company S.C. Johnson & Son Inc. in 1992.

Goddard's stag's head trademark, number 188.

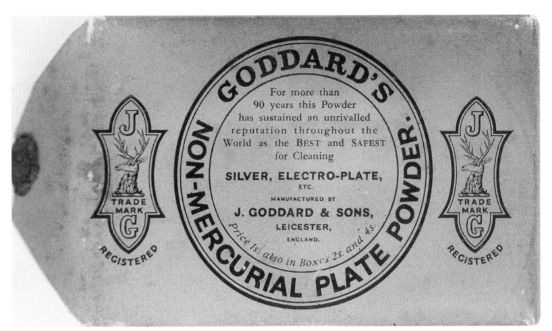

Packaging from Goddard's plate powder from about 1910 includes the original trademark. (*The Robert Opie Collection*)

Mander's trademark number 4,546.

MANDER'S PAINT

In 1773 brothers Benjamin and John Mander set up a chemical manufacturing works in Wolverhampton and started to make carriage varnish. The varnish business expanded and in 1845 the partnership became known as Mander Brothers. The firm continued to prosper through the nineteenth century by manufacturing paint and then printing ink, with branches in London, Paris, Florence, Vienna and Berlin.

Mander Brothers became a household name. The first trademarks were filed in 1876 for varnishes and japans (numbers 4,544–6). The Mander family supported local causes and social reform, helping to set up free libraries, chapels and schools, later serving as magistrates and in other official roles, with one Mander even becoming a member of parliament. In 1911 Charles Mander was made a baronet.

Manders plc continued to manufacture in Wolverhampton until it was broken up in

INSTRUCTIONS FOR USE ON OTHER SIDE
Makers Mander Brothers, Wolverhampton
LONDON, DEPÔT 165 OXFORD ST W.

A 1902 Mander's trademark (number 246,955) for Olsina paint shows the gold medals won.

1994. The American company Flint Ink took over the coatings and printing inks business in 1997 and the Mander Shopping Centre now occupies the site in central Wolverhampton where once the business flourished.

MAPLE'S FURNITURE

John Maple started a small furniture shop in London's Tottenham Court Road in the nineteenth century but it was his son John Blundell Maple, born in 1845, who developed the business into a major store. The firm Maple & Company applied for a trademark for its Beaver Carpet (number 45,848) in 1885 and this was followed by others.

The business was incorporated as a limited liability company, with a capital of £2 million, in 1890, with John Blundell Maple as chairman. Maple was knighted in 1892 and made a baronet in 1897 after having served as a member of parliament. The store

204

went into receivership in 1997 and some of the assets including the trademarks were purchased by the Allders retailing group.

Maple's trademark number 45,848.

MAPPIN & WEBB'S SILVERWARE

On 10 April 1876 John Mappin applied for two trademarks on behalf of Mappin & Webb, the first of which (number 4,810 for M Trustworthy) had been used since 1860 and is still

Mappin & Webb's trademark number 4,810 is still in use.

A 1906 Mappin & Webb trademark for Crocodile machine knives.

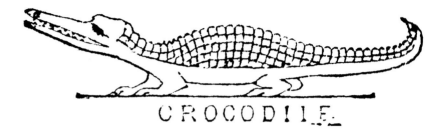

A Mappin & Webb advertisement for Sterling Silver and Prince's Plate published in 1895. (*Illustrated London News Picture Library*)

registered for cutlery and other products today. The firm is now an upmarket jeweller based in Regent Street, London, but it derives from a silversmith's workshop set up in Sheffield in 1797 by Jonathan Mappin. In 1868 John Mappin, a descendant of Jonathan, invited his brother-in-law George Webb to join the business and Mappin & Webb was born. At the same time another branch of the family operated as

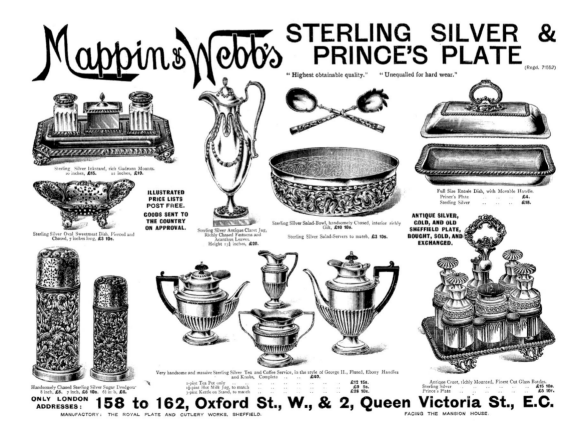

Mappin Brothers, but this company was bought out by Mappin & Webb in 1902.

The firm now has seventeen registered trademarks, including the original mark. The newest trademark, applied for in 1995 (number 2,026,381), is identical to the original M Trustworthy mark but has extended the goods to which it can be applied to cutlery, silver and electro-plated hollow-ware and giftware and jewellery.

MINTON'S POTTERY

Thomas Minton started a pottery business in Stoke-on-Trent in about 1793. He became famous for Minton ware, blue-printed cream earthenware majolica, bone china and Parian porcelain, and is remembered today for his introduction of the willow pattern design. In the 1820s he started production of bone china.

Minton's 1876 trademark (number 2,975).

After Thomas's death in 1836 his son Herbert succeeded him in the firm and is credited with enhancing its reputation by enlisting the services of artists and skilled artisans. In 1845 Michael Daintry Hollins became a partner in the tile-making side of the business, which became known as Minton Hollins & Co. After Herbert died in 1858 the firm was run by his nephew Colin Minton Campbell, who continued the innovative and artistic tradition.

In 1876 the firm applied for a trademark for china (number 2,975) consisting of

a crown on a globe. By 1913 this symbol had evolved to include laurel leaves and the words Est. 1793 (number 350,391). By 1946 the globe had gone and the crown was based on an M design (number 641,786). These and other Minton trademarks are still used today, although Minton became part of the Royal Doulton Group in 1968. The Minton name is now registered as a trademark in forty countries and sales of Minton ceramic tableware and giftware in the UK amounted to £6.3 million in 1996.

NAIRN'S LINOLEUM

Kirkcaldy in Scotland was, towards the end of the nineteenth century, the world's largest source of linoleum floor covering and Nairn was the biggest of the Kirkcaldy manufacturers. Linoleum was made by pressing a mixture of linseed oil and ground cork into a jute cloth and it became very popular before the age of plastic flooring.

Michael Nairn, who was born in Kirkcaldy into a family of master weavers, started to produce canvas to sell to the

English floor-cloth trade in 1828 and in 1847 set up his own factory to manufacture floor-cloths by applying size and a form of paint to canvas. After Michael died in 1858, Michael Nairn & Co. continued to expand. His widow Catherine, his son Robert and a manager formed a partnership to run the business. They were joined in 1861 by another son, Michael Barker Nairn, who was granted a number of British patents for his inventions to do with floor-cloths, power looms and linoleum (GB 548 in 1865, GB 2,951 and 3,081 in 1867, GB 35 in 1875 and GB 5,725 in 1881). In the 1870s Nairn & Co. built a massive six-storey factory in Kirkcaldy, which was finally closed in the 1980s.

The company was one of the first to apply for a trademark in January 1876, for Nairn's floor-cloths and linoleum (number 440). The trademark, which is based on a Scottish thistle design and was claimed to have been in use since 1864, was only taken off the register in 1988. The successor company, Forbo-Nairn, is now the UK's only manufacturer of linoleum and also produces other flooring materials.

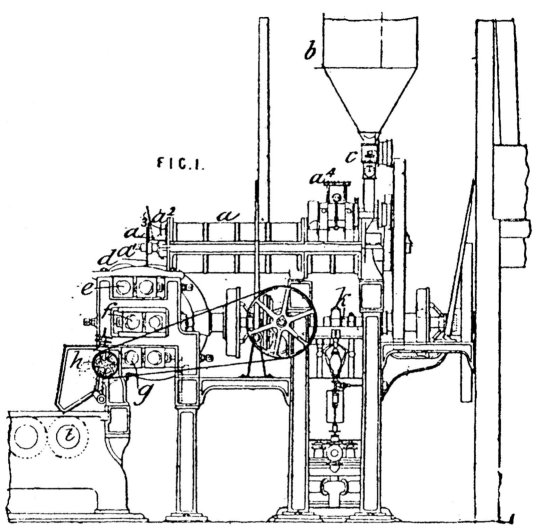

FIG.1.

PRICE'S CANDLES

After the collapse of his father's business in 1812, William
Wilson moved from Scotland to London and set up as a
merchant trading with Russia. He then started a business to
produce candles with a partner. In 1830 William and his
partners, John Studholme Brownrigg, John Cockerell and Sir
George Gerard de Hochpied Larpent, obtained a licence for a
process to separate coconut oil into solid and liquid
components (James Soames patent GB 5,842 of 1829) and
went on to invest in coconut plantations in Sri Lanka. The

partners used this technique and distillation to produce a harder and pure white fat called stearine, which burned brightly without smoke or smell. Up to this time candles had either been made from beef tallow or from beeswax, and their manufacture was a far from glamorous process.

The firm that the partners set up was called E. Price & Co. and it is thought that they used a trading name, rather than their own names, because of the poor image of the candle-manufacturing business. The invention by William's son George and William Jones, a chemist engaged by him, of the steam distillation of fatty acids had a great effect on the company, as did the later invention of the steam distillation of glycerine. In 1847 the name of the company was changed to Price's Patent Candle Co.

Price's soon began to sell the by-products of candle-making, glycerine and a liquid fat called oleine, which was used as a lubricating oil in the textile industries. The firm also began to distil the first petroleum oil to make paraffin wax for candles and then started selling the by-products. The original factory in Vauxhall, London, closed in 1855 but others were opened in Battersea and Liverpool.

From 1876 onwards the company registered a raft of trademarks, the first of which were numbers 2,467–93. Number 2,467 for the mark Belmont, after the Belmont Works in Battersea, recently expired but those for Sherwood and Palmitine are still in force.

Price's 1876 trademark (number 2,488).

Nr. **2788.** ℘. 159. **Price's Patent Candle Company Limited,** London, Belmont Works, Battersea, Surrey, und Bromborough Pool Works, Cheshire; Vertr.: Robert R. Schmidt u. Henry C. Schmidt, Berlin, Potsdamerstr. 141. Anmeldung vom 18. 10. 94. Eintragung am 15. 2. 95.

Geschäftsbetrieb: Seifen= und Lichtefabrik. Waarenverzeichniß: Lichte und Oel.

Top: An 1876 trademark showing Price's candle works (number 2,489).

Above: Price's 1895 German Ship brand trademark.

By the end of the nineteenth century Price's was the world's largest candle manufacturer with goods being exported throughout the British Empire. Trademark number 2,488 shows a tropical scene promoting 'candles made expressly for hot climates'. With British sales beginning to be affected by other newer lighting sources, Price's set up candle factories in Johannesburg, Shanghai, Chile, Rhodesia, Morocco, Pakistan, New Zealand and Sri Lanka to serve local demand. In 1919 Price's was taken over by Lever Brothers Ltd, which was conveniently next door to Price's Liverpool factory at Port Sunlight!

RECKITT'S STARCH

Isaac Reckitt was born in 1792, the fifth of thirteen children. With his elder brother he began a milling business in Boston, Lincolnshire, and then started his own corn business in Nottingham. In 1840 he rented (and then purchased in 1848) a starch factory in Hull, which is still the main UK headquarters of the business. By the time Reckitt displayed his wares at the 1851 Great Exhibition he was employing fifty-one people.

LAMP OIL

is prepared with the utmost care from the finest materials that it is possible to obtain.

——Yet it costs riders no more than any other standard brand and it is suitable for any cycle lamp.

——Its wide popularity and reputation for excellence are based on splendid quality, and charred wicks and smoky reflectors are unknown.

——Just ask for Price's Cycle Lamp Oil next time and note the improvement.

PRICES' COMPANY LIMITED

BATTERSEA, LONDON, S.W.,

Supply Free Samples for Trial.

A 1918 advertisement featuring the Ship trademark.

Top: Reckitt's 1876 trademark (number 7,390).

Above: Reckitt's 1900 Robin starch trademark (number 230,326).

The firm Reckitt & Sons was taken over by Isaac's three sons after his death in 1862 and went on to become one of the most successful businesses in Hull in the second half of the nineteenth century and into the twentieth. The firm diversified into laundry blue, lead stove blacking and later a range of other products.

In 1876 the firm applied for trademarks for Reckitts' Patent Starch (numbers 7,390 and 7,392), both of which had been in use for ten years, and for Reckitts' Paris Blue (number 7,391). The starch trademarks are still on the trademark register today. After many years of joint ventures with J. & J. Colman Ltd, the firms merged to form Reckitt & Colman Ltd in 1938. In 1999 Reckitt & Colman plc and Benckiser N.V. merged to become the world's biggest household cleaning products firm, Reckitt Benckiser plc. Among the best-known Reckitt's trademarks today are Robin starch, Brasso polish and Dettol disinfectant.

214

SALTER'S SCALES

Salter's Staffordshire knot trademark (number 40,629).

Richard Salter, a spring maker, began making 'pocket steelyards', or scales, in the late eighteenth century in the village of Bilston, near Wolverhampton. By 1825 his nephew George had taken over the firm, which then became George Salter & Co. The firm later set up scales production in West Bromwich, then in Staffordshire.

The firm's first trademarks using the Staffordshire knot emblem (numbers 40,629–30) were registered in 1884 for 'spring balances and spring weighing machines, roasting jacks, revolving show stands for shop windows and other machines actuated by coiled or band springs, steam etc. gauges, sand and box and other smoothing irons'.

In 1972 the company was purchased by Staveley Industries plc, which also bought the Weigh-Tronix company of America and other weighing businesses. In 1998 the weighing businesses de-merged to become the Weigh-Tronix Corporation but in 2002 Salter Housewares was bought out from the group by its management. It was sold again in 2004 to the US-based HoMedics company.

SALVATION ARMY

In 1865 William Booth founded the East London Christian Mission for the poor and destitute. In a report on the work of the mission in

Salvation Army
trademark number
36,066.

1878 he referred to it as a 'volunteer army' but his son Bramwell objected to the term volunteer as he felt compelled to do God's work, so William crossed out the word volunteer and replaced it with the word 'salvation' – and the Salvation Army was born.

In 1884 William Booth applied for a series of trademarks (the first of which were numbers 36,066–70) for 'Salvation Army – Blood and Fire' for its sales of earthenware, porcelain, musical instruments, watches and many other products. Trademarks 36,066 and 36,069 are still registered today, as are other similar marks from 1884 and 1891. Today the organisation uses a red shield logo as its main trademark. The organisation in Britain now generates 14 per cent of its income of over £180 million each year through trading activities and it operates in over a hundred other countries.

"Everite"

H. SAMUEL'S CLOCKS AND WATCHES

Harriet Samuel took over her father-in-law's clock-making business in Liverpool in 1862 and soon set up manufacture and mail order at 97 Market Street, Manchester. By 1884 trademarks for Acme and Climax had been registered for H. Samuel watches (numbers 38,832–3).

H. Samuel's trademark number 570,767 was first used in 1923.

Harriet's son developed the retail business and a shop was opened in Preston in 1890, followed by others throughout Lancashire. By 1912 the business had moved to Birmingham and Harriet's grandsons had taken over the firm. In 1948 the firm became a public company and soon there were two hundred stores in the UK. In the late 1970s Harriet's great-grandson took over as chairman and acquired the James Walker Group of jewellers in 1984. The firm was acquired by Ratner's jewellers in 1986 but this was renamed the Signet Group in 1993 after sales plummeted following derogatory remarks made by the then chairman, Gerald Ratner, about the quality of the products sold.

The Climax trademark only expired in 1997 and the name Ratner, once an important brand, has disappeared. However, other trademarks from the first half of the twentieth century, including the well-known Everite (number 570,767), live on.

SINGER'S SEWING MACHINES

Isaac Singer, who was born in Schaghiticoke, New York, in 1811, built the first commercially successful sewing machine in the 1850s. The Singer machine was powered by a foot treadle but it used the same lockstitch that Elias Howe had patented in 1846. Howe successfully

Singer's 1876 trademark (number 43) has an S formed
by a thread.

A German Singer trademark of 1895 showing an S girl
and the original trademark inset.

Nr. **8322.** N. 250.
G. Reidlinger, Hamburg. Anmeldung vom
21. 3. 95. Eintragung am
15. 7. 95.

Geschäftsbetrieb:
Fabrikation von Nähmaschinen, Nähmaschinentheilen und Nähmaschinenzubehör und Handel damit.

Waarenverzeichniß:
Von The Singer Manufacturing Company in
New-York hergestellte Nähmaschinen.

sued Singer for patent infringement in 1854 and shared in Singer's profits.

By 1855 Singer had become the world's largest sewing machine company and expanded overseas, starting in Paris, France. Singer teamed up with his lawyer, Edward Clark, who originated the hire-purchase plan so that even people with little income could own a Singer sewing machine. In 1867 Singer opened its first factory outside the United States, in Glasgow, Scotland.

The Red 'S' girl trademark was first introduced in 1870 and was soon to become one of the best-known logos in the world. Isaac Singer died at Torquay in England in 1875 just before the first British trademark application was made on 1 January 1876 (number 43). In the 1960s Singer began to diversify, acquiring Packard Bell Electronics, the General Precision Equipment Corporation and other companies making electrical equipment and office machinery.

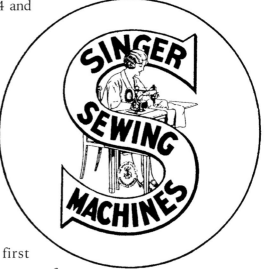

This Singer S girl trademark from 1932 is still registered (number 141,604). *Below:* A quite different Sphinx mark was registered by Singer for sewing machines in 1903 (number 253,365).

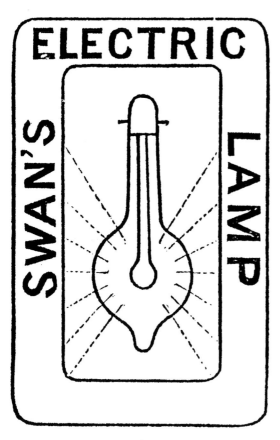

A.D. 1880. Nov. 27. No 4933.
SWAN'S SPECIFICATION.

SWAN'S ELECTRIC LIGHT

Joseph Swan was born in Sunderland in 1828. He began an apprenticeship with a pharmacist at 13 and then joined a firm of manufacturing chemists where he patented the first commercially feasible process for carbon printing in photography (patent GB 503 of 1864). Next Swan invented the dry plate in 1871, followed by the development of bromide photographic paper in 1879.

Swan is best known for his work on the carbon-filament incandescent electric lamp, the first demonstration of which was performed by Swan at the Literary and Philosophical Society of Newcastle upon Tyne on 3 February 1879, and for which he took out a patent in 1880 (GB 4,933). By 1881 he had started his own company, the Swan Electric Light Company, and was producing the first commercial lamps, 1,200 of which were used to illuminate the Savoy Theatre in London to the astonishment of the audiences.

In 1881 the company registered a trademark (number 25,726) but within two years Swan had teamed up with Edison for the commercial exploitation of lamps using the EdiSwan trademark. Swan was elected to the Royal Society in 1894 and was knighted in 1904.

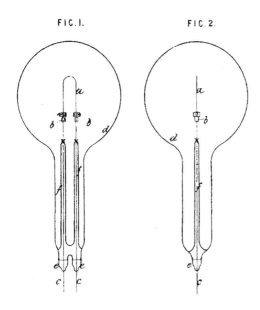

FIG.1. FIG.2.

Top, left: Swan's trademark number 25,726.
Left: Swan's patent for the incandescent electric lamp.

WEDGWOOD'S POTTERY

Josiah Wedgwood was born in 1730 into a family of potters. After his father's death in 1739 he started as a thrower in the pottery of his brother Thomas, to whom he was later apprenticed. Sadly, when he was 12 an attack of smallpox seriously weakened his knee, which later had to be amputated, so that he was unable to use his right leg to turn a potter's wheel. Thomas unkindly refused Josiah a partnership in the business, so Josiah worked for

TRADE MARK.

Wedgwood's trademark number 8,024.

A catalogue showing Wedgwood's stoneware, *c.* 1880. The Bow trademark shown at the top of the advertisement is that of the agents. (Illustrated Catalogue of China, Glass, Earthenware, Lamps etc./*Mary Evans Picture Library*)

222

several other people, including the renowned potter Thomas Whieldon.

In 1759 two relatives leased him Ivy House in Burslem, Staffordshire, where he started his own pottery business, financially helped by his marriage to a distant cousin Sarah Wedgwood, who brought with her a large dowry. Wedgwood's work was of very high quality and soon he was receiving orders from the nobility, including Queen Charlotte, who was persuaded to allow Wedgwood to name his cream earthenware Queen's Ware. In 1768 Wedgwood developed a black porcelain called Black Basalt and later introduced his most successful innovation, Jasperware, which is still produced today, typically in blue and white.

When Wedgwood died he left a fortune of half a million pounds and a thriving business, now Wedgwood Ltd. Wedgwood's earliest trademarks were registered in 1876, the first for the name Wedgwood (number 2,823) and the second for a vase design (number 8,024). Both are still registered today.

WHITELEY'S STORE

William Whiteley was born at Agbrigg, near Wakefield, Yorkshire, in 1831, the son of a corn merchant. He was apprenticed at 16 to a firm of drapers in Wakefield and in 1852 worked in a draper's shop in London. In 1863, with savings of £700, he opened his own fancy drapery shop in Westbourne Grove, Bayswater, London, and within a year he was employing fifteen staff. By 1866 he was selling general drapery and gradually added more and more departments so that soon he claimed the store could supply anything.

By 1876, when he applied for his first trademark (number 6,355), he had been using the term 'Universal Provider' for five years. The trademark covered an extensive range of goods from artist's materials to wind instruments. The firm obtained a listing on the London Stock Exchange in 1899, by which time the business employed over six thousand staff. Tragically, however, on 24 January 1907 a man claiming to be William Whiteley's illegitimate son entered the store and murdered him. His legitimate sons then took over the business and a magnificent new store was opened in 1912. It was sold in 1927 to Gordon

Selfridge but in the 1950s it began to decline and closed in 1981. However, in 1989 a new Whiteley's shopping centre opened behind the old façade.

ROYAL WORCESTER PORCELAIN

In 1751 Dr John Wall, a surgeon, and William Davis, an apothecary, transferred the ceramic works set up in 1749 by Benjamin Lund in Bristol to Worcester, on the banks of the River Severn, where they perfected the production of soft paste porcelain. By 1756 Robert Hancock was working at Worcester and was the first to apply transfer prints on to porcelain. The porcelain produced was admired for its ability to withstand boiling water without cracking and for its translucency. Robert Chamberlain, who was believed to have been Dr Wall's first apprentice, opened an independent decorating factory nearby in about 1783 and later the businesses merged and expanded into the Severn Street site which has been used ever since. In 1789 the company was given a

Right: Royal Worcester trademark number 2,686.

Below: Royal Worcester's Severn Street factory, *c.* 1870. (*Worcester Porcelain Museum*)

royal warrant and subsequently the word Royal was added to the name of the firm.

The company registered a trademark (number 2,686) in 1876 for its porcelain and pottery and this mark, along with others from the nineteenth century, is still registered. The '51' on the mark refers to the year 1751 when the original pottery was set up. In the last years of the nineteenth century Royal Worcester produced a new material, Parian ware, which revolutionised the making of figures. In 1976 Royal Worcester joined with ceramic manufacturer Spode to become Porcelain and Fine China Companies Ltd, which now owns the Royal Worcester trademark rights.

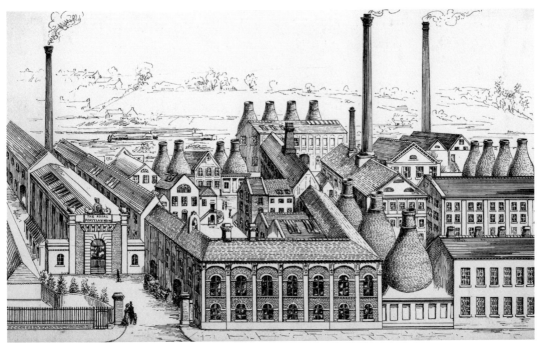

6

AGRICULTURAL, HORTICULTURAL AND INDUSTRIAL MERCHANDISE

Trademarks were not so important for heavy industries that did not sell into mass markets. Nevertheless, iron and steel firms like Carron, the Earl of Dudley and Firth did register some trademarks in the nineteenth century. Bessemer, the inventor of one of the key steel-making processes, was another to register a trademark, which in this case illustrated his tilting converter. Like much of British heavy industry, these firms and their marks have largely disappeared.

Manufacturers of tools such as Marples, Nettlefolds, Rabone and Spear & Jackson sold their products to a wider market and were keen to have their brands recognised and respected. Their names, if not their original trademarks, have survived in various ways.

The chemical industry was growing fast, though the number of marks registered was relatively small. Albright & Wilson, May & Baker and Nobel were among those which registered their marks, along with foreign companies like Badische Anilin- & Soda-Fabrik and Solvay, which had made important developments and wanted the benefits of British trademarks.

The last quarter of the nineteenth century was a time when agricultural produce was beginning to be imported on a

Ransome started to make ploughshares in the eighteenth century but developed the brand to be synonymous with lawnmowers, as this advertisement from the early 1930s illustrates. (*The Robert Opie Collection*)

large scale. Millers like Bibby were having to diversify to survive but seedsmen like Suttons and Webbs increasingly catered for local horticulture and export. Ransome's were long-standing agricultural machinery manufacturers but they started to specialise more and more in lawnmowers as the century turned.

Many cement manufacturers were registering their trademarks in the 1870s and 1880s and these were generally of circular design. It is perhaps unsurprising that when many of these firms amalgamated in 1900 the resulting company chose a Blue Circle logo. What is surprising is that the Trade Mark Registry allowed the trademark of Wm Tingley & Son (number 33,532) to be altered to show the new name.

ALBRIGHT & WILSON'S CHEMICALS

Arthur Albright was born in Oxfordshire in 1811 and in 1827 moved to Bristol, where he was apprenticed to his uncle as a chemist. In 1840 he joined the firm John & Edmund Sturge,

Albright & Wilson's trademark number 2,915.

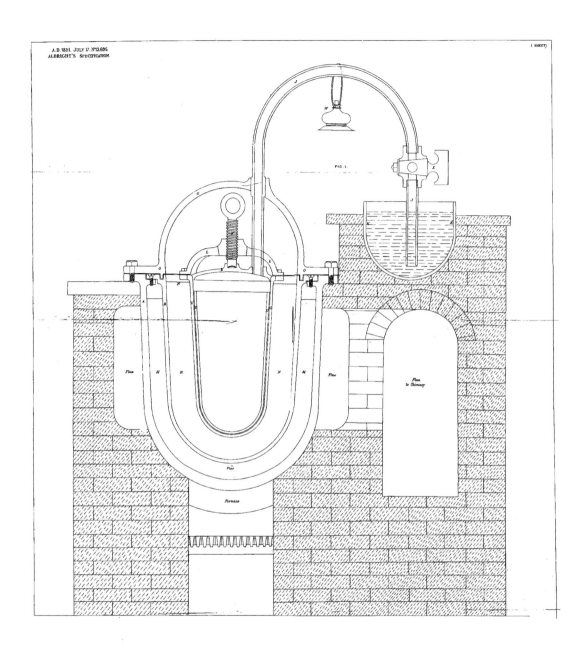

Albright's patent GB 13,695 of 1851 for phosphorus manufacture.

manufacturing chemists in Birmingham. In 1844 the firm started to produce phosphorus, which was used in the making of matches, and in 1851 Albright was granted a patent for his improved method. At this time production was transferred to Oldbury near Birmingham.

John Wilson was born in 1834 in Kendal and at the age of 16 he was sent to work in a warehouse in Manchester. In 1856 he became a partner in business with Arthur Albright, forming the

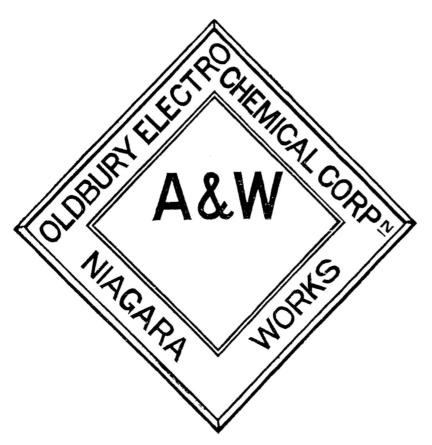

A 1905 trademark for Albright & Wilson, by then with works in Oldbury and New York State (number 276,917).

firm Albright & Wilson. Arthur Albright applied to register simple trademarks for the firm in 1876 (numbers 2,915–16) for phosphorus, chlorate of potash and sulphur.

Several generations of Wilsons and Albrights served the company, which prospered especially during the First World War when there was an increased need for phosphorus for munitions. In 1948 the firm became a public company and by 1951 it employed four thousand people in the UK, Ireland, North America and Australia. In the late 1960s it built plants at Belledune and Long Harbour in Canada but these turned out to be disastrous investments; the situation was rescued through the firm's partial acquisition by the American company Tenneco, which took full control in 1977. After reflotation in 1995, it was taken over by the French firm Rhodia four years later.

BADISCHE ANILIN- & SODA-FABRIK'S CHEMICALS

Badische Anilin- & Soda-Fabrik (BASF) of Ludwigshafen, Germany, was founded in 1865 by Friedrich Engelhorn to produce coal tar dyes. In 1873 the company merged with the Stuttgart firms of Rudolph Knosp and Heinrich Siegle and new trademarks were required. In 1876 the firm applied for four British trademarks

BASF trademark for aniline colours (number 33,391).

230

A BASF German trademark of 1895 with an Indian theme.

Nr. 7875. B. 482. **Badische Anilin= & Soda=Fabrik, Ludwigshafen a. Rh., Aktiengesellschaft,** Mannheim, mit Zweigniederlassung in Ludwigshafen a. Rh. Anmeldung vom 6. 10. 94 / 20. 6. 90. Eintragung am 2. 7. 95.

Geschäftsbetrieb: Fabrikation und Verkauf von Farben und chemischen Produkten.

Waarenverzeichniß: Farben und chemische Produkte.

This 1907 trademark shows an oriental theme and the Stuttgart horse and the Bavarian lion (number 298,099).

(numbers 2,911–14) for aniline dyes and artificial alizarin. All four trademarks showed either the Stuttgart horse on a shield or the Bavarian lion holding a shield with the coat of arms of the city of Ludwigshafen, then part of the kingdom of Bavaria. One trademark (number 2,912) showed both symbols. In 1883 the firm applied for British trademarks for aniline dyes, artificial alizarin and other chemicals (numbers 33,391–3 and 34,172–5), featuring Chinese scenes as well as the Bavarian horse. Since 1922 the firm has used geometric shapes and letters for its corporate trademark, apart from a brief return to the horse and lion after the Second World War.

In 1897 the firm had a major breakthrough when it succeeded in synthesising indigo blue dye. Since then BASF has diversified into other chemicals and by 2005 its sales reached €42.7 billion with eighty-seven thousand employees on five continents, including at the Ludwigshafen headquarters.

231

BESSEMER'S STEEL

Henry Bessemer was born in Hertfordshire in 1813, the son of a type-caster, and made his fortune by inventing brass powder used in 'gold' paint. He went on to make numerous other inventions for industrial processes such as glass-making, sugar refining and ordnance manufacture, and had taken out forty-six patents by the time of his most famous invention at the age of 43.

Bessemer's most successful invention was that of a steel-making process which was patented in 1856 (GB 44). This involved blowing air through the molten steel to remove carbon and thus

Below, left:

Bessemer's Converter trademark, number 12,904.

Below, right:

Bessemer's patent of 1856 (GB 44).

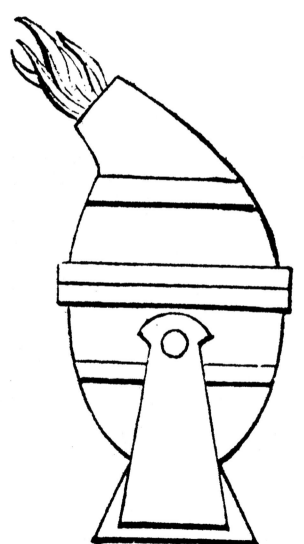

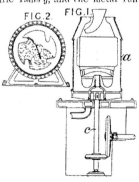

Bessemer or pneumatic processes; converter furnaces; blast and cupola furnaces; cementation. — Cast iron is refined and converted into malleable iron and steel by subjecting it to heat and to the action of air and steam. According to the first method, the molten metal is run through a series of small cupolas or blast furnaces in which it is broken up and heated by the fuel, and also subjected to the blast. Or two furnaces *a,* side by side, as shown in Fig. 4, with telescoping blast pipes *s,* are alternately raised and lowered by hydraulic rams *g,* and the metal run from one to the other until it is sufficiently refined. By the third modification, the metal and fuel are held in a horizontal revolving drum to which air is supplied through the trunnions; the interior may be plain, or formed into pockets, as shown in Fig. 2, to lift and drop the metal. In the fourth modification, the metal and fuel are contained in a drum *a,* Fig. 1, on a vertical axis *c,* which can be driven at such a speed as to lift the metal on to the walls by centrifugal action. Blast may be introduced centrally or laterally to act on the fuel and metal. Fig. 1 shows one of the three forms illustrated in the Specification. The refined metal may be cast into moulds and may be further treated by cementation for the manufacture of rods, bars, and plates.

create a much stronger product. He went on to develop a tilting steel converter which gained wide acceptance throughout the world. Bessemer & Co. Ltd registered two trademarks showing the tilting converter (numbers 12,904–5) in 1877 for iron and steel, machinery, tools, cannons, etc.; they had been in use since 1862.

BIBBY'S ANIMAL FEEDSTUFFS

In 1820 Edward Bibby became the tenant at Conder Mill near Quernmore, Lancaster, and ten years later he was able to buy it. The mill passed to one of his sons and then to two of his grandsons, Joseph and James, who from 1878 ran the business as J. Bibby & Sons. About this time, when there was a recession in arable farming and there was less flour milling to be done, the firm started to produce compound animal feed. It is claimed that Bibby was first to produce calf meal.

Bibby's trademark number 34,305.

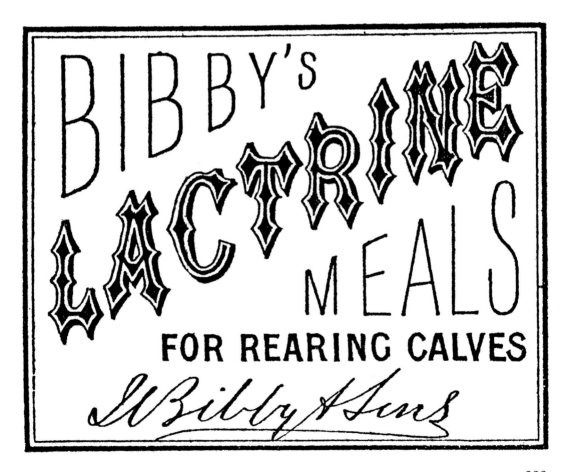

233

In 1883 the company registered a trademark for Lactrine meals for rearing calves (number 34,305), followed by other marks for wheaten flour and other calf feeds in 1884. In 1885 Condor Mill was destroyed by fire but the business continued at Fleet Square Mills, Lancaster, and a second mill was opened in Liverpool, where production increased to 3,000 tons per week within ten years.

Over the following decades the firm diversified into seed crushing, soap manufacture, vegetable oil refining and paper production. In 1968 it acquired Princes Foods Ltd. Bibby subsequently became part of ABN (Associated British Nutrition), which is owned by Associated British Foods plc. Recently Bibby has transferred its ruminant feed business and trademarks to Pye Farm Feeds.

BLUE CIRCLE CEMENT

In the second half of the nineteenth century there were many small cement manufacturers in Kent, such as William Tingley & Son at

Blue Circle's trademark number 33,532 (as it was originally registered).

the Frindsbury Cement Works in Rochester. In 1883 this company registered its first trademark (number 33,532) for Portland cement. Many companies at this time used circular marks that could be easily burnt on to the ends of the barrels used to pack the cement.

Large amounts of capital, which the small firms did not possess, were required to build efficient rotary kilns and so in 1900 Tingley and two dozen or so other small cement manufacturers and their subsidiaries merged to form Associated Portland Cement Manufacturers (1900) Ltd. It is said that one of the directors drew a circle with a blue pen around the names of all the merged companies and thus the blue circle brand came into being. Later the date 1900 was dropped from the name and the company used Blue Circle as its trading name. In the late 1970s it became Blue Circle Industries plc.

Unusually, trademark number 33,532 was officially altered in 1925 to reflect the change in name, and the new form of the mark

Blue Circle's trademark number 33,532 (as it is registered today).

is still registered today. In 2001 Blue Circle Industries was taken over by the French company Lafarge, the world's leading producer of cement. The UK cement business has kept its famous Blue Circle brand for cement.

CARRON IRON

John Roebuck, who was originally from Scotland, trained as a doctor but became more interested in chemistry and the purification of silver and gold. Together with Samuel Garbett and William Caddell, a wealthy ship-owner, he decided to set up an iron works in Scotland. The partners found a site on the River Carron to the north of Falkirk, where iron ore and coal were plentiful. They set up a partnership in 1759 with Roebuck's three brothers and Cadell's son. Despite early difficulties, pig iron and various other types of iron were made.

Carron's trademark number 26,496.

In 1771 the firm became the Carron Company and two years later it was incorporated by royal charter. By this time it was a major manufacturer of guns. Almost a century later in 1866 the firm launched the Carron Bath, which was to become ubiquitous in Britain's bathrooms. In 1881 the company applied for three trademarks (numbers 26,494–6) for pig iron, iron castings and bricks. Trademark number 26,494 had been in use since 1759. It consisted of the Carron Arms of crossed cannons with the motto *Esto perpetua* ('May it live forever').

At the end of the nineteenth century the firm's modern smelting plant enabled it to maintain

MORAY COOKING STOVE, 29×19×13 ins.
W · H · B

Specially suitable for use in Kitchens with bad going vents or for Fishing Boats.   With Sheet Iron Oven 13 × 7½ × 10⅝ ins., having hinged Door in halves; small Fire lined with Brick, with hinged Door and sliding Ventilator below to regulate draught.   Hob or Hotplate has loose Covers and forms an admirable Boiling Table.   Flue can go direct into flue pipe when quick fire is wanted, or go round Oven for Cooking; Oval Nozzle at back 7 × 3 ins. for pipe; Shovel, Raker and Lifting Hook.

Supplied also with Wrought Iron Guards or Rails and with Sheet Iron Funnel 24 ins. long.

supremacy in the industry and by 1913 the Carron company's interests included collieries, coke ovens, ironstone mines, limestone mines, refractory brick works, foundries, blast furnaces, plating shops, galvanising, porcelain, vitreous and stone enamelling shops, non-ferrous foundries, ships and warehouses.

Part of a Carron's Catalogue of Wrought and Cast-Iron Steamers' Hearths, Stoves, etc., of 1884.

In 1965 the firm diversified into plastic baths. Carron reorganised in the 1970s but failed to make a profit after 1979. In 1982 receivers were called in and only a few parts of the business, notably Carron Phoenix and Carron Bathrooms, survived.

CARTER'S TESTED SEEDS

In 1879 James Carter, Dunnet and Beale of 237 and 238 High Holborn, London, registered the 'Trocadéro – Carters Grass Seeds' trademark for their agricultural and horticultural seeds (number 20,331). The trademark shows the old Palais du Trocadéro in Paris, which was built for the 1878 World's Fair – one assumes that Carter's grass seed was used for the lawns.

The business is said to have started in 1804 and by 1880 its patrons included Queen Victoria, the Prince of Wales, the Sultan of Turkey, the King of Portugal and the King of Italy. In about 1910 the firm moved from its premises in High Holborn to Raynes Park in

Carter's Trocadéro trademark (number 20,331).

Carter's 1885 trademark for 'The Best and Cheapest' seeds (number 49,295).

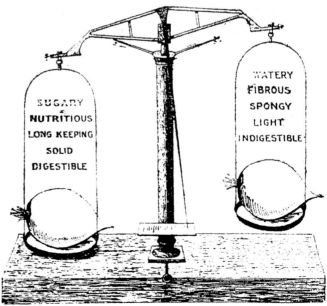

Carter's 1901 trademark (number 236,154) for agricultural and horticultural seeds (guess which is Carter's seed!).

south-west London. The firm became a limited company in 1930 under the name Carters Tested Seeds Ltd and is now, with Suttons, part of the international company Vilmorin, the largest packet seed distributors in the world. The Carters Tested Seeds trademark is still protected although the original trademark (number 49,295) is not.

COLT'S FIREARMS

Colt's trademark for rifles and pistols (number 10,476).

Samuel Colt may not have invented the revolver but from his US patent of 1836 for the famous Colt .45 he played a key role in developing the concept. He took out other patents, including

ones in England in 1851 (GB 13,527) and in Scotland (in 1850). Samuel Colt exhibited his pistols in London at the Great Exhibition of 1851 and was soon importing firearms from America before his London factory started production in 1854.

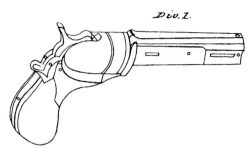

Samuel Colt's 1836 American patent for a revolver.

In 1877 Colt's Patent Firearms Manufacturing Co. registered two British trademarks for rifles and pistols (numbers 10,476–7), which are no longer registered. The first of these shows a rampant colt carrying a broken spear and the second the words Colt London. New Colt Holding Corporation of America now holds four British trademarks for firearms, including one similar to the original rampant colt, and Colt International Licensing Ltd owns many similar trademark logos for other products.

EARL OF DUDLEY'S IRON

Brierley Hill near Dudley in the West Midlands had been an iron manufacturing area since before the eighteenth century and the Round Oak steel works there can be traced back to 1784, when blast furnaces were built next to the canal constructed in the 1770s. The Round Oaks works was inherited by Lord Ward (later the Earl of Dudley) in 1835 and he built railways from his coal mines to feed the works. According to the 1868 book *Dudley: Illustrated By Photographs*, 'the works comprise four forges, containing besides the full

Earl of Dudley's trademark number 4,099.

Dudley and its iron works from the castle in 1853. (*Illustrated London News/Mary Evans Picture Library*)

complement of puddling and ball furnaces, four helve hammers of seven tons each, one huge steam hammer fifty tons, four shears, and four trains of rolls. [It was] a vast Cyclopean workshop.'

In 1876 the earl applied for a trademark for his iron (number 4,099), for which use was claimed since 1858, the year in which new works were built by his principal agent, Richard Smith. The trademark initials L.W.R.O. presumably signify 'Lord Ward, Round Oak'. The works employed over three thousand people at its peak and until just before closure in 1982.

FIRTH'S STEEL

Thomas Firth was born in Pontefract, Yorkshire, in 1789 and as a young man worked as a smelter in Sheffield. He later became head smelter at Sheffield firm Sanderson Brothers & Co., where the two eldest of his seven sons, Mark and Thomas, joined him. His sons left in 1842, dissatisfied with their wages, and set up

Firth's trademark
number 27,326.

Firth's 1907 trademark for shells and projectiles (number 288,585).

their own iron-smelting business in Charlotte Street, Sheffield. Thomas Sr and a few workers from Sanderson soon joined them.

By 1846 the business had grown and employed twenty-five or so staff. Thomas Sr died in 1850, by which time the business had expanded and was moving to the Norfolk works in Sheffield. Mark then took over the company, assisted by his brothers. The firm became the leading gun forgers in the world but was adversely affected by the depression between 1876 and 1878.

The firm Thomas Firth & Sons applied for a trademark in 1881 (number 27,326); it had been in use since 1851 and only expired in 1994. The company's main claim to fame is the invention by Harry Brearley in 1912 of stainless steel. Brearley found that a chrome alloy steel was much more rust-resistant than anything seen before and named it 'rustless steel', soon to be called 'stainless steel' by one of the Sheffield cutlery manufacturers. In 1967 Thomas Firth & Sons became one of the fourteen major UK steel companies that formed the British Steel Corporation, which itself became part of Corus in 1999, and then part of the Indian company Tata in January 2007.

KYNOCH'S AMMUNITION

George Kynoch started to manufacture percussion caps at the Lion Works, Witton, Birmingham, in 1862 and later manufactured metallic ammunition. In 1883 he applied for a series of trademarks using lion and bird logos (numbers 32,134–8). Use was claimed for the first trademark back to 1867. In 1884 the business was changed to a limited company, G. Kynoch & Co. Ltd, but five years later George Kynoch was ousted from the management and in 1891 he died in South Africa.

By 1897 the company name had changed to Kynoch Ltd and by the early years of the twentieth century the firm had ten factories in Birmingham, Kynoch Town in Essex, Barnsley and Ireland, and

Kynoch's lion trademark, number 32,136.

244

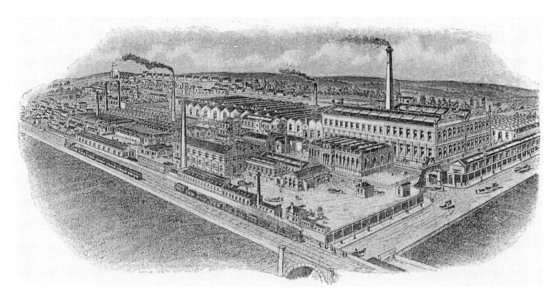

Kynoch's Lion Works at the end of the nineteenth century. (*The Kynoch Journal*, December 1899– January 1900)

A Kynoch 1902 trademark neatly uses ammunition to form the letter K (number 244,432).

the goods produced included explosives, engines, paper, soap, candles, brass, copper and all kinds of shells. After the First World War the company was merged, along with Eley and other ammunition makers, into Explosives Trades Ltd, which later became Nobel Industries.

In 1926 Nobel became part of the newly formed Imperial Chemical Industries and the Kynoch factory at Witton was retained as the ammunition manufacturing centre. In 1962 the Metals Division of ICI was reorganised as a separate company known as Imperial Metal Industries (Kynoch) Ltd. IMI became independent in 1977 and in 1993 the Ammunition Division became separately incorporated as Eley Ltd, which currently owns the Kynoch brand.

MARPLES' TOOLS

William Marples Jr joined his father's business making joinery tools in Rockingham Street, Sheffield, in 1821 when he was 12 years old. By 1828 he was trading under his own name from Broomhall Street and in 1837 transferred to bigger premises, known as Hibernian Works, in Broomspring Lane. About this time he adopted the Irish harp as a logo and only in 1887 changed to a shamrock (trademark numbers 61,480–1).

Marples' trademark number 61,480.

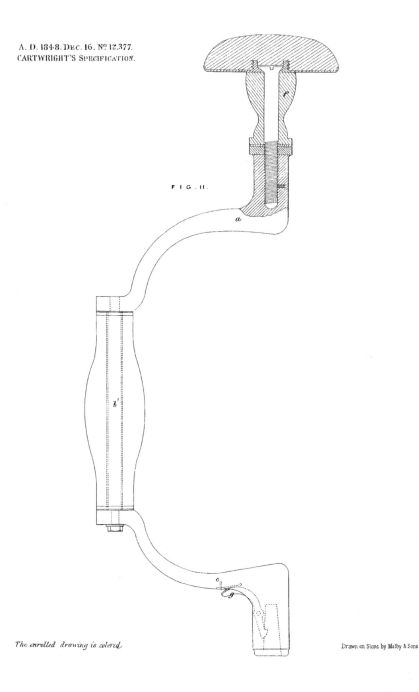

A. D. 1848. Dec. 16. Nº 12.377.
CARTWRIGHT'S SPECIFICATION.

F I G . II .

The enrolled drawing is colored.

Drawn on Stone by Malby & Sons.

Cartright's patent for a brace which Marples bought and manufactured as the Ultimatum.

In 1848 John Cartwright had taken out a patent for a carpenter's brace (GB 12,377), the rights for which Marples bought. The brace, which Marples called the Ultimatum, was gradually improved. In 1856 Marples moved to a workshop in Westfield Terrace, which the firm was to occupy for 116 years. In about 1860 William's sons Edwin Henry and William Kent became partners in the firm Wm Marples & Sons, and in 1878 trademarks were registered for E. Henry & Co. and Wm Kent (numbers 15,590–1). It was William Kent who applied for trademarks for edge tools and cutlery in 1883 (numbers 31,362–4).

The business remained in the Marples family until 1962, when it was purchased by W. Ridgeway & Sons and C. & J. Hampton Ltd. When the Sheffield works were sold for redevelopment in 1972 production transferred to Dronfield. The trademarks are now owned by the Irwin Industrial Tool Company Ltd.

MAY & BAKER'S CHEMICALS

In 1834 John May, with his two partners Joseph L. Pickett and Thomas S. Grimwade, started to manufacture chemicals for use in the pharmaceutical industry in Battersea, now London. In 1839 May took on a new chemist, William Garrard Baker, as a partner and the business became May & Baker. In 1884 the firm applied for three trademarks (numbers 35,440–2) for anti-corrosives, anti-foulers and chemicals for medicine, pharmacy, photography, philosophical research, agriculture, horticulture, veterinary use and sanitary use.

The company scientists developed sulphonamide drugs in the 1930s and became a major producer of a number of

May & Baker's trademark number 35,440.

important types of pharmaceuticals, including anti-bacterials and anti-malarials as well as agrochemicals, photochemicals and fine chemicals. The firm was taken over in 1927 by the French chemical company Rhône-Poulenc (and then became part of Aventis Pharma), although it continued to trade as May & Baker until the 1980s.

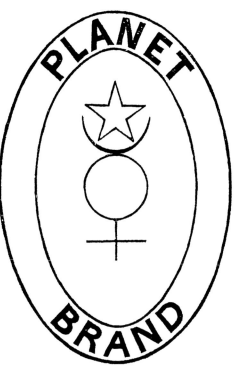

Right: A 1905 trademark for May & Baker's Planet brand (number 277,823).

Below: Technicians preparing a new drug at May & Baker's laboratory in Dagenham, *c.* 1945–70. (*Hulton-Deutsch Collection/Corbis*)

MORGAN'S CRUCIBLES

The five Morgan brothers started a business as importers, exporters and merchants some time before 1856 in what is now the Barbican in the City of London. Among the items they imported were ceramic crucibles (used for making metals and other materials), and after seeing superior American-made crucibles at the Great Exhibition of 1851 they became sole agents for the British Empire for crucibles from the New Jersey manufacturer Joseph Dixon & Co. In 1856 the brothers bought the manufacturing rights from the American company and a small factory in Battersea, London, where they erected a new kiln. Business for the Patent Plumbago Crucible Company, as it was then known, was good.

Morgan's trademark number 27,458.

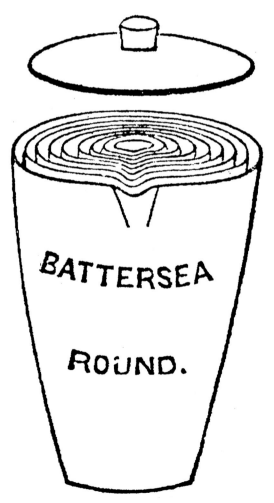

In 1882 several trademarks were registered (numbers 27,285, 27,454 and 27,457–9) by what was then the Morgan Crucible Co. In 1890 the firm became a public limited company with two Morgans on the board, chairman Octavius Morgan and member Edward Morgan. Early in the twentieth century the company started production of carbon brushes for electric motors. After the First World War the firm acquired the crucible business of Doulton & Co. but the post-war slump, and later the Great Depression, hit sales badly.

The company prospered in the Second World War and its Battersea factory suffered little bomb damage. After the war a new plant was opened on the Wirral in Cheshire. The Battersea site was still too small and in the 1970s production was transferred to a greenfield site near Swansea in South Wales and the Battersea factory closed. Two of the original trademarks

(numbers 27,458–9) for Battersea Round and Battersea Triangle are still owned by what is now the Morgan Crucible Company plc.

A 1905 Morgan Crucible salamander trademark (number 270,301).

NETTLEFOLD'S SCREWS

Nettlefold & Company was set up in Smethwick by John Sutton Nettlefold in 1854 to make screws using new American machinery. His son Joseph Henry Nettlefold managed the business and turned it into one of the world's leading manufacturers of screws. Nettlefold opened the Castle ironworks in Hadley, Shropshire, in 1871 and soon it was making wire and 400–500 tons of bar iron each week, although production was taken back to Smethwick in 1886 because of the high costs in Shropshire. In 1876 Joseph Nettlefold applied for a series of

Nettlefold's castle trademark, number 2,774.

trademarks (numbers 2,774–7) for screws, iron wire, rolled iron, etc., all showing a castle logo. At that time the firm was also trading under the names the Imperial Wire Co. and the Castle Iron Co.

The firm was taken over by Guest, Keen & Company Ltd in 1902 to form Guest, Keen, Nettlefolds Ltd, with Mr Edward Nettlefold joining the board. GKN, as it became known, expanded rapidly through the acquisition of other companies during the early part of the twentieth century to become a major UK

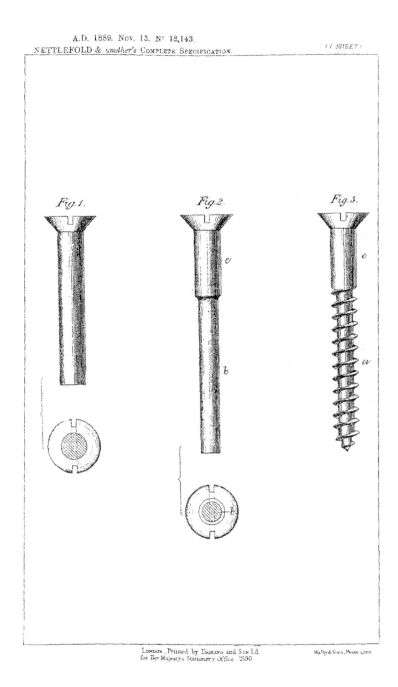

Fig. 1.

Fig. 2.

Fig. 3.

London. Printed by Darling and Son Ld.
for Her Majesty's Stationery Office. 1890

Malby & Sons, Photo-Litho

Hugh Nettlefold's 1889 patent for making screws.

engineering and manufacturing company with current sales of £3.6 billion.

Trademark number 2,774, which was first used in 1871, only expired in 2002 but other Nettlefold marks are still used by GKN. The firm still has operations at the Hadley Castle works.

Nobel's trademark
number 10,997 for
dynamite.
Below: Nobel's 1902
trademark for
gunpowder (number
244,632).

NOBEL'S DYNAMITE

Alfred Nobel was born in 1833 in Stockholm, Sweden, but early in his life his family moved to St Petersburg in Russia. Alfred was interested in both science and the arts but was sent abroad to train as a chemical engineer, returning to Sweden in 1863 to concentrate on developing nitroglycerine as an explosive. His brother Emil was killed in a nitroglycerine explosion in 1863 and subsequently experimentation with it was made illegal in Stockholm.

Alfred continued to experiment outside Stockholm to make the explosive safer and within a few years produced dynamite, which is a stable mixture of nitroglycerine and silica. He made a number of other inventions, including the blasting cap used as a detonator. In 1870 he set up his Nobel's Explosives firm at Ardeer, Scotland, and by 1877 had applied for a trademark for dynamite (number 10,997).

The firm, with three other major chemical businesses, was transformed into Imperial Chemical Industries Ltd

ALFRED NOBEL.

Alfred Nobel, from A.W. Cronquist (*Alfred Nobel, hans far och hans bröder, etc.*, Stockholm, 1898)

(ICI) in 1926. When Nobel died in 1896, it came as a surprise to all that his fortune was to be used for prizes in Physics, Chemistry, Physiology or Medicine, Literature and Peace – the Nobel Prizes.

PILKINGTON'S GLASS

When the St Helens Crown Glass Company was set up in 1826 with capital from three of the most influential families in St Helens, Lancashire, it was the sole producer of flat glass in Britain. The families were the Bromilows, the Greenalls and the Pilkingtons. William Pilkington was one of the original shareholders and he was later joined by his elder brother Richard.

Pilkington's
trademark number
13,100.

The firm was renamed Greenall & Pilkington in 1829 and
Pilkington Brothers in 1849 after the withdrawal of Peter
Greenall.

In the 1870s Pilkington Brothers set up a new factory to
produce plate glass on the outskirts of St Helens and in 1877 the
firm registered its first trademark (number 13,100), which
expired only in 2003. The cross in the centre of the trademark is
still used in many of the current Pilkington trademarks.

Over the years the firm has patented many aspects of glass
manufacture but in the twentieth century the most significant
development was the invention in the 1950s of the float-glass
process which became the universal method for making plate
glass and flat glass for windows. The firm continued at St
Helens as a private family firm until 1970, when it became
Pilkington plc, which was recently taken over by the Japanese
NSG group.

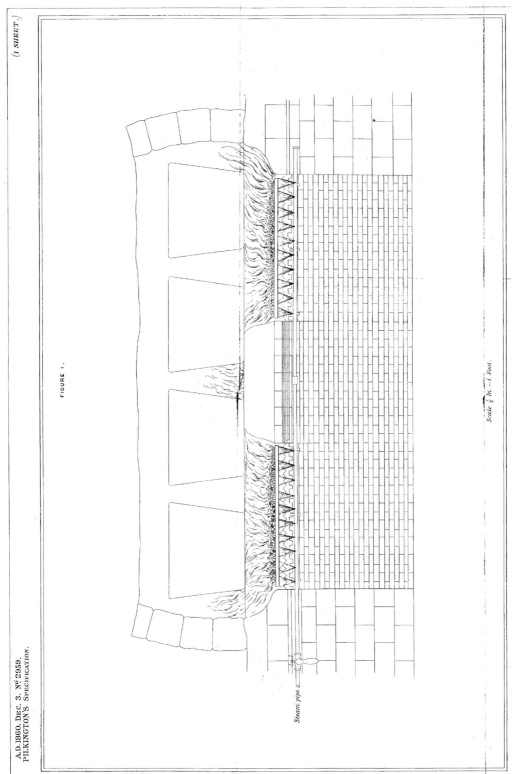

A.D.1860. Dec. 3. Nº 2959.
PILKINGTON'S SPECIFICATION.

FIGURE 1.

Steam pipe.

Scale ½ In. — 1 Foot.

William Pilkington's patented furnace for melting glass (GB 2,959 of 1860).

257

RABONE'S TOOLS

John Rabone & Sons, rule and tool maker, has its origins in Birmingham in 1784. John was born in 1803 and took over the business in 1817; his son, also John, joined the firm in 1845. In 1872 their newly patented spirit levels and rules were exhibited in Moscow, followed by other exhibitions in Vienna, Sydney and Melbourne. The firm moved to Hockley Abbey in Birmingham in 1871. John Jr's sons Harry and Arthur joined as partners in 1873 and 1877 respectively, after which the firm became John Rabone & Sons.

Rabone's trademark number 3,413.

JOHN RABONE & SON'S

PATENT ADJUSTABLE PLUMB AND SPIRIT LEVELS.

WARRANTED CORRECT.

BY ROYAL LETTERS   PATENT.   DRAWN ONE THIRD SIZE.

Adjusting Plumb and Level, Arch Top Plate, Side Views.

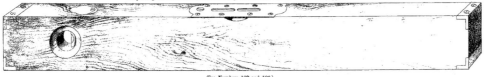

(See Numbers 101 and 105.)

Adjusting Plumb and Level, Arch Top Plate, Side Views, Full Brass Tipped.

(See Numbers 102 and 106.)

Adjusting Plumb and Level, Arch Top Plate, Brass Lipped Side Views, Full Brass Tipped.

(See Numbers 103 and 107.)

IMPROVED TRIPLE STOCK LEVEL, MADE OF THREE PIECES OF WOOD JOINED TOGETHER.

Adjusting Plumb and Level, Triple Stock, Arch Top Plate, Brass Lipped Side Views, Full Brass Tipped.

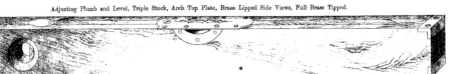

(See Numbers 104 and 108.)

ENTERED AT STATIONERS' HALL, 1872.

In 1876 applications were made for four trademarks (numbers 3,413–16) for Vulcan, Atlas, Hockley Abbey and J. Rabone & Son Patentees Hockley Abbey. Vulcan was a Roman god and the manufacturer of art, arms and iron, and Atlas was a Greek Titan, a symbol of strength.

The Rabone family controlled the business until about 1962 and in 1963 it merged with toolmaker James Chesterman & Co. of Sheffield and the firm became Rabone Chesterman. Although a new factory was opened in Summer Hill, Birmingham, in 1984, business is still done at Hockley Abbey.

Rabone's spirit levels from an 1872 catalogue.

259

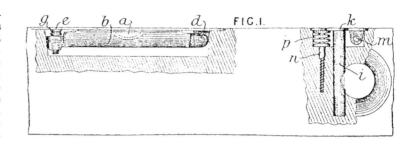

Rabone's 1872

patent for a spirit

level (GB 1,989).

Ransome's

trademark number

12,371.

RANSOME'S AGRICULTURAL MACHINERY

Robert Ransome was born in 1753, the son of a Quaker schoolmaster. He was apprenticed to a Norwich ironmonger before going into business on his own. In 1789, with capital of £200, he moved to Ipswich in Suffolk to a new foundry where he made ploughshares. His chilling process to produce cast iron with a hard under surface and a softer upper layer was a technical breakthrough which produced self-sharpening ploughs. He obtained several patents for his inventions.

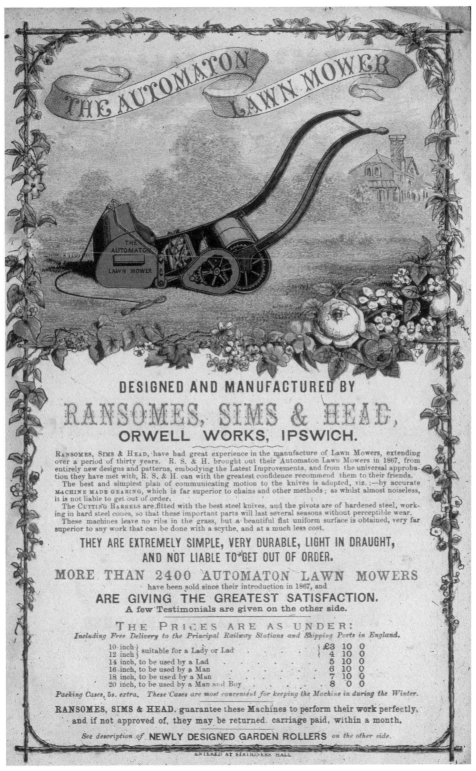

A leaflet for Ransome's Automaton lawnmower from the 1870s. (*The Robert Opie Collection*)

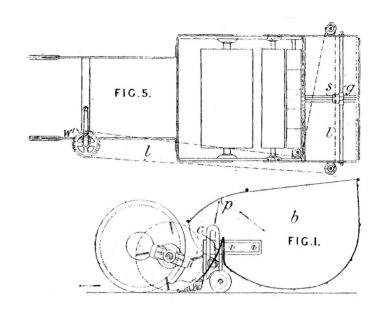

Lawn-mowers.—Relates to detail improvements in the means for collecting the cut grass and depositing it in heaps on the ground. A concave *c*, Fig. 1, is arranged behind the cutter barrel, and throws the stream of grass upwards against a plate *p* which deflects it into the grass box *b*. The plate *p* forms a part of the box *b*. In large machines, the grass box is emptied periodically by means of a plate *s*, Fig. 5, sliding on a guide-bar *g*. The plate *s* is operated by a chain *l* passed over guide-pulleys to a sprocket-wheel w^1 mounted on the handles, within reach of the driver.

James Edward Ransome's 1900 lawnmower patent (GB 21,049).

In 1808 Robert's son James joined the firm, which then became Ransome & Son, and from 1812 until 1826 the famous engineer William Cubitt was employed by the firm, which had started bridge-building and mill-wrighting. In 1830 Robert's grandson James Allen became a partner and developed other agricultural implements, including lawnmowers, for the firm. A new lawnmower works was opened in 1872.

In 1877 a series of trademarks was registered for ploughs, ploughshares, lawnmowers and haymaking machines (numbers 12,369–88) by the firm, which at that time was known as Ransome, Sims & Head of the Orwell Works, Ipswich. Over a hundred years later Ransomes plc is one of the best-known names in British agricultural engineering and is still based in Ipswich.

RUGBY CEMENT

The original Rugby works at Newbold produced lime but after the discovery in 1824 that burning impure limestone produced cement it started to produce Crown cement. It was run as a family concern by local landowner Thomas Walker, whose son George Henry Walker opened a works at New Bilton, Rugby, which he called the Victoria Lime and Stone Company.

Rugby Cement
trademark number
8,728.

By 1876 the firm had started to make Portland cement and had applied for a trademark (number 8,728) as the Rugby Portland Cement Company. Early in the twentieth century the Walker family continued to run the business and invested in new rotary kilns, but despite this the company was not very profitable. After the depression of the early 1930s the business was modernised and there followed a period of acquisition of other cement companies.

By 1970, Rugby Cement was producing 2.5 million tonnes of cement per year and another period of investment and acquisitions followed. Early in 2000 the firm was taken over by the RMC Group plc, which started life in 1930 as a ready-mixed concrete supplier. The original trademark for lime and cement is still registered and used today.

SCHERING'S CHEMICALS

In 1851 Ernest Schering purchased a chemist's shop, the Green Pharmacy, in Berlin and in 1871 it became a public limited company, Chemische Fabrik auf Aktien. An affiliate company, Schering & Glatz, was soon operating in New York and in 1920 the Schering Corporation subsidiary was set up in America. This was nationalised during the Second World War and later merged with Plough Inc. to become Schering Plough, which has remained completely separate from the German company.

During 1877–8 Chemische Fabrik auf Aktien applied for British trademarks for Celloidin and Celloidin-collodium forms of nitro-cellulose (numbers 12,773 and 14,460–1). The company continued to expand, establishing new factories and a laboratory. In 1927 the company amalgamated with the Berlin Chemische Fabrik Kahlbaum to form Schering-Kahlbaum AG, which became Schering AG when there was a change in ownership ten years later.

Schering's trademark number 14,460.

264

After the Second World War the business was dismantled and the trademarks and other assets confiscated but in 1950 the business was re-established. It now produces diagnostic and radio-pharmaceuticals, fertility control and hormone therapy products, dermatology treatments and therapeutics for disabling diseases. Sales are now over £5 billion.

SOLVAY'S CHEMICALS

Ernest Solvay was born in 1838 at Rebecq-Rognon in Belgium. He developed an interest in chemistry and was the inventor, with his brother Alfred, of the Solvay process for producing sodium carbonate from salt, ammonia and carbon dioxide. The invention was patented widely including in the UK in 1863 (GB 3,131). In the same year Ernest set up Solvay & Cie to exploit the invention but it took ten years to perfect the process, during which time bankruptcy threatened several times.

In the 1870s factories were set up in England, France, Germany, Russia and the United States. The first British trademark using an S logo was applied for in 1878 (number 14,007) and is still registered by the Solvay business today. Ernest Solvay lived until 1922 and during his lifetime founded the Institute of Physiology

Solvay's trademark number 14,007.

Solvay's trademark number 14,007 is still in use today. (*Solvay*)

in Brussels and supported many universities. The company later produced peroxide chemicals and PVC plastics, and in the 1950s moved into pharmaceuticals.

SPEAR & JACKSON'S TOOLS

The tool-making firm Spear & Jackson was set up in 1760 by a draper named John Love, who started up a new business to make crucible steel in Sheffield with Mr Manson. In the event the business made saws rather than steel. Love was joined in partnership by Alexander Spear, a wealthy merchant from Wakefield. By 1814 the business was being run by Alexander's nephew John Spear, and despite some difficult years was exporting saws to Europe and America by 1820. John then took on Samuel Jackson, who in 1830 became a partner in Spear & Jackson. The firm exhibited at the 1851 Great Exhibition and won a medal for its 5ft cast circular saw.

Spear & Jackson's trademark number 4,451.

In 1862 Samuel Jackson pressed a Select Committee to set up a trademark registration system but his advice went unheeded until the following decade. In 1876 the firm registered its first

A 1907 Spear & Jackson trademark (number 292,888) for agricultural and horticultural machinery showing leap-frogging men (presumably not Mr Spear and Mr Jackson).

trademarks (numbers 4,451–8), which had then been in use for twenty-five years. The first of these trademarks is still on the register today. In 1985 Sheffield-based James Neill Ltd, which owned the Eclipse brand of tools, bought Spear & Jackson and in 1995 the company was renamed Spear & Jackson plc. Today Spear & Jackson's headquarters are still in Sheffield and the firm is known for its blades and garden tools.

SUTTON'S SEEDS

The House of Sutton was founded as a corn merchant in 1806 by John Sutton in King Street, Reading. In 1832 he was joined by his sons Martin and Alfred, and in 1836 Martin became a partner and the firm became Sutton & Son. A few years later the business was transferred to the Market Place, when the sons persuaded their father to start in the flower and vegetable seed trade. Martin

started a nursery and greenhouse in Queens Road and by mid-1838 he was selling greenhouse plants. In 1840 a seed-testing station was set up and in 1873 new offices and warehouses were built in Market Place, Reading.

Two trademarks were registered in 1876 (numbers 2,934–5). The first, for Sutton & Sons good seeds, is still registered, although originally it stated 'Carriage free', a phrase that has since been replaced by 'For all climates'. Alterations are allowed to British trademarks

Above: Sutton's first trademark (number 2,934) from 1876 is similar to Webb's first mark.

Right: Sutton's 1876 mangle trademark (number 2,935).

only if they do not substantially affect the identity and in this case this seems to have been permitted in 1946. Other trademarks were registered in 1878, 1881 and 1886; the last of these, for Sutton's seeds, is also still registered.

In 1962 Sutton moved premises in the Reading area, relocated again in 1976, this time to Torquay in Devon, and then in December 1998 moved to brand-new premises in Paignton, Devon. At one time Sutton was part of the AB Volvo Group but is now part of the international company Vilmorin, the largest packet seed distributors in the world. Vilmorin also owns Carters Seeds.

TWYFORD'S WATER CLOSETS

In 1849 Thomas Twyford, a descendant of the potter Joshua Twyford from Hanley, Stoke-on-Trent, established two factories where wash-basins and water closet pans were made. In the same year his first son Thomas William was born in Hanley. During the early 1880s Thomas William designed and manufactured the first one-piece wash-out pedestal closet sold as the Unitas.

In 1884 a trademark was registered for the Unitas name (number 40,447) and this has remained on the register to the present day. Other trademarks followed, including Twyford's

Twyford's National water closet trademark (number 52,513).

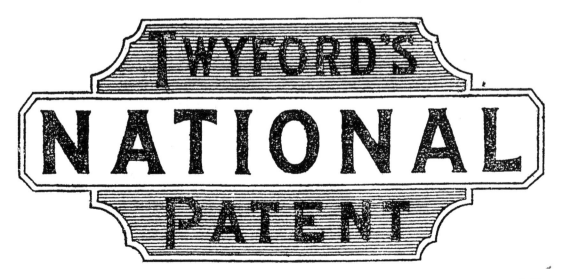

Closets fitted with washing-basins, designed for the use of Mohammedans, who are prohibited from using toilet paper (cleansing by washing being enjoined). In front of the basin *a*, which may be of any type, a washing-basin *b* is fixed. This basin is provided with a flushing-scroll b^2 and spreader b^3, communicating with the scroll of the basin *a* by an orifice a^5. It is also provided with a waste-pipe *d*, which leads the water back again to the main basin. The simultaneous flushing of the basins is thus effected. In plan, the closet has the shape of the figure 8, the constriction occurring between the two basins being intended for the accommodation of the user's legs.

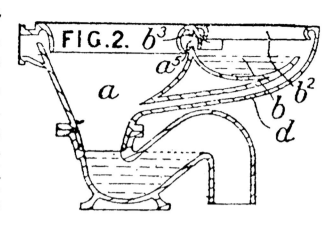

FIG.2.

Thomas William Twyford's 1888 patent for a combined WC and bidet (GB 9,163).

National Patent (number 52,513) and the Deluge (number 54,121).

Twyfords became a public limited company in 1919, two years before Thomas William's death. In 1971 Twyfords joined Reed International Ltd to form the Reed Building Products Division, which was bought in 1985 by Caradon Ltd, which in turn was purchased by the MB Group to form MB Caradon.

WEBB'S SEEDS

Edward Webb set up his business as a seed merchant in the middle of the nineteenth century at Wordsley near Stourbridge in the West Midlands. In 1876 Edward Webb & Sons was one of the earliest applicants for a registered trademark (number 928), which covered agricultural seeds and artificial manures. About 1894 the firm took over, and later expanded, the bone manure works of Proctor & Ryland in Saltney, near Chester.

By the end of the nineteenth century Webb's seeds were well known throughout the country and the firm had been appointed seedsmen to Queen Victoria. Early in the twentieth century William Webb, one of Edward's grandsons, was running the business. In 1925 a trial ground for testing seeds was set up at Wychbold in Worcestershire. Webbs merged with the seed firm Bees in the 1960s and transferred to Chester. In 2004 Westland Horticulture, based in County Tyrone, Northern Ireland, bought Unwins Seeds, which at that time owned the Webb's brand.

Webb's trademark for 'prize seeds, grasses, roots and manures' (number 928).

WHITWORTH ENGINEERING

Joseph Whitworth was born at Stockport, Cheshire, in 1803. At the age of 18 he ran away to Manchester and worked in a factory as a mechanic and then worked in London for Maudslay and Field, well-known engineers of the day. He returned to Manchester in 1833 to set up in business on his own and produced machine tools with better accuracy. He invented a method of machining very flat surfaces and a very accurate micrometer but is often remembered for his introduction of standard screw threads. At his works at Openshaw, near Manchester, Whitworth also designed rifles and artillery.

He converted the business into a limited liability company in 1874, and in 1876 applied for a trademark (number 5,897) showing the wheatsheaf logo that had been in use from 1865. A

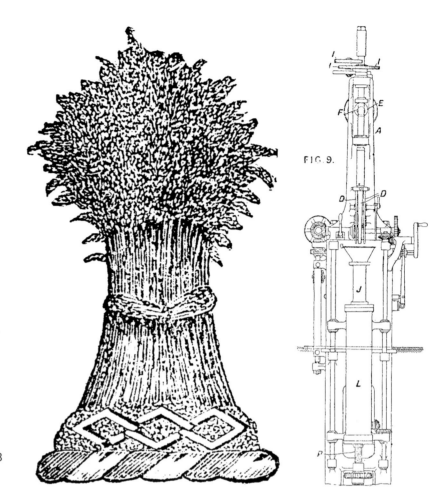

Right: Whitworth's wheatsheaf trademark, number 5,897.

Far right: Whitworth's 1870 patent for casting rifled projectiles (GB 1,745).

FIG. 9.

wheatsheaf appears in the Whitworth coat of arms. In 1897 the business merged with William Armstrong's engineering firm in Elswick, Newcastle, which in turn amalgamated with the Siddeley Deasy Company in 1919 to become Armstrong Siddeley.

7

MEDICINES AND TOILETRIES

Pills, Potions and Perfumes

In Victorian times people relied on patent medicines to treat all manner of illnesses and as there was no scientific basis on which to judge how effective they were, many firms thrived by promoting their products on the strength of testimonials and heavy advertising. Trademarks were an important component of advertising.

Names of patent medicines like Beecham's, Milk of Magnesia and Eno's were as familiar to many people at the end of the nineteenth century as they are to the older generation today. Since the Second World War, though, there have been huge scientific advances and resulting growth in prescription drugs, such as antibiotics, and some of the companies involved in these developments have evolved from those early makers of patent remedies. Today's drug trademarks are usually scientific-sounding names rather than the more interesting graphic marks of years gone by.

Many of the medicine makers in this chapter merged as drug manufacture became more complex and costly. Allen & Hanbury, Beecham, Burroughs Wellcome, Eno and Glaxo have all ended up as part of GlaxoSmithKline, now one of the world's major pharmaceutical companies.

Many soap manufacturers have merged, too. Crosfield, Lever and Pears are all part of the Anglo-Dutch Unilever company. Some early trademarks for soap have survived, but even more have disappeared. Pears soap, produced as an upmarket product, is still in our shops, although Wright's Coal Tar Soap is now very hard to find and Lever's Sunlight soap has fallen out of favour.

A trademark for Eno's Fruit Salts from 1908 (number 305,117).

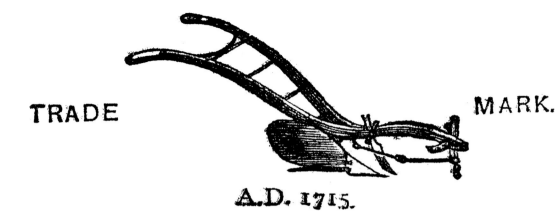

TRADE   MARK.

A.D. 1715.

Allen & Hanbury's
plough trademark
(number 3,628).

ALLEN & HANBURY'S MEDICINES

Silvanus Bevan, an apothecary and Fellow of the Royal Society, started a pharmacy at the Old Plough Court, Lombard Street in London in 1715; over a century later it would become Allen & Hanbury. William Allen became an employee in 1792 and five

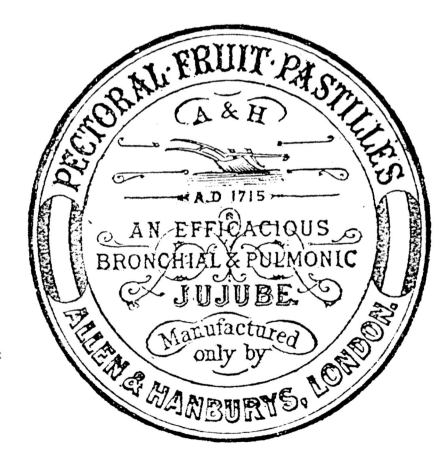

An 1879 trademark
for Allen &
Hanbury's fruit
pastilles (number
20,317).

274

Allen & Hanbury's
1904 trademark
using the letter A
(number 265,839).

years later took over the business. He was one of the most famous Quakers of his time and later helped found the Pharmaceutical Society. In 1824 Daniel Bell Hanbury and Cornelius Hanbury were taken into partnership and the Hanbury family then ran the firm, which became Allen & Hanbury, for many generations.

In the 1870s the main products were cod liver oil, malt products, pastilles, jujubes and milk food for infants. Cornelius Hanbury applied for a trademark in 1876 for cod liver oil, tinctures, extracts, pills, cachets and confectionery (number 3,628), using a plough logo to represent the pharmacy at Plough Court. Soon many other trademarks were registered. By 1923, when the firm started to manufacture insulin, the business's annual turnover had reached over £1 million. In 1958 the firm merged with Glaxo Laboratories, which later became Glaxo Holdings plc.

BEECHAM'S PILLS

Thomas Beecham was born in 1820 in Curbridge, Oxfordshire. At the age of 8 he became a farmer's boy but at 20 moved to Lancashire and became a market trader. By 1842 he was selling Beecham's pills and other medicines at markets around Wigan and then he acquired premises in St Helens where he opened his first factory in 1858. The business prospered through advertising and testimonials and by 1875 he was exporting his remedies to Africa and Australia.

Beecham was one of the first to apply for a trademark in January 1876 (number 1,416) for his patent pills. This trademark had by then already been in use for sixteen years. Thomas had two sons, Joseph and William, who succeeded him in the business when he died in 1907. From the 1880s the firm publicised the pills on a record scale through fun advertisements.

Beecham's Powders were launched in 1926 but the business got into difficulties soon after, at which point the firm was sold and the family connection ended. The name was then changed to Beecham Pills Ltd and the new firm was amalgamated with the makers of Veno's cough medicine and Germolene antiseptic. During a period of expansion in 1938–9 it bought Macleans toothpaste, Lucozade health drink, Eno's Fruit Salts and Brylcreem hair dressing to add to its portfolio of brands.

During the 1950s and 1960s the company was one of the leaders in antibiotics,

Beecham's trademark number 1,416.

Nr. 5841. B. 705. Tho=
mas Beecham, St. Helens
(England); Vertreter: Dr. Joh.
Schanz und Max Wertheim,
Berlin. Anmeldung vom 13.
10. 94/6. 2. 90. Eintragung
am 30. 4. 95.

Geschäftsbetrieb: Fabri=
kation nachbenannter Waaren.

Waarenverzeichniß: Me=
dizinische Präparate

Above: A trademark almost identical to the British mark was registered by Beecham in Germany in 1895.

Right: Advertisement showing Beecham's Pill Manufactory in St Helen's, Lancashire, in 1893. (*London Illustrated News Picture Library*)

discovering Amoxycillin. In 1989 the firm merged with the American drug company Smith Kline to form SmithKline Beecham, which in turn merged in 2000 with Glaxo Wellcome. Production of Beecham's pills, which contained nothing more than ginger, coriander, soap, aloes, rosemary oil, juniper oil, anise oil, capsicum oleoresin, ginger oleoresin and light magnesium carbonate, ceased in 1998.

BURROUGHS WELLCOME'S DRUGS

The Burroughs Wellcome company was set up in 1880 by two American pharmacists, Silas Burroughs, then aged 35, and Henry Wellcome, aged 27. Burroughs was born in Medina, New York, worked in several pharmacies and graduated in 1877. He was soon working as a sales representative for John Wyeth & Brother. Wellcome was the son of a farmer-preacher from Wisconsin. At 13 he helped in the family drug store in Minnesota and later took a post with a firm of pharmaceutical chemists in nearby Rochester before joining another drug house. After two years he joined McKesson & Robbins selling gelatine-coated pills in America and later moved to London as their sole overseas agent; here, in 1879, he registered a British trademark for Capsuled Pills (number 22,389).

Below: Burroughs' trademark (number 20,167) for the Kepler Malt Extract Co. *Bottom:* Burrough's trademark for a bismuth and strychnine preparation (number 20,264).

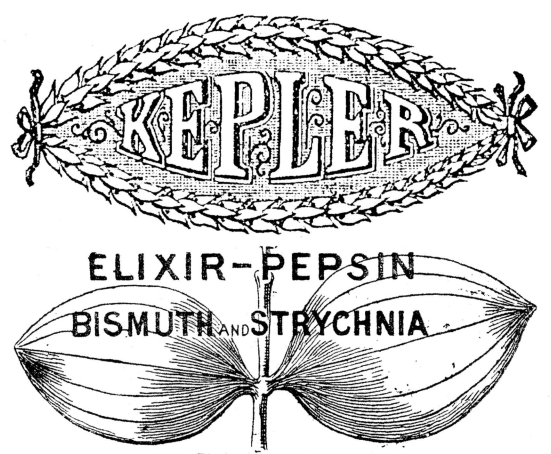

THE STRYCHNOS NUX VOMICA

CAPSULED-PILLS

Burroughs joined Wellcome in London and in 1879 registered one trademark (number 20,167), which only expired in 2005, on behalf of the Kepler Malt Extract Co. of Snow Hill, London, and others in his own name (including number 20,264 for a bismuth and strychnine preparation). He was soon selling 'compressed medicines', for which Wellcome coined the trademark Tabloid in 1884 (numbers 36,154–5, which are still registered). It is said that the word Tabloid came to him at 4.30 in the morning by combining the words 'tablet' and 'alkaloid'. By 1901 Wellcome was taking action against infringers of the trademark.

Burroughs liked travelling and the good life but died in 1895. Wellcome was a frugal but philanthropic man, setting up the Wellcome Foundation in 1924 to take over all of the company interests. By 1979 the Foundation had distributed £56 million for the relief of suffering and disease. The company did well in the first quarter and the second half of the twentieth century and by 1980 sales had reached £400 million through successful drugs like Zyloric and Septrin and through veterinary medicines. In 1995 the Glaxo company and Wellcome merged and in 2000 GlaxoSmithKline was formed through the merger with SmithKline Beecham. The Foundation, now the Wellcome Trust, continues separately as a major charity.

CARTER'S LITTLE LIVER PILLS

Below: Carter's 1885 trademark (number 48,916).

Opposite, top: A 1906 trademark for Carter's pills lists the complaints it alleviates (number 286,923).

Opposite, bottom: A 1910 advertisement highlighting the 1906 trademark. (*Mary Evans Picture Library*)

The Carter Medicine Company was set up in America in 1880 to sell Carter's Little Liver Pills and soon it was selling the pills in Britain from Holborn Viaduct in London. The 'purely vegetable' pills were advertised as being good for a torpid liver, bilious headaches and much else.

In 1885 the company applied for three trademarks (numbers 48,914–16), of which numbers 48,915 and 48,916 are still registered. The pills disappeared from chemist's shops after it became difficult to prove to the public that they were a cure for so many ills. Carter's Laxative, though, is still sold in America in packets bearing a big L logo similar to the packaging of the original Little Pills. The company became Carter-Wallace in 1965 and was taken over in 2001 by Church & Dwight Co., makers of Arrid deodorant and Arm and Hammer toothpaste.

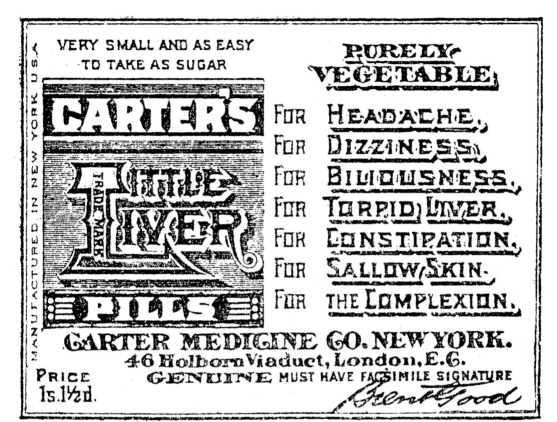
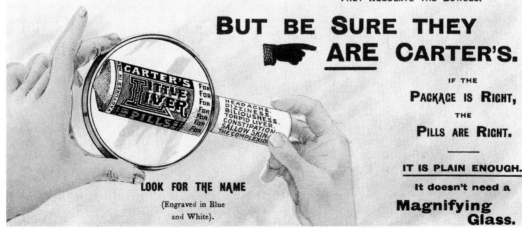

4711 COLOGNE

In 1693 Jean-Paul Femini from Cologne acquired the formula for an eastern concoction of lemon and rosemary known as Aqua Mirabilis Coloni. A family member, Jean-Marie Farina, started to produce the Eau de Cologne in 1742 and one of his German descendants, Johann Maria Farina, later sold the formula for the Cologne to perfumer Wilhelm Mülhens.

Mülhens had opened a shop in 1792 and the address was 4711 Glockengasse so the number became the trademark. In 1886 Die Eau de Cologne & Parfumerie-Fabrik applied for two British trademarks (numbers 50,146–7) for the perfume, and the first of these is still registered today by Mülhens GmbH & Co. KG. Seven generations of Mülhens ran the firm until it was sold in 1994 and became part of the Wella company. Though there were, and still are, many producers of eau de Cologne, today 4711 Eau de Cologne is the world's oldest continuously produced fragrance and is available in bottles with labels similar to those produced over a hundred years ago.

Mülhens' 4711 trademark (number 50,146) from 1886.

This trademark for Mülhens' Eau de Cologne (number 50,146) is not familiar today.

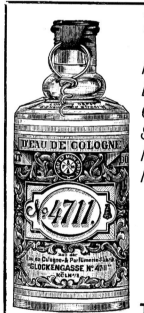

Buy the **4711 Eau de Cologne**

It is the
Best
Genuine,
Strongest,
Most Lasting,
Most Refreshing
and Invigorating.

INSIST UPON

MÜLHENS' "4711" BRAND.

REFUSE ALL SUBSTITUTES.

Of most Dealers in first-class Perfumes.

Case of Six Bottles carriage paid for 13s.; or Sample Bottle, 2s. 6d. post free.

THE 4711 DEPOT, 62, NEW BOND STREET, W.

An 1897 advertisement for 4711 Cologne. (*Mary Evans Picture Library*)

JOSEPH CROSFIELD'S SOAP

Joseph Crosfield started manufacturing soap at Bank Quay, Warrington, Lancashire, when he was 21 years old in 1815, and for over a hundred years Joseph Crosfield & Sons remained a successful family business. Joseph was the fourth

son of a Cumberland Quaker, who had started as a grocer in Warrington and, with partners, opened a sugar refining business. Joseph sank £1,500 into a soapworks but did not see much profit in the first few years, especially when the duty on hard soap was increased from 2¼ to 3 pence per pound weight in 1816. When Joseph died in 1844 the business had grown considerably and his son George carried on the firm. In 1848 another brother joined and the firm became Joseph Crosfield & Sons.

In 1877 the firm's first trademark was registered for Pale Perfection soap (number 11,100) and in the following year Marbled Blue was registered (number 14,253). The word pale was dropped from the former brand in 1885 but in 1909 its registration met with opposition from rival Lever Brothers. The High Court and the Appeal Court decided that Perfection was not distinctive and registration was refused.

In 1909 the firm acquired rights to the Persil soap product in the UK and this soon became successful. The key advantage of Persil was the invention by German chemists of adding peroxide to washing powder in the form of perborate. In 1907 Persil had been registered as a trademark in the UK by the German concern Henkel.

In 1919 Crosfield was acquired by its chief competitor, Lever Brothers, subsequently to become Unilever. Crosfield operated as a separate company until 1964, when the production of soap powders, including the Persil brand, was transferred to Lever Brothers and Crosfield concentrated on its speciality chemicals business. In 1997 Crosfield was bought by the company ICI and then in 2001 it was sold off and became Ineos Silicas.

SOLE MANUFACTURERS

JOSEPH CROSFIELD & SONS, LTᴰ WARRINGTON.

"PERFECTION." GREAT SOAP — MAKERS ALSO OF THE OTHER

BRITISH MANUFACTURE.

"PINKOBOLIC" SOAP. FINEST QUALITY.

BRITISH MANUFACTURE.

"PERFECTION." GREAT SOAP — MAKERS ALSO OF THE OTHER

A HEALTH SAFEGUARD
THE BEST DISINFECTANT SOAP
FOR EVERY HOUSEHOLD PURPOSE
& LAUNDRY USE

BRITISH MANUFACTURE.

"PINKOBOLIC"
SOAP.
FINEST QUALITY.

BRITISH MANUFACTURE.

THIS LABEL IS ISSUED ONLY BY JOSEPH CROSFIELD & SONS, LIMITED.

A trademark for Crossfield's Pinkabolic disinfectant soap from 1907 (number 297,222).

CUTICURA MEDICINE

The company Weeks & Potter of Boston in America was formed in about 1852 to market medicines and remedies. These included Sanford's Radical Cure and the 'Cuticura System of Curing Constitutional Humors'. George Robert White, who started at the firm as a boy and worked his way up until he owned the company, is credited with inventing the name Cuticura. When White, a

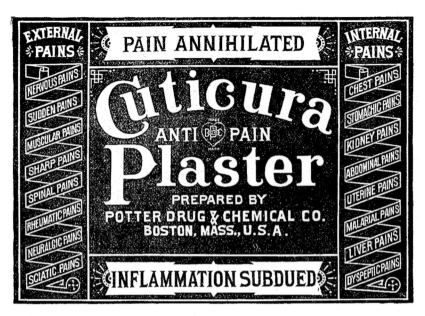

Above, left: Cuticura trademark number 48,323.

Above, right: A Cuticura 1886 trademark for an anti-pain plaster (number 48,320).

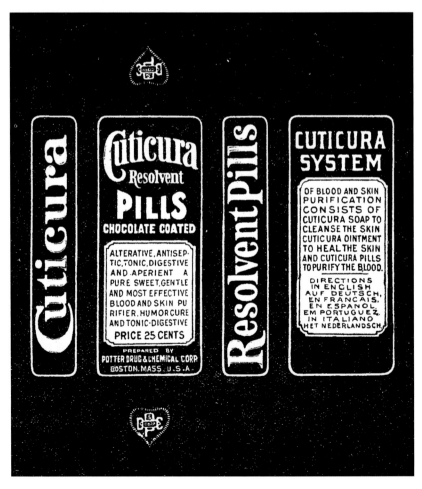

A Cuticura trademark for chocolate-coated pills from 1907 (number 292,582).

bachelor, died in 1922 he had made a fortune and left $50,000 for a memorial to himself, which was built in Boston.

The Cuticura trademark was registered in America in 1878 and in Britain in 1885 for medicine for human use (numbers 48,322–4) by the Potter Drug and Chemical Co., which was described as the successor to Weeks & Potter. The American company was taken over by the German firm Henkel but in 2000 Cuticura Laboratories Corporation reintroduced Cuticura anti-bacterial soap, medicated shampoo, body-wash and the like.

CUXSON GERRARD'S CORN CAP

In 1878 Mr Gibbs and Mr Cuxson set up in Birmingham as wholesalers of medical supplies to doctors and pharmacies. Ten years later the company applied for a trademark (number 75,965) for chemicals used in medicine and pharmacy, and another, Dorothy, for diagnostic instruments (number 76,352).

Cuxson Gerrard's trademark number 75,965.

Later Mr A.W. Gerrard joined the firm as a sleeping partner. Mr Gibbs left the firm when it was discovered that he had started making pill boxes in direct competition next door! Gerrard had been a laboratory assistant at Guy's Hospital in London and then by 1868 a pharmacist. He became head of the pharmaceutical department at London's University College Hospital and then set up as a retail pharmacist in 1884. In about 1905 Gerrard became active in the firm, by that time called Cuxson Gerrard, and began to build up the firm's business in surgical dressings. After the First World War the partners split and the Gerrard family ran the business.

A 1930s display card for Cuxson Gerrard's Carnation corn caps. (*The Robert Opie Collection*)

In about 1922 Gerrard invented the corn cap. Saying that it reminded him of a flower, he called it Carnation, a name that was not registered as a trademark until much later but went on to became the firm's most famous brand.

ELLIMAN'S EMBROCATION

Elliman's trademark number 55,090.

James Elliman started out as a draper in Chandos Street in Slough, Berkshire, but as a sideline he produced medicaments produced to formulations passed down by his ancestors. One of the remedies was a liniment which became popular among his friends for soothing their aching limbs.

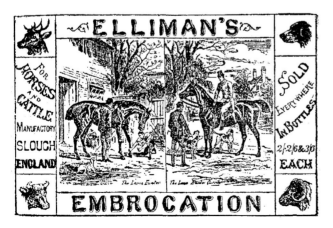

In 1847 James started the manufacture and distribution of the embrocation on a larger scale and in 1878 Elliman Sons & Co. applied for two trademarks

ELLIMAN'S ROYAL EMBROCATION

LEADER WANTS SOME OF THAT EMBROCATION

(numbers 14,435–6) for Elliman's Royal Embrocation and Elliman's Universal Embrocation. These trademarks are now owned by Thornton & Ross Ltd of Linthwaite near Huddersfield, along with marks from 1886 for embrocation for horses and cattle (numbers 55,090–1). The firm also owns well-known brands such as Settlers antacid medicine and Eucryl toothpaste.

An illustration from The uses of Elliman's embrocation for horses, dogs, birds, cattle, *1906.* (*Thornton & Ross*)

ENO'S FRUIT SALT

James Crossley Eno was born in 1827 and as a young man served as an apprentice in a pharmacy at Sandhill, Newcastle, and then as dispenser at the Newcastle upon Tyne Infirmary. From there he took over the pharmacy business of John Burrell in Groat Market, Newcastle. He started to sell his remedies for biliousness and constipation from his pharmacy in the 1850s.

In 1876 he applied for four trademarks (numbers 3,321–4), in use since 1872, for his 'fruit salt, saline or powder and digestive granules' using the motto 'Truth and Light' and a Sun logo.

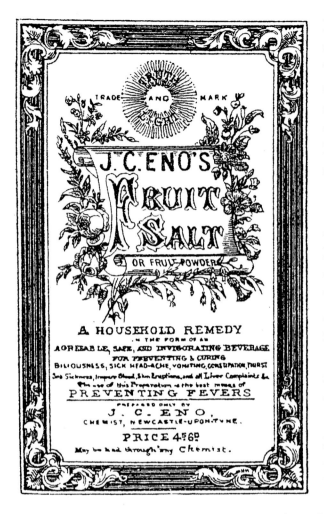

Eno's trademark number 3,322.

Business was good, particularly as sailors from Newcastle spread the word of the benefits of his fruit salt, and within a year or two he opened a factory at Hatcham, New Cross, in London. The new factory had space for expansion and operated for over forty years.

Eno used advertising extensively (see for example colour plate 8) and fought to retain the right to the Fruit Salt trademark when it was questioned whether this term was valid under the 1875 Trade Marks Act. Eventually the House of Lords ruled that the words Fruit Salt were so closely linked to Eno that nobody else could use the expression unless they used it in such a way that there was no possibility that the public would associate it with Eno's. In 1938 the Beecham Group Ltd (now GlaxoSmithKline) took over Eno Proprietaries. Many trademarks are still registered, including Eno, Fruit Salt and Eno's Fruit Salt.

J.C. & J. FIELD'S TOILETRIES

The firm started life as Field's candle-makers on Lambeth Marshes, now part of London. Probably the earliest record of the family firm is the retirement of Thomas Field from the Worshipful Company of Wax Chandlers in 1581. In 1800 the business was known as John & Charles Field and after another twenty years John, from the next generation, joined and it became J.C. & J. Field.

In 1876 Arthur Field and his partners, Frederick Field and John Kingsford Field, applied for a number of trademarks (numbers 3012, 3014 and 3021–2) on behalf of the firm, described as candle manufacturers, for Ozokerit candles, illuminating oil and

perfumed soap. Ozokerit is a natural mineral wax which occurs in Eastern Europe. During the following two years further trademarks were registered, including one for Ozokerine pomade and for toilet soap (number 14,549), at which point the firm was described as a wax chandler.

Top: J.C. & J. Field's trademark number 3,021 from 1876.
Above: J.C. & J. Field's 1878 trademark (number 14,549) for toilet soap.

In 1888 Messrs Field absorbed Messrs Ogleby and non-Field family members joined the firm. In 1900 it successfully defended its Savonol trademark for soft soap in the courts against a company using the name Savoline. It was later taken over by the company Benckiser and the brand disappeared from use.

GILLETTE'S RAZORS

King Camp Gillette was born in 1855 in Wisconsin, USA. His father was an inventor and later a patent agent and King, though for many years a travelling salesman, was something of an inventor himself. Ironically, by 1894 he had become bitter and wrote an anti-capitalist book, *The Human Drift*, in which he denounced business and the rich. 'I advocate a system where money and all representative value would be eventually done away with', he stated.

Gillette's 1906 trademark (number 285,723).

In about 1895 Gillette came up with the idea for a disposable safety razor and worked for many years trying to sharpen thin sheets of metal to perfect the idea. He found a financial backer in William Nickerson, with whom, in 1901, he set up the American Safety Razor Company and applied for patents in America. He also applied for a patent in Britain in 1902 (GB 28,763). The firm sold the razors cheaply to encourage purchases and by 1904 over 12 million blades were sold. Soon Gillette became a millionaire.

In 1906 the Gillette Safety Razor Company applied for a British trademark for King C. Gillette razors and razor blades (number 285,723) and this

The trademarked portrait of King C. Gillette still appeared in this 1930s display. (*The Robert Opie Collection*)

remains registered today. In 1908 Wilkinson Sword tried unsuccessfully to register Gilledge as a trademark for a stropper to resharpen blades. King Camp Gillette died on 9 July 1932 but the Gillette name lives on. Today the Gillette Corporation also sells products under other well-known brand names including Braun, Oral-B, and Duracell.

GLAXO PHARMACEUTICALS

Joseph Nathan was born in 1835 to a poor Jewish family in the East End of London. After his mother died in 1852 he left for Melbourne, Australia, to seek his fortune from prospecting for gold but instead opened a store to serve the gold-diggers. In 1856 he set off for Wellington in New Zealand, which then had a population of only 3,200. Five years later he set up a partnership with his sister's husband, Jacob Joseph, and this lasted until

Glaxo trademark
number 423,166.

1873, at which time he started his own merchant's business, Joseph Nathan and Co. In 1882 he started refrigerated shipping to export butter and soon he was exporting frozen meat, becoming chairman of the Wellington Meat Export Company. He also became involved in the development of railways in New Zealand and expanded into dairy factories.

By 1904 the company had developed a process for producing dried milk which was sold at first under the name Defiance and then, because Lacto could not be registered, Glaxo. The Glaxo name was registered as a British trademark for milk foods in 1906 (number 287,350) and this mark still remains in force. The phrase 'Glaxo builds bonny babies' was used in a 1908 advertising campaign without much success but was registered in 1922 as a trademark (number 423,166). The Glaxo Baby Book, created in 1908 by Joseph's son Alec, was a more successful promotional tool. At first, sales and profits from the dried milk were meagre but by 1912, when Joseph Nathan died, the turnover was huge.

Joseph's sons took control and Glaxo soon became a household name, particularly through the company's direct contact with doctors and mailings to mothers. In 1924 Glaxo produced its first pharmaceutical product, a vitamin D preparation, and after the Second World War it helped to develop penicillin. In 1996 Glaxo (which was the name of the company as well as a trademark from 1947) merged with Burroughs Wellcome and in 2000 with SmithKline Beecham to become GlaxoSmithKline, the world's largest pharmaceutical company.

GUERLAIN'S PERFUME

In 1828 Pierre-François-Pascal Guerlain opened a perfume shop on the Rue de Rivoli in Paris and in 1840 he moved to the fashionable Rue de la Paix. Together with his two sons Aimé and Gabriel, he gained a good reputation for the business and even provided royalty with his scents. After Pierre's death his sons took over the firm.

Aimé applied for a series of British trademarks in 1876 (numbers 6,780–5) for perfume and perfumed soap. The first shows an angel over flags and the rest are a series of labels.

Guerlain's first trademark (number 6,780).

GUERLAIN

Guerlain's trademark for face powder (number 6,782).

The House of Guerlain continued as a family business until 1994 and has produced more than 626 perfumes, including Shalimar, Jicky and Mitsouko. Jicky was created by Aimé in 1889 and is said to be named after a girl who broke his heart when he was a student in England. The firm was acquired in 1994 by the LVMH group, a multinational investment corporation specialising in luxury brands including Moët champagne and Hennessey cognac.

JEYES' FLUID

In 1877 John Jeyes took out his first British patent for a substance for preservative, antiseptic, lubricating and other purposes. This was the beginning of the Jeyes business producing disinfectant fluid and the product, Jeyes Fluid, is still sold today. John Jeyes produced his disinfectant in response to the poor social conditions created by poverty, disease and pollution in Britain and the medical profession adopted the fluid because it could be swallowed by patients without ill-effect.

In 1881 Jeyes Sanitary Compounds Co. Ltd, which had been set up in Richmond Street, Plaistow, London, applied for a trademark for disinfectant (number 26,957) and though this is no longer registered other Jeyes trademarks are still actively used by the Jeyes Group Ltd. The company was acquired by Cadbury

Jeyes' trademark
number 26,957.

A Jeyes' trade card from about 1900. (*Mary Evans Picture Library*)

Schweppes in 1972 but bought out by its management in 1986, only to be later acquired by another company followed by a second management buyout in 2002.

LEVER'S SOAP

William Hesketh Lever was the son of a wholesale grocer in Bolton and Wigan, Lancashire, and he was already a wealthy man when at the age of 33 he decided to start soap manufacture with his brother James. Lever went to a trademark agent in Liverpool to come up with an easy-to-remember name for his soap but was disappointed with the names suggested; then he had a flash of

Lever's Sunlight trademark number 43,406.

33,151. LAUNDRY SOAP. LEVER BROTHERS, LIMITED, Port Sun-light, England. Filed Feb. 23, 1899.

Essential feature.—The representation of a swan. Used since January, 1879.

An American Lever trademark from 1899.

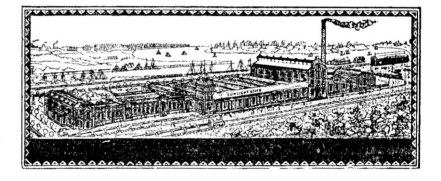

A 1900 British trademark for Sunlight soap made in Germany by Lever (number 232,591).

inspiration when the name Sunlight occurred to him. Two trademarks were duly registered in 1884 (numbers 35,315–16). Sunlight was also registered for starch (number 43,406).

The following year Lever leased a small soap works in Warrington where soap was made from a mixture of coconut or palm kernel oil, cottonseed oil, resin and tallow. Sales were good and in order to expand production he built a new factory beside the River Mersey at a marshy site he called Port Sunlight.

Production started in 1889 and continues there to this day. Lord Leverhulme, as Lever had become, died in 1925, by which time Lifebuoy, Lux and Vim had been added to the range of goods produced by Lever Brothers. At about this time the firm acquired numerous companies, including A. & F. Pears, the Erasmic Co., Joseph Crosfield's, Price's Patent Candle Co. and John Knight Ltd. Turnover of the business, now Unilever, was over £26 billion in 2005.

LISTERINE MOUTHWASH

Listerine was originally a disinfectant for surgical procedures and only later became the name of a mouthwash. In 1879 the disinfectant was formulated by Americans Dr Joseph Lawrence and Jordan Wheat Lambert. They named their new product Listerine after the English surgeon Sir Joseph Lister, who had introduced antiseptic surgery in 1865. It was reported that Lister objected to the use of his name for the product but this did not stop the registration of the word by the Lambert Company as a trademark in Britain in 1882 (number 27,665).

This mark and others for Listerine are still registered by the Warner-Lambert Company, which in 2000 merged with drug company Pfizer. Jordan Lambert's son Gerard apparently coined the term 'halitosis' for abnormally bad breath from the Latin *halitus* in an advertising campaign. In another campaign in the 1930s the phrase 'always a bridesmaid, never a bride' was created for Listerine mouthwash.

Listerine trademark number 27,665.

301

PEARS' SOAP

In 1789 Andrew Pears moved from his native Cornwall to London where he became a successful barber. Recognising the need for a soap that was less harsh than the products then available, he perfected a process to remove impurities and added a delicate perfume to produce a transparent soap. The soap continued to be manufactured by Pears and in 1835 he was joined in the business by his grandson Francis, and the firm became A. & F. Pears, operating from premises just off London's Oxford Street. Andrew retired three years later and in 1862 Francis set up a new factory in Isleworth, Middlesex. Francis's son Andrew and son-in-law Thomas Barratt soon came into the business and started to revolutionise it.

Pears' 1878 trademark number 15,642.

Thomas steadily increased sales by a series of audacious publicity ventures and bold endorsements. In 1877 the firm applied for three trademarks (numbers 10,673–5). The first of these, for the Pears name, had been in use since 1789 and was registered until 1996 when it was merged with trademark number 1,093,334. A trademark registered in 1878 (number 15,642) featured a boy being washed with the caption 'You dirty boy'. The most famous Pears trademark, though, was 'Bubbles', registered in 1894. The Bubbles advertisement featured the 1886 painting by the English artist Sir John Everett Millais of a curly-headed boy blowing a soap bubble, originally entitled *A Child's World*. Barratt was a pioneer of modern advertising and through his work Pears Transparent Soap became a major product at home and abroad. After his death A. & F. Pears Ltd became part of Lever Brothers and production later moved to Port Sunlight.

YOU DIRTY BOY.

Pears' trademark showing 'A negro child in a bath being washed by a white child' would be considered politically incorrect today (number 21,039).

An artistic Pears' trademark for toiletries from 1900 (number 232,523).

PHILLIPS' MILK OF MAGNESIA

English chemist Charles Henry Phillips moved to Glenbrook near Stamford, Connecticut, and set up the Phillips Camphor and Wax Company. He invented a suspension of magnesium hydroxide in water for use as an antacid and laxative in 1873. He took out trademarks for the name Milk of Magnesia for this product in Britain (number 20,460) in 1879 and in America in 1894. He also took out a second British mark (number 20,461) for other proprietary medicines.

The blue bottles containing the medicine became very familiar. Less well-known from the 1930s and 1940s are Phillips Milk of Magnesia Cleansing Cream and Phillips Milk of Magnesia Texture Cream, which were applied externally to improve the complexion.

Phillips' trademark number 20,461.

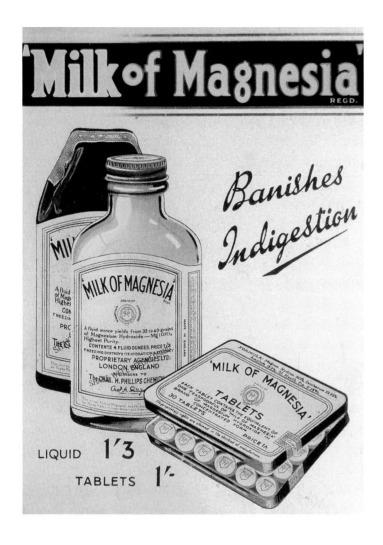

A 1930s advertisement for Phillips' Milk of Magnesia. (*The Robert Opie Collection*)

The Charles H. Phillips Company was run by Henry's four sons after his death in 1882 until 1923, when it was acquired by Sterling Drug Inc. The brand is now owned by Bayer Healthcare in America and by GlaxoSmithKline in Britain.

POND'S EXTRACT

In 1846 chemist Theron T. Pond distilled a healing potion from witch hazel bark. He had produced the remedy for numerous ailments with the assistance of a medicine man from the Oneida tribe of American Indians, and he sold the product as Pond's Extract. In 1849 Pond formed the T.T. Pond Company but he sold

Right: Pond's 1876 trademark, number 2,787.

Below: Pond's packaging from about 1930 still used the 1876 trademark. (*The Robert Opie Collection*)

PREPARED EXCLUSIVELY BY THE

POND'S EXTRACT COMPANY, NEW YORK AND LONDON.

out shortly before his death in 1852. The company set up a factory in Connecticut and later moved its sales offices to New York.

The extract sold well and in 1876 two British trademarks were registered for the patent medicine under the name Pond's Extract (numbers 2,786–7) by the Ponds Extract Co. of Oxford Street, London, and New York. These marks, for which use was claimed from 1846, were registered until 2002.

The company developed Pond's Vanishing Cream and Pond's Cold Cream in the first decade of the twentieth century. In 1955 the company merged with Vaseline manufacturer Chesebrough Manufacturing Company to become Chesebrough Ponds, which was later bought by Unilever.

SAVORY & MOORE'S PHARMACY

Savory & Moore started as a chemist's shop set up by Thomas Paytherus in London in 1794. Thomas Field Savory joined the firm in 1797 and became a partner in 1806, as did Thomas Moore. The pharmacy shop in Bond Street prospered under the name Savory & Moore. Another shop was opened in 1849 near Belgrave Square, London, to serve the area around Buckingham Palace. The shop closed in 1968 and the contents were given to the Wellcome Trust, which passed them to the Medical History Museum in

Savory & Moore's trademark number 6,171 for American dentifrice.

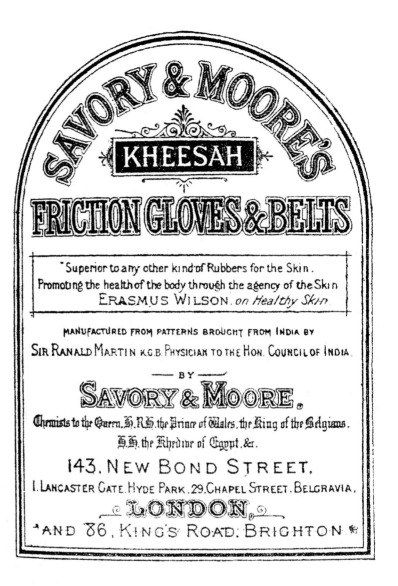

Savory & Moore's trademark number 6,176 for friction gloves and belts.

Melbourne, Australia, where they were used in a reconstruction of a mid-Victorian pharmacy.

In 1876 Savory & Moore applied for a series of trademarks (numbers 6,162–4 and 6,166–82) for American dentifrice, tooth powder, medicines and perfumes, etc. The trademarks show the firm then had three shops in London and one in Brighton and were chemists to Queen Victoria. Although these marks have lapsed, newer marks for the Savory & Moore name are owned by one of the UK's leading pharmacy multiples, Lloyds Pharmacy Ltd, which took over the business in 1992.

Savory & Moore's 1903 trademark for nutrient food (number 255,039).

VICTORY V LOZENGES

During the middle of the nineteenth century Dr Edward Smith of Bolton prepared special lozenges which he gave to his patients to relieve coughs and settle stomach upsets. Demand increased and he started to sell the 'Cough No More Lozenge'. To manufacture the lozenges he took over a bankrupt drug factory at Nelson in Lancashire from Thomas Fryer & Co., and asked his younger brother William Carruthers Smith to be manager. They decided to use the name Victory Chlorodyne Lozenges after seeing the Victory Spinning Mill in Bolton and recognising the connection with Admiral Lord Nelson. Later the name was changed to Linseed Liquorice V Lozenge Victory and the patent remedy became a confection.

In 1885 William Smith, on behalf of Thomas Fryer & Co., manufacturing confectioners, registered two trademarks for

Top: Victory trade-mark number 40,848.

Above: Detail from an advertisement from about 1910 for Thomas Fryer, showing changes from the original Victory trademark. (*The Robert Opie Collection*)

confectionery (numbers 40,847–8), the first for Victory and the second depicting a cannon being fired. By 1911 the name of the well-known sweets had become Victory V Lozenges. The sweets no longer contain chloroform, if they ever did, but are still popular. They are now made by Ernest Jackson, a subsidiary of Cadbury Trebor Bassett, and Cadbury still holds the registration of trademark number 40,487.

WOODWARD'S GRIPE WATER

William Woodward was born in Lincolnshire in 1828 and as a youth spent seven years as an apprentice pharmacist. After a year in London he set up his own pharmacy in Nottingham. Noting that the medicine given by local doctors for malaria, which was then endemic in the marshes of the east of England, had the side-effect of soothing babies' indigestion, he developed the formula for relieving babies' gastric pain.

He probably coined the mark Gripe Water after the old name for a pain in the bowel, gripe. In 1876 he registered trademarks for Gripe Water (number 100) and for a sketch of the 'The Infant Hercules Strangling the Serpents' after the 1786 painting by Sir Joshua Reynolds (number 99). Both are still on the trademark register, as is a 1983 trademark for Woodward's Glucose D featuring the Infant Hercules.

Woodward's Infant Hercules trademark (number 99).

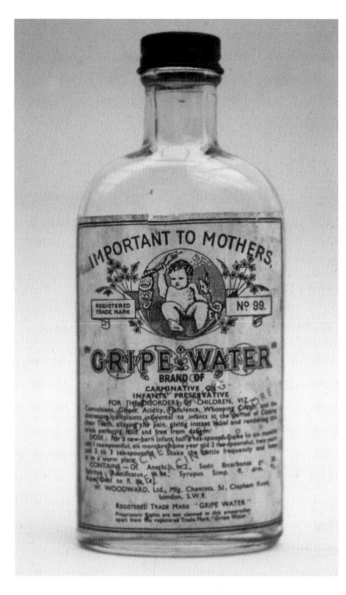

William died in 1912 and his son William Harrison Woodward took over the business. Woodward's Gripe Water is the favourite remedy for babies' colic throughout the world today and still contains dill seed oil as the main ingredient. Now it is manufactured by condom-maker SSL International plc.

WRIGHT'S COAL TAR SOAP

W.V. Wright & Co. was set up in 1867 as a wholesale druggist by William Valentine Wright and his wife at 11 Old Fish Street Hill, London. William had been apprenticed in the drug trade in Ipswich, Suffolk, and then came to London and worked at a pharmacy in Oxford Street. When he was 23 he became a partner with Mr Curtis at Old Fish Street Hill and started to produce Liquor Carbonis Detergens, later

An early bottle of Woodward's Gripe Water showing the trademark. (*The Robert Opie Collection*)

setting up under his own name as W.V. Wright & Co.

The company became Wright, Sellars & Layman in 1875 when Wright required partners to help in the drug department and Wright, Layman & Umney the following year after the retirement of Mr Sellars, but it was as William V. Wright & Co. of Southwark Street, now in south London where he had moved in 1863, that trademarks (numbers 7,418–20) were applied for in 1876. The best-known of these marks is number 7,419 for Wright's Coal Tar Soap, and this is still on the trademark register.

COAL TAR SOAP,
WRIGHT'S

Wright's trademark number 7,419 for perfumed soap.

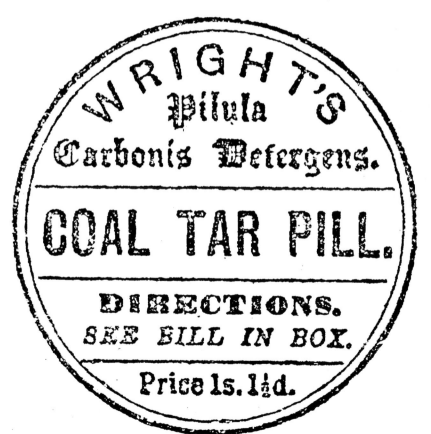

Wright's trademark number 7,418 for coal tar disinfectant.

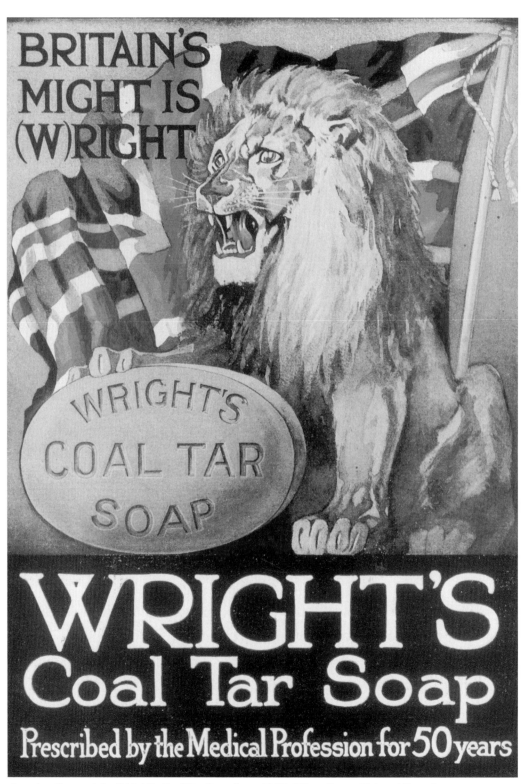

An advertisement for Wright's Coal Tar Soap from 1917. (*Mary Evans Picture Library*)

William died in 1877 and the business was subsequently managed by his son, with his widow owning the business until it was sold. Early in the twentieth century the soap was being advertised as having 'Forty years reputation as a preventative of measles, scarlet-fever [and] small-pox'. In 1995 the trademarks were bought by the London International Group plc, then by Smith & Nephew, and, following a management buyout in 2001, by Accantia Toiletries Ltd. The soap is still widely sold.

8

PASTIMES

Games, Music, Stationery and Tobacco

Mass-produced toys did not really exist in the nineteenth century and items such as dolls and toy soldiers were generally locally made. Only at the start of the twentieth century did the country see the introduction of trademarked toys like Meccano. Card games were immensely popular and De la Rue built a successful business on printed playing cards, for which it registered many trademarks. The playing of sports became more popular as leisure time increased and firms like Slazenger and Lillywhite became well known.

Photography, invented around the middle of the nineteenth century, became easier and cheaper. The Kodak Brownie, introduced around 1890, was the first mass-produced camera. 'Pull the string, turn the key, press the button' and, according to the advertisements, the picture was taken. Celluloid became synonymous with moving film though the trademark was used first for items like dentures and billiard balls.

Music was undergoing something of a revolution at the end of the nineteenth century. Steinway became a big name in pianos through its innovations but the real change was in the growth of recorded music. The Gramophone Company grew from

John Carter's elegant trademark for the Literary Machine (number 25,565).

THE

LITERARY   MACHINE.

nothing into one of the biggest names in the record business in the twentieth century, successfully using the evocative picture of a dog listening to a gramophone recording of his master's voice as its trademark.

In the office and at home people used Dickinson paper, Stephens ink, Remington typewriters, Singer sewing machines and perhaps even Gestetner duplicators. Though John Carter's trademark for the Literary Machine (number 25,565) from 1881 was beautifully drawn, his business of making easels did not long survive. Instead people bought their artist's materials from Reeves and from Winsor & Newton.

Smoking was a pastime that grew and grew, promoted even by royalty. The brands of today were very much in evidence in the early trademarks. Benson & Hedges, Gallaher, Lambert & Butler, Ogden, Philip Morris, John Player and Wills were heavy users of advertising and the trademark system.

BENSON & HEDGES CIGARETTES

Benson & Hedges was started in 1873 when Richard Benson and his uncle William Hedges set up a tobacco business at 13 Old Bond Street, London, and within three years Edward, Prince of Wales had given the firm its first royal warrant. The firm introduced the idea of selling tobacco sealed in tins instead of loose by weight. In 1883 the company applied for its first trademark for Cairo Citadel cigarettes (number 32,550). These

Benson & Hedges Cairo Citadel trademark, number 32,550.

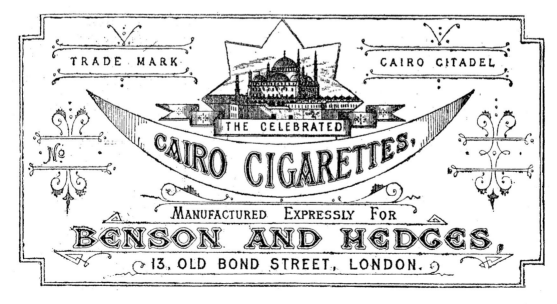

Egyptian-style cigarettes were introduced at the request of the Prince of Wales, who had toured Egypt on behalf of the royal family and brought back Egyptian tobacco.

Richard Benson left the business in 1885 and Alfred Paget Hedges succeeded his father. Benson & Hedges Ltd opened branches in America and Canada in the 1900s, which were much later acquired by Philip Morris. In 1955 Benson & Hedges Ltd and its British trademarks were bought by Gallaher Ltd and in the following year British American Tobacco purchased the overseas business and trademark rights. The trademark Cairo Citadel (number 58,831) is still owned by Benson & Hedges.

CELLULOID PLASTIC

Today the name Celluloid is synonymous with motion picture film but in the nineteenth century it was the name given to

Celluloid trademark number 29,846.

An 1893 advertisement for Celluloid collars, cuffs and shirt bosoms. (*Corbis*)

diverse products made by the Celluloid Manufacturing Company of America. In 1856 Englishman Alexander Parkes had developed a synthetic ivory which he called Parkesine, made from cellulose treated with nitric acid and a solvent. The synthetic material could be moulded when heated but the resulting products tended to warp and crack.

It was American John Wesley Hyatt who perfected the product in 1863 using camphor as the solvent in its production. Hyatt's Celluloid Manufacturing Company started making billiard balls and dentures and in 1882 the firm applied for a British trademark (number 29,846), already in use for ten years, for Celluloid musical instruments, dental plates, cutlery, clothing, stationery items, and billiard and pool balls, etc.

American Hannibal Goodwin applied for a US patent in 1887 for a transparent roll-film made from nitro-cellulose and camphor but this was not granted until 1898. Meanwhile in 1889 the Eastman Kodak Company was granted a patent for a roll-film of nitrocellulose with a gelatine coating. Movies provided a rapidly expanding market for nitrocellulose film and the name Celluloid became a household word.

DE LA RUE'S PLAYING CARDS

In 1793 Thomas De La Rue was born in Guernsey in the Channel Islands and at the age of 10 he was apprenticed as a printer to his brother-in-law. In 1818 he moved with his family to London and set up shop as a paper manufacturer.

Thomas introduced letter-press printing into playing card production and his patent was granted in 1832 (number 6,231 for making and ornamenting playing cards). His firm started printing postage stamps in 1855 and banknotes in 1860. These two products, along with playing cards, continued for years as the main items of the De La Rue business.

Warren William De La Rue, on behalf of the company, was one of the first to apply for British trademarks in 1876. A series of marks were registered, the very first being number 210 for playing cards. In 1969 the playing card business was sold out to games manufacturer Waddington, while the rest of the business continues under the De La Rue name to this day.

De La Rue's first trademark (number 210).

An 1876 trademark for De La Rue's Victoria playing cards (number 8,325).

An 1878 De La Rue trademark for Henry VIII playing cards (number 12,641).

JOHN DICKINSON'S STATIONERY

John Dickinson was not yet 15 when he was apprenticed to the stationers Thomas Harrison of Leadenhall Street in London in 1797. Seven years later he was admitted to the Stationers' Company and started trading as a stationer in Walbrook in the City of London. After a year he moved to Ludgate Street.

He was clearly an inventor since between 1807 and 1847 he applied for fourteen patents concerned with paper. His 1809 patent (GB 3,191) describes a process for producing paper with improved finish compared to that made on the recently introduced continuous Fourdrinier paper-making machines. In

John Dickinson's
Reliance trademark
(number 14,638).

the same year he acquired Apsley Mill at Hemel Hempstead, Hertfordshire, with finance from George Longman. Soon further mills were opened in the same area and further innovations were introduced into paper making. In 1850 machines to produce gummed envelopes were introduced and by 1876 three million were produced each week.

John Dickinson died in 1869 but in 1878 the firm he had started applied for two trademarks (numbers 14,637–8) for

John Dickinson's 1901 Goalie trademark for paper, stationery and bookbindings (number 241,759).

Reliance paper and stationery. In 1910 the company adopted the Lion Brand as its logo and in 1918 it acquired Millington & Sons, originators of Basildon Bond. The company amalgamated in 1966 with Robinsons to form the Dickinson Robinson Group Ltd (DRG), one of the largest stationery and packaging companies in the world. This was followed by a period of acquisitions, the sale of parts of the business and a change of ownership. In 1999 the firm left Apsley Mill to relocate to Cambridgeshire. Today, however, John Dickinson Stationery Ltd is a subsidiary of DS Smith plc and owns many well-known stationery trademarks.

GESTETNER'S DUPLICATORS

David Gestetner was a Hungarian who came to London and then emigrated to America. He had already invented and patented printing transfer ink and a method of producing copies when in 1881 he patented the Cyclostyle pen with a rotating toothed stylus (GB 2,450), which cut stencils used for duplicating writing. A series of patents from 1897 to 1905 (US 584,787, GB 23,406 of 1900, GB 25,373 of 1901, GB 14,303 of 1902 and GB 18,257 of 1905) describe his key inventions in rotary duplicating machines, on the basis of which Gestetner built his office copier business.

In 1884 he registered two trademarks, the Gestetner and his signature, for 'Stationery and apparatus for producing facsimile copies of writings and designs' (numbers 37,761–2). The

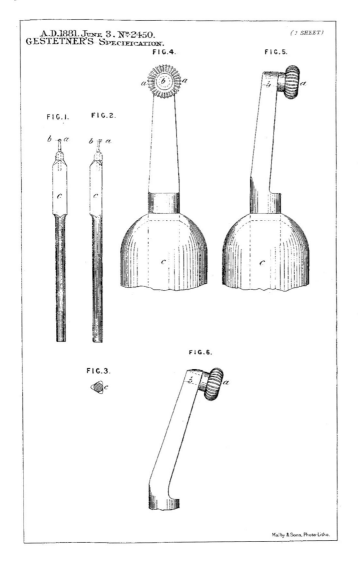

A.D.1881. JUNE 3. Nº 2450.
GESTETNER'S SPECIFICATION.

(1 SHEET)

FIG.4.

FIG.5.

FIG.1.   FIG.2.

FIG.6.

FIG.3.

Malby & Sons, Photo-Litho.

Gestetner's Cyclostyle pen patent, GB 2,450 of 1881.

Gestetner company, incorporated in the US in 1881, continues to this day as part of the Savin Corporation and is now one of the world's leading companies producing copier-printers incorporating cutting-edge digital technology. In the UK and other parts of the world Gestetner is part of the NRG Group.

HIS MASTER'S VOICE RECORDS

The Gramophone Company was set up in London in 1897 by William Barry Owen, a former director of the American National Gramophone Company, and Trevor Williams. The company started to produce gramophone records and machines to play them.

Two years later the artist and photographer Francis Barraud showed the company a photograph of a picture he had painted of his brother's dog Nipper listening to a phonograph. Soon a deal was struck and Barraud repainted the phonograph as a gramophone and assigned the picture and copyright to the company for £100 in January 1900. On 28 December 1900 the company filed an application for a trademark (number 235,053) consisting of a representation of the painting, and one of the best-known of all British trademarks began its life. The picture began to be used and in 1910 the words His

HMV trademark number 235,053.

HIS MASTER'S VOICE

Master's Voice were registered as a trademark. At the same time the mark was used in America by the Victor Talking Machine Co. (see colour plate 12).

By this time the company had built a recording studio in Hayes, Middlesex, and in 1921 a new shop was opened in Oxford Street, London. In 1931 the company merged with the Columbia Gramophone Company as EMI (Electrical and Musical Industries) and the Abbey Road Studios in London opened. From 1989 EMI was owned by Thorn Electrical Industries but demerged in 1996. Over the years the company recorded many famous people, including Sir John Barbirolli and the Beatles. The trademarks for His Master's Voice and Nipper are still registered and used today by HMV in Britain and by RCA in America.

A less appealing trademark, compared to British mark number 235,053, was registered in America by the Victor Talking Machine Company (later RCA) to which HMV had assigned the rights.

ILFORD FILM

Alfred Harman was born in 1841 and by 1863 he was advertising his services for photographic printing. In 1864 he set up his own business in Peckham, South London, doing

OPEN THESE PLATES ONLY IN THE DARK ROOM.

THE

ILFORD

DRY PLATES.

THE BRITANNIA WORKS COMPANY,

ILFORD, LONDON, E.

KEEP THEM IN A DRY PLACE.

Ilford trademark
number 51,304.

photographic work, including printing and copying slides. By 1878 he had applied for a patent (GB 2,174) for 'producing enlarged photographs with artistic finish'. He soon acquired a house in Ilford, Essex, using a cellar and the ground floor for his business; here, with the help of two men and three boys, he produced dry photographic plates.

He traded as Britannia Works Co. and in 1883 built a factory to cope with the expanding sales. He had appointed Marion & Co. of 22–23 Soho Square, London, as his agents and they registered the trademark Britannia Dry Plates (number 22,414) as their own. As a result Harman decided to use the trademark Ilford in 1886 and by 1901 he had changed the company name to Ilford, Ltd (including the comma at the insistence of the local authority). A paddle-steamer logo continued to be used in the Ilford trademarks until after the Second World War. In 1898 the firm changed to a public company and Harman left, though he was subsequently involved in many company matters before his death in 1913.

After being part-owned by the chemical company ICI and then by the Swiss company CIBA from 1969, Ilford was taken over by the Japanese firm Oji Paper in 2005. In 1976 the firm moved from its site in Ilford but the Ilford name is still registered for photographic products today.

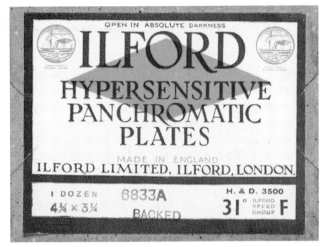

Ilford packaging from about 1920 using the paddle-steamer trademark. (*Science & Society Picture Library*) *Below:* Keswick Pencil Works trademark number 2,438.

KESWICK PENCILS

Keswick in Cumbria has been home to pencil-making ever since deposits of graphite were discovered nearby in Borrowdale in the sixteenth century. Pencils were made locally in cottages, and records show that from 1832 factories were set up in the town with four in existence in 1851.

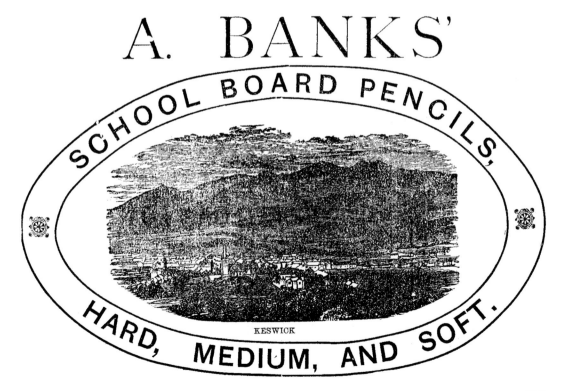

One of the early manufacturers in the town was Ann Banks, who ran the Keswick Pencil Works. In 1877 J.D. Wivell, on behalf of the company, applied to register a trademark (number 2,438). The firm no longer exists but the nearby works of the Cumberland Pencil Company still produces pencils under the Derwent brand.

KODAK CAMERAS AND FILM

George Eastman was born in 1854 in upstate New York but the family moved to Rochester, NY, in 1859. His father died soon after the move and there was little money to spare. George had to start work as an office boy at the age of 14. Later he started to experiment with photography and by 1880 he had invented a gelatine dry plate composition, patented a machine for preparing the plates and begun commercial production. The following year he set up the Eastman Dry Plate Company with Henry A. Strong.

Within a few years cameras using film were sold with the slogan, 'You press the button – we do the rest'. In 1888 George came up with the trademark Kodak, chosen he said 'because I knew a trade name must be short, vigorous, incapable of being misspelled to an extent that will destroy its identity and, in order to satisfy the trademark laws, it must mean nothing'. An office had opened in London's Oxford Street by the time the Eastman Photographic Materials Company applied for a British trademark for Kodak photographic apparatus in 1888 (number 75,818). Other trademarks followed, including number 152,483 using a

Kodak trademark number 152,483.

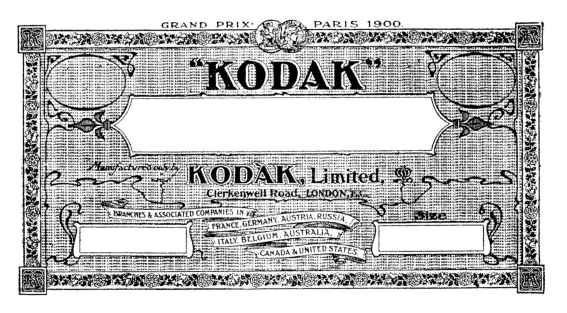

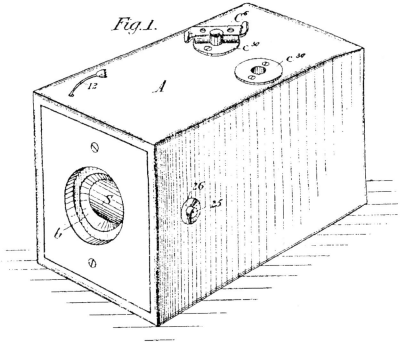

Kodak 1905 trademark for photographic paper (number 269,772).

Kodak 1888 box camera patent (GB 6,950).

Cannon logo and, in 1890, number 230,797 for the Brownie camera.

The Brownie sold for $1 and made photography affordable for almost everyone. Eastman made a fortune, much of which was given away; among the institutions he funded was the Eastman

Dental Hospital in London. Eastman suffered a progressive disabling disease and committed suicide in 1932. Today the Eastman Kodak Company has sales of over $14 billion and worldwide its brand is valued at $4.9 billion.

LAMBERT & BUTLER'S TOBACCO

Charles Lambert, the son of a snuff miller from Beddington in Surrey, set up a business manufacturing cigarettes, pipes and cigars with Charles Lambert in 1834. They started first in St John Street, Clerkenwell, London, and then after two years moved to Drury Lane, London.

In 1876 Charles Butler Jr registered a series of trademarks (numbers 6,151–5) on behalf of Lambert & Butler. Others were

Lambert & Butler's
1877 trademark
(number 10,853).

registered in 1877 (10,852–3 and 12,076) for tobacco, cigars and cigarettes. During the Tobacco Wars of 1900–2, when the American Tobacco Company tried to obtain a major part of the British tobacco business, Lambert & Butler joined forces with twelve other British companies to form the Imperial Tobacco Company. After the amalgamation Imperial concentrated on the British market, in exchange for use of American Tobacco's brands in Britain, and a new company called British American Tobacco was set up to export all the brands.

In 1973 the companies exchanged trademarks and so today the Lambert & Butler name is owned in Britain and elsewhere by Imperial Tobacco, though the original registrations have been allowed to expire.

Lambert & Butler's 1901 trademark, still employing the Sphinx logo (number 239,413).

LILLYWHITE'S CRICKET BATS

The Lillywhite family is renowned in cricketing history, the most famous member probably being James Lillywhite Jr, who was born in 1842. In 1876/7 he was in the English side touring Australia, and played at Sydney and Melbourne. It was James who in 1863 opened the Lillywhite's sports shop in London, which later moved to its present site in Piccadilly.

In 1881–2 two trademarks were registered by C. Lillywhite & Co. of Newgate Street, London, the first for cricket bats, lawn tennis or racquet bats (number 25,552) and the second for the Compound cricket bats (number 28,364). The first trademark shows a Lion and Kangaroo device rather than the usual Lion and Unicorn, presumably as a reference to Australia and the New

Lillywhite's first
trademark (number
25,552) showing a
mixture of sport and
heraldry.

South Wales coat of arms. the 'Compound' may refer to the Gutta Percha rubber compound that was introduced into Europe in 1843.

By 1895 the company was trading in Tunbridge Wells but the connection with the cricketing family and the Piccadilly store is uncertain. Lillywhite's original Piccadilly store has changed hands many times but still sells cricket bats and other sports equipment.

OGDEN'S TOBACCO

Thomas Ogden opened a small tobacco shop in Park Lane, Liverpool, in 1860 and had soon established several branches in the city. By 1866 he had set up a factory in St James's Street.

In 1877 Thomas Ogden of 65 Cornwallis Street, Liverpool, applied for three trademarks (numbers 20,450–2) for tobacco. Number 20,451 has a castle logo, which also appears in some later trademarks. The well-known St Bruno trademark was first used in 1896. By 1899 all manufacturing was moved to Boundary Lane, Liverpool, which is still Ogden's base. At this time Ogden's was putting a quarter of its profits into advertising, despite being only 'a tinpot firm', to quote one of the rival salesmen of the time.

Then in 1901 James B. Duke, a ruthless tycoon and founder of the American Tobacco Company, landed at Liverpool, went directly to Ogden's factory and bought it for £818,000. However, the Ogden's business was transferred back into British hands in 1902, shortly after the formation of the Imperial Tobacco Company, as part of a deal to end the Tobacco Wars between British and American manufacturers.

Top, left: Ogden's Bird's Eye trademark number 20,450.

Top, right: Ogden's 1888 trademark for snuff, showing the castle logo (number 229,528).

Right: Ogden's 1900 trademark for cut plug tobacco (number 228,994).

PHILIP MORRIS' TOBACCO

In 1847 Philip Morris opened a shop in Bond Street, London, selling hand-rolled Turkish cigarettes, and by 1854 he was manufacturing them. When Philip died in 1873 the firm was run by his widow Margaret and brother Leopold. In 1879 Philip Morris & Company applied for its first trademark (number 20,869), showing a 'twin bears' logo, which is still on the British trademark register.

The firm became Philip Morris & Company & Grunebaum in 1885 when Leopold brought in a partner but then it reverted back to Philip Morris & Co. Ltd after two years. In 1894 majority control was taken from the company's creditors by William Curtis Thomson and his family and by 1902 the company was owned fifty–fifty between the British and American partners. A new firm was set up in Virginia in 1919 to acquire the American Philip Morris Company under the name of Philip Morris & Co. Ltd Inc.

The original Philip Morris trademark, number 20,869.

336

In 1919, too, the firm started to use its Coronet logo and within a few years the famous Marlboro brand had been introduced. In the second half of the twentieth century the US company diversified into food, drink and other businesses and by 1980 total group revenues approached $10 billion. The holding company of Philip Morris Incorporated is now known as the Altria Group.

A 1902 Philip Morris trademark for 'Twin Bear Mixture' (number 246,483). *Below:* Player's 1891 trademark featuring Hero (number 154,011).

PLAYER'S CIGARETTES

John Player was born in 1839, the son of a solicitor from the small market town of Saffron Walden in Essex. He went to the city of Nottingham in 1862 to take up a job as a draper's assistant and later set up shop on Beastmarket Hill as an agent for a company producing agricultural manure and seeds, selling tobacco as a sideline. Then in 1877 he bought the tobacco business of William Wright, which at that time employed 150 people in Broadmarsh, Nottingham.

Hero is missing from this 1888 Players' trademark (number 72,210).

By November 1877 Player had applied for his first trademark (number 13,645), which depicted Nottingham Castle. Player's most famous trademark is that depicting the head of a sailor Hero, which was first registered in 1883 with the sailor alone, and then, five years later, in a lifebelt frame with Player's Navy Cut superimposed. In 1891 two ships, thought to be HMS *Britannia* and HMS *Dreadnought*, were added (trademark number 154,011). Originally Hero had one stripe on his shirt collar but the trademark was registered with two. By the time it was pointed out that the correct number of stripes was three, it was too late to change the trademark. Other variations were used but in 1927 it was decided to rationalise the position and create a standard sailor to be used on all packaging, display and advertising

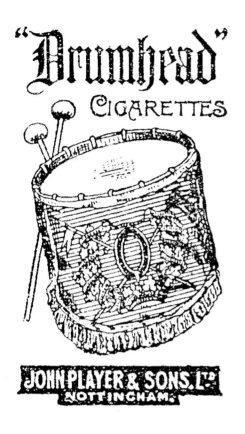

John Player & Sons, Ltd

material, and a painting was commissioned from A.D. McCormick.

In 1881 land was purchased at Radford, Nottingham, and three new factory blocks were erected. The Castle tobacco factory started production in 1884 but a few weeks later John Player died at the age of 45. After his death the firm was run by a group of close friends until his two sons John Dane and William Goodacre took control in 1893. As a defence against the American tobacco companies during the Tobacco Wars of 1900–2, Players, with a capital of £601,456, combined with twelve other companies into the Imperial Tobacco Company. Today Player's cigarettes are still manufactured at factories in Nottingham.

A Player's trademark from 1900 still features Nottingham Castle (number 225,266).

REEVES & SONS' ARTIST'S PAINTS

A business supplying dry cakes of premixed artist's colours was set up in London in 1766 by William Reeves and he was soon joined by his brother Thomas. The brothers split up but Thomas

Reeves & Sons' 1876 British trademark number 2,899.

Below, left: Reeves' 1925 US trademark registered in the rest of the world in the 1990s. (© *ColArt Fine Art & Graphics Ltd*) *Below, centre:* Reeves' 1935 Israeli trade-mark. (© *ColArt Fine Art & Graphics Ltd*) *Below, right:* Reeves' 1962 British trade-mark. (© *ColArt Fine Art & Graphics Ltd*)

continued as a colourman and later his firm traded as Reeves & Woodyer and then Reeves & Sons. Thomas's son William John continued in the business after Thomas's death in 1799.

In 1876 a trademark was registered by the company for a Greyhound or Hunting Dog logo (number 2,899) for artist's colours, mathematical instruments, pencils and miscellaneous artist's materials. The mark, which had been in use since 1786 and continues today (as number 2,901), was taken from the Ryves family crest by William John Reeves. The Hunting Dog (or Alaund) originally had five gold coins (rather than spots).

Over the years the trademark was redesigned and the coins in the logo were reduced to the current three gold coins purely from artistic whim. The cushion was removed from underneath the dog and the design simplified for increased brand-name association. This major change in design was initiated in 1925 in the USA but did not occur in the rest of the world until the mid-1990s, some seventy years later. The change may have been made to simplify the

REEVES

Reeves' 1981 Argentinian trademark. (© *ColArt Fine Art & Graphics Ltd*)

Reeves' 1995 British trademark. (© *ColArt Fine Art & Graphics Ltd*)

Reeves' 1998 Chinese trademark. (© *ColArt Fine Art & Graphics Ltd*)

341

TRADE MARK

REEVES & SONS, LTD.

Est. 1766

Manufacturers of

ARTISTS' OIL & WATER COLOURS

TEMPERA COLOURS

POSTER COLOURS

ARTISTS' BRUSHES

CANVAS

SKETCH BOOKS

and BLOCKS, Etc.

REEVES & SONS, LTD., 18, ASHWIN STREET DALSTON. LONDON, E.8

Reeves' 1927 advertisement featuring the Greyhound logo trademark. (© *ColArt Fine Art & Graphics Ltd*)

printing of the logo on product labels and also to give a more modern look to the products following the change of ownership from Reckitt & Colman to AB Wilhelm Becker of Sweden in 1991.

The Reeves brand is now owned by Wilhelm Becker through Colart Fine Art & Graphics Ltd. Colart also owns the Winsor & Newton brand.

REMINGTON'S TYPEWRITERS AND SEWING MACHINES

After successfully making his own flintlock rifle in 1816, Eliphalet Remington received requests to make guns for others and so started a business manufacturing rifles. In 1828 he moved the firm to the current location of Remington's firearms plant in Ilion, New York. The partnership of E. Remington & Sons was incorporated as a stock company in 1865. The company was also

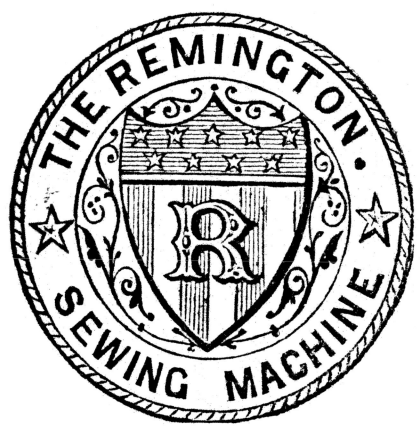

Remington's Stars
and Stripes
trademark, number
8,828.

An 1887 French
trademark for
Standard Remington.

4044. — M. p. être apposée sur des machines à écrire, déposée le 22 juin 1887, à à 2 h. 40, au greffe du tribunal de commerce de la Seine, par la *Société* dite : *The Standard type writer manufacturing Company*, dont le siège est à Ilion (Etats-Unis d'Amérique).

Cette marque a 0.057 de diamètre. Elle s'imprime en toutes couleurs.

producing sewing machines when eight years later it diversified into typewriter manufacture.

In 1876 Remington applied for a British trademark (number 8,828) for steam engines, boilers, pneumatic machines, hydraulic machines, locomotives, sewing machines, weighing machines, machine tools, mining machinery and fire engines. E. Remington

& Sons had made a steam streetcar for Salt Lake City in July 1874 so it was natural for the firm to include steam engines in the goods covered by the trademark.

In 1886 the typewriter business was sold and became the Remington Typewriter Co., soon to take over Standard and other typewriter firms, while the firearms business became the Remington Arms Company. Remington Typewriter Company merged with the Rand Kardex Corporation in 1927 to become Remington Rand Inc., which started to produce shavers in 1937. In more recent years there have been a series of mergers and sales of parts of the business.

SLAZENGER'S TENNIS RACKETS

Slazenger's trademark number 35,566.

Tennis, of sorts, was played in ancient Greece and in the twelfth century in France but the modern game of lawn tennis is credited to Major Walter Wingfield of Pimlico, Middlesex, now London,

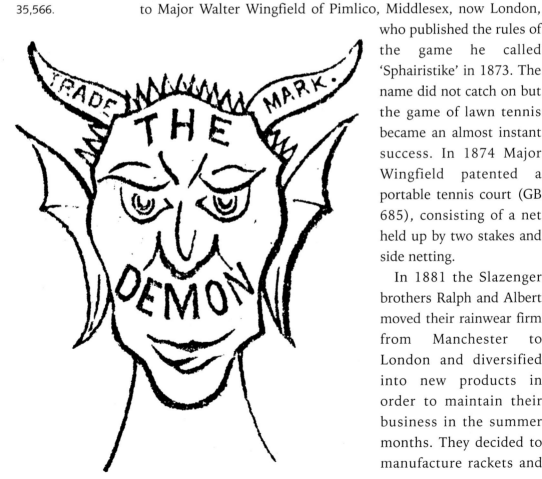

who published the rules of the game he called 'Sphairistike' in 1873. The name did not catch on but the game of lawn tennis became an almost instant success. In 1874 Major Wingfield patented a portable tennis court (GB 685), consisting of a net held up by two stakes and side netting.

In 1881 the Slazenger brothers Ralph and Albert moved their rainwear firm from Manchester to London and diversified into new products in order to maintain their business in the summer months. They decided to manufacture rackets and balls for the new game and in 1884 Slazenger & Sons registered the Demon trademark (number 35,566) for 'tennis, racket, cricket and other games'. Slazenger made golf balls as well as rackets, as shown in colour plate 13.

The firm came to prominence when its tennis balls and equipment were adopted by the All England Lawn Tennis Club for the Wimbledon Championship in 1902; they have been used at the event ever since. The 1884 trademark is no longer registered but the firm's Demon trademark of 1922 for games and playthings (number 426,331) is still owned by Slazengers Ltd.

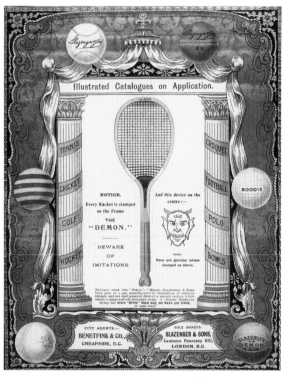

An advertisement from 1900 for the Demon tennis racket. (*The National Archives*)

STEINWAY'S PIANOS

Henry Steinway was a German cabinetmaker who emigrated to the USA. In 1853, capitalising on a strike by workers at the leading piano maker in New York, he and his sons started to produce pianos. Within a decade Steinway & Sons was the world's largest piano manufacturer.

In 1855 Steinway pianos received gold medals at American and European exhibitions and in 1867 the company was awarded the French Grand Gold Medal of Honour. The firm was very innovative and many US and foreign patents were granted to the family business. In 1859 a patent was granted to Henry Steinway for improved over-stringing of the grand piano (US patent 26,532). Henry died in 1871 and his sons C.F. Theodore and William took over operations.

Steinway & Sons.

Steinway's 1883 trademark demonstrates a simple grandeur (number 29,544).

345

It was William who helped establish a showroom in London in 1875. Eight years later Steinway & Sons registered a British trademark (number 29,544) for pianofortes for which they claimed use since 1853. This mark is no longer registered, though other Steinway trademarks, such as numbers 45,605 and 45,607, first registered in 1885, are. Today Steinway & Sons makes 5,000 pianos a year for sale worldwide.

STEPHENS' INK

In about 1832 Dr Henry Stephens (1796–1864) invented a Blue-Black Writing Fluid, later developed into a permanent writing ink similar to today's formulations. In 1837 he was granted a patent

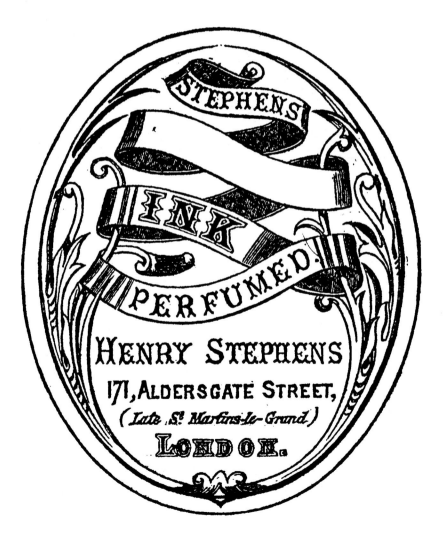

Stephens' trademark number 3,143.

with Ebenezer Nash for 'manufacturing colouring matter and rendering certain colours more applicable to dyeing, staining, and writing', and another for 'ink stands or ink holders, and pens for writing'.

His son, Henry Charles Stephens (1841–1918), known as 'Inky', continued the development of the family business. He was a member of parliament for Finchley, London.

A raft of trademarks, in the form of labels, were applied for in 1876 (numbers 3,135–53) for ink and gum, etc. These are no longer registered but other Stephens' trademarks, some dating back to 1930, are still used. A few Stephens' stationery items are still available, including bottles of Indian Drawing Ink. The brand is now owned by Royal Sovereign Ltd, part of DRG.

Stephens' trademark (number 241,444) from 1901 (see colour plate 15 for a label based on this trademark).

WIGGINS TEAPE PAPER

The paper merchant business of Wiggins Teape was set up originally as Edward & Jones in Aldgate, London, in 1761. In 1876 Richard Teape applied for six trademarks, used since 1861, on behalf of himself and his partner John Carter for Wiggins Teape & Co. (numbers 5,572–7). At some point around this time the firm was known as Wiggins, Teape, Carter & Barlow.

Wiggins Teape Greyhound trademark, number 5,575.

W T & C°

EXTRA STRONG

3009

Wiggins Teape started manufacturing its own paper in 1880 at a mill at Downton, near Salisbury, but this was sold and in 1889 the company bought a mill at Withnell Fold, near Chorley in Lancashire. Later the firm was to own a large number of paper mills in Britain and abroad. The firm's well-known Conqueror trademark was introduced in 1906.

In 1970 the firm became part of the British American Tobacco conglomerate but in 1991 it merged with paper maker Arjo and the resulting merchant's business was renamed Antalis in 1999, becoming the biggest paper merchant in Europe. In 2000 Antalis was absorbed by Worms & Cie, a French industrial and financial group.

A Wiggins Teape's 1878 trademark that could be used on paper as a watermark (number 14,900).

W.D. & H.O. WILLS' CIGARETTES

Henry Overton Wills was born in Salisbury, Wiltshire, in 1761 and by 1786 he was a partner in the tobacco firm of Wills, Watkins & Co. in Mary-le-Port Street and Redcliff Street, Bristol. The firm changed its name to W.D. & H.O. Wills in 1815 when Henry's sons, William Day and Henry Overton Jr, took over. The brothers, like their father, were staunch Nonconformists and supported the Congregationalists by giving to their charities and helping to establish chapels in Bristol. The third Henry Overton

349

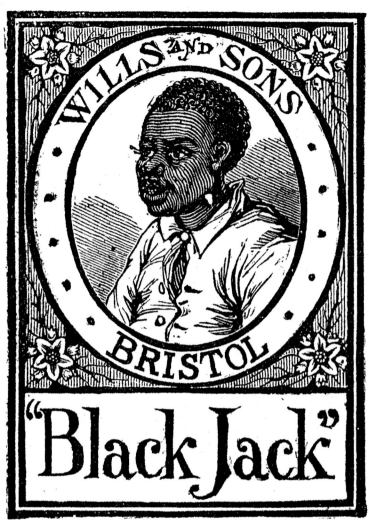

Wills' trademark number 5,909 showing its distinctive eight-pointed star.

Wills joined the firm in 1846, as later did many of his ten surviving siblings.

In May 1876 the firm applied for a series of trademarks (numbers 5,908–12) and the first of these was registered until 2002. By the end of 1877 Wills had registered a long list of marks including Aquidneck (another name for Rhode Island), Best Bird's Eye Tobacco, Bishop Blaze, Black Jack, Early Bird, El Necociante, Fabrica de Tabacos, Firefly brand, Gold Flake, Golden Grain and Star symbol. Soon Wills was leading the way in branding. The famous Woodbines brand was launched in 1888 and sold at a price of five for a penny. There was a dispute

between Wills and a manufacturer selling cigarettes under the trademark Star of Hope, which came to the High Court of Justice in 1893. As a result, one of Wills' Star trademarks (number 52,425) was ordered to be struck off the Trade Mark Register because the word Star on its own was said to be common in the tobacco trade.

When the company amalgamated with other British tobacco manufacturers to form the Imperial Tobacco Company in 1901 it was the dominant firm, being valued at just under £7 million. The Wills siblings became very wealthy, and donated much money to worthy causes including museums, libraries, hospitals and Bristol University. The Wills brand was withdrawn in Britain in 1988.

Wills' Star trademark (number 52,425) was registered in 1886 but taken off the register by the High Court.

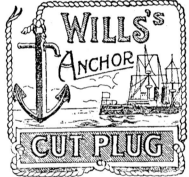

Wills' Anchor Cut
Plug trademark from
1900 (number
227,349).

WINSOR & NEWTON'S ARTIST'S COLOURS

Chemist William Winsor and artist Henry Newton set up a
business in London to sell artist's colours in 1832. They took a
scientific approach to improve the materials, using glycerine to
produce pan watercolour paints and then developing the syringe
for storing paint in 1840 (patent GB 8,394), which led to tube
paints. Winsor & Newton was appointed supplier to Queen
Victoria in 1841.

In 1876 the company registered its trademark (number 2,293)
consisting of a winged sea-lion or Griffin, for which they claimed
use back to 1851. They were the first colourmen to publish

Winsor & Newton's Griffin trademark (number 2,293).

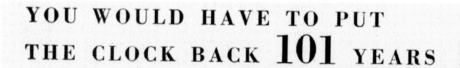

YOU WOULD HAVE TO PUT
THE CLOCK BACK 101 YEARS

. . . to realise why it is that the artist of to-day finds such consistent satisfaction in Winsor & Newton's Colours. For the publication of Winsor & Newton's "Selected List" of colours sets the seal of success on over 100 years of continuous research. Finely ground from the purest quality mineral ingredients, and of unsurpassed brilliance, all colours in the selected list may be regarded as permanent under all normal atmospheric conditions.

SEND FOR WINSOR & NEWTON'S POCKET CATALOGUE SHOWING THE SELECTED LIST OF PERMANENT COLOURS.

WINSOR & NEWTON LTD.
37, Rathbone Place, W.1.   Phone: Museum 7624 (5 lines)

TRADE MARK

Ars probat artificem

A Winsor & Newton advertisement from 1934 using the Griffin logo. (© *ColArt Fine Art & Graphics Ltd*)

A 1982 Winsor & Newton advertisement using the Griffin logo. (© *ColArt Fine Art & Graphics Ltd*)

permanence ratings for their colours and details of the chemical composition of their pigments in 1892. The processes, though, remained secret. The company is now part of Swedish firm Wilhem Becker, which also owns other artist's materials suppliers including Reeves & Sons.

A 1906 Winsor & Newton trademark using a newt logo (number 287,342).

BIBLIOGRAPHY

INTRODUCTION

Hewish, John, *Rooms near Chancery Lane – The Patent Office under the Commissioners, 1852–1883* (London, British Library, 2000)

Newton, David, *Trademarks – an introductory guide and bibliography* (London, British Library, 1991)

Room, Adrian, *Dictionary of trade name origins* (London, Routledge & Kegan Paul, 1983)

A century of trademarks (London, The Patent Office, 1976)

1 TRANSPORT

Bell Punch Ticketing
Modern Transport, 26 June 1948

Commer Vehicles
Carverhill, G., *The Commer Story* (Crowood, 2002)

Crossley's Engines
Eyre, M., Heaps, C. and Townsin A., *Crossley: the story of a famous engineering business and the cars, buses, lorries, aeroplanes and railway locomotives which it manufactured* (Hersham, OPC, 2002)

Humber's Cars
Bullock, John, *The Rootes brothers: story of a motoring empire* (Sparkford, P. Stephens, 1993)

Demaus, A.B., *The Humber Story: 1868–1932* (Gloucester, Sutton, 1989)

Lucas Lamps
Bunce, Gordon, *Lucas in Birmingham* (Stroud, Sutton, 2003)

Bunce, Gordon, *Lucas: Birmingham and Beyond* (Stroud, Sutton, 2004)

Nockolds, Harold, *Lucas, the first hundred years*, vol. 1 *The king of the road* and vol. 2 *The successors* (Newton Abbot, David & Charles, 1976 and 1978)

Raleigh Cycles

Bowden, Gregory Houston, *The Story of the Raleigh Cycle* (London, W.H. Allen, 1975)

Lloyd-Jones, Roger and Lewis, M.J., *Raleigh and the British Bicycle Industry: an economic and business history, 1870–1960* (Aldershot, Ashgate, 2000)

http://homepage.ntlworld.com/catfoodrob/choppers/history/history1.html

Rover Cars

Pinkerton, J. and Roberts, D., *A History of Rover Cycles* (Birmingham, D. Pinkerton, 1998)

2 CLOTHING, FOOTWEAR AND TEXTILES

Aertex Underwear

Cellular Clothing Co. v. Maxton and Murray, *Reports of Patent Cases*, vol. XVI, no. 19 (1899), 397–410

Aquascutum Coats

Campbell, Patrick, *The Aquascutum Story* (London, Aquascutum Ltd, 1976)

Cash's Name Tapes

http://www.jjcash.co.uk/history.htm

Christy's Hats

Barbour, William, *The Chronicles of Canal Street. From BC (before Christy's) to 1868* (Stockport, Swain & Co., 1965)

Early's Blankets

Plummer, Alfred and Early, Richard E., *The Blanket Makers, 1669–1969: a history of Charles Early & Marriott (Witney) Ltd* (London, Routledge & Kegan Paul, 1969)

http://www.witneyblanketstory.org.uk

K Shoes

Crookenden, Spencer, *K Shoes: the first 150 years 1842–1992* (Kendal, K Shoes, 1991)

Lister's Silk

Keighley, M., *A Fabric Huge: The Story of Listers* (London, James & James, 1989)

Macintosh's Raincoats

Macintosh, Charles, *Trade Price List of Caoutchouc or India Rubber Articles, manufactured and sold by C. Macintosh and Co.* (Manchester, 1853)

Wolsey Socks

Baren, Maurice, *How Household Names Began* (London, Michael O'Mara, 1997)

3 DRINKS

Allsopp's Beer

Bushnan, John Stevenson, *Burton and its bitter beer* (London, W.S. Orr, 1853)

Bass Beer

Molyneux, William, *Burton-on-Trent: its history, its waters, and its breweries* (London, 1869)

Owen, Colin C., *The Greatest Brewery in the World – a history of Bass, Ratcliff & Gretton* (Chesterfield, Derbyshire Record Society, 1992)

Trade Mark Owners Association centenary 1886–1986, ed. Les Powell (London, TMOA, 1986)

Carlsberg Beer

http://www.carlsberg.co.uk

Chartreuse Liqueur

http://www.chartreuse.fr

Cockburn's Port

Cockburn, Ernest H., *Port Wine and Oporto, etc.* (London, Wine & Spirit Publications, 1949)

http://wine.about.com

Courvoisier Brandy

http://www.courvoisier.com

Eldridge Pope Beer

Seekings, John, *Thomas Hardy's Brewer: the story of Eldridge, Pope & Co.* (Wimborne, Dovecote, 1991)

Gaymer's Cider

http://www.vaugrat.demon.co.uk/Gaymer/wmgaymer.htm

Gilbey's Gin

Kidd, J., *Gilbeys, Wine and Horses* (Cambridge, Lutterworth, 1997)

Waugh, Alexander Raban, *Merchants of Wine, Being a centenary account of the fortunes of the House of Gilbey* (London, Cassell & Co., 1957)

Gonzalez Byass Sherry

Old Sherry. The story of the first hundred years of Gonzalez Byass & Co. Ltd, 1835–1935 (London, Gonzalez Byass, 1935)

http://www.gonzalezbyass.com

Greene King Beer

Wilson, R.G., *Greene King: a business and family history* (London, Bodley Head, 1983)

Wilson, R.G., 'Edward Greene (1815–1891)', *Journal of the Brewery History Society*, vol. 62, 1990, 23–5

Heering's Cherry Liqueur

http://www.distillers.dk

Heidsieck's Champagne

http://www.riwine.com

Hennessy's Cognac

http://www.hennessy-cognac.com

McEwan's Beer

Keir, David, *The Younger Centuries. The story of William Younger & Co. Ltd, 1749 to 1949* (Edinburgh, William Younger and Co., 1951)

Mumm's Champagne

http://www.champagne-mumm.com

Schweppes' Carbonated Drinks

Trade Mark Owners Association centenary 1886–1986, ed. Les Powell (London, TMOA, 1986)

Stone's Ginger Wine

Wainwright, David, *Stone's Ginger Wine. Fortunes of a family firm 1740–1990* (London, Quiller, 1990)

http://www.stonesgingerwine.com

Tennent's Lager

http://www.archiveshub.ac.uk/news/tennents.html

Whitbread's Beer

Whitbread's Brewery. 1740–1920. An illustrated history, etc. (London, Whitbread & Co., 1920)

http://www.spartacus.schoolnet.co.uk/BUwhitbread.htm

Worthington's Beer

Molyneux, William, *Burton-on-Trent: its history, its waters, and its breweries* (London, 1869)

William Younger's Beer

Keir, David, *The Younger Centuries. The story of William Younger & Co. Ltd, 1749 to 1949* (Edinburgh, William Younger and Co., 1951)

http://www.archiveshub.ac.uk/news/wyounger.html

4 FOOD

Allinson's Flour

    Allinson, Thomas Richard, *A system of hygienic medicine, or the only rational way of treating disease* (London, F. Pitman, 1886)

Bovril Beef Drink

    Bennett, Richard, *The Story of Bovril* (Bovril, 1953)

Carr's Crackers

    Forster, Margaret, *Rich desserts and captain's thin: a family and their times 1831–1931* (London, Chatto & Windus, 1997)

McDougall's Flour

    The McDougall Brothers and Sisters: the children of Alexander McDougall of Manchester [pamphlet], 1923

5 HOUSEHOLD GOODS

Avery's Scales

    Leigh-Bennett, E.P., *Weighing the World* (Birmingham, W. & T. Avery, 1930)

Berger's Paint

    Farnol, John Jeffery, *A portrait of a gentleman in colours. The romance of Mr. Lewis Berger* (London, Sampson Low & Co., 1935)

Bryant & May's Matches

    Beaver, Patrick, *The Match Makers* (London, Melland (for Bryant & May), 1985)

Chubb's Locks

    Chubb, George Hayter and Churcher, Walter Graham, *The House of Chubb 1818–1918* (London, Herbert Jenkins, 1919)

Codd's Bottle Stopper

    www.bottlebooks.com

Doulton's Pottery

    Eyles, Desmond, *The Doulton Lambeth Wares* (London, Hutchinson, 1975)

    Eyles, Desmond, *Royal Doulton, 1815–1965. The rise and expansion of the Royal Doulton Potteries* (London, Hutchinson, 1965)

Price's Candles

    Price's Patent Candle Company, *A Brief History of Price's Patent Candle Company Limited, Belmont Works, Battersea, London, and Bromborough Pool Works, near Birkenhead* (London, Waterlow & Sons, 1891)

    Price's Patent Candle Company, *Still the candle burns* (Privately printed, 1947)

6 AGRICULTURAL, HORTICULTURAL AND INDUSTRIAL MERCHANDISE

Albright & Wilson's Chemicals

King, Wilson, *Arthur Albright, born March 12, 1811. Died, July 3, 1900. Notes of his life* (Birmingham, The Guild Press, 1901)

Threlfall, Richard E., *The story of 100 years of phosphorus making: 1851–1951* (Oldbury, Albright & Wilson Ltd, 1951)

Bessemer's Steel

Bessemer, Henry, *Sir Henry Bessemer, F.R.S.: an autobiography* (London, Engineering, 1905)

Bibby's Animal Feedstuffs

Bibby, J. B. and Bibby, C. L., *A Miller's Tale: a history of J. Bibby & Sons Ltd, Liverpool* (Liverpool, J. Bibby & Sons, 1978)

Blue Circle Cement

Trade Mark Owners Association centenary 1886–1986, ed. Les Powell (London, TMOA, 1986)

Carron Iron

Watters, Brian, *Where iron runs like water!: a new history of Carron Iron Works 1759–1982* (Edinburgh, John Donald Publishers, 1998)

Earl of Dudley's Iron

Dudley: illustrated by photographs (Dudley, W.H. Laxton, 1868)

Firth's Steel

Marshall, A.C. and Newbould, Herbert, *The history of the Firths* (Sheffield, Thomas Firth & Sons, 1924)

100 Years in steel. Being an account of the history and progress of the firms of John Brown & Co. Ltd. and Thos. Firth & Sons Ltd., from their earliest beginnings until the celebration of the centenary, 1937 (Sheffield, T. Firth & J. Brown, 1937)

Marples' Tools

Eaton, Reg, *The ultimate brace: a unique product of Victorian Sheffield* (Erica Jane Publishing, 1989)

Morgan's Crucibles

Bennett, Richard, *Battersea Works 1856–1956* (London, Morgan Crucible Company, 1956)

Rabone's Tools

Hallam, Douglas J., *The First 200 years: a short history of Rabone Chesterman Limited* (Birmingham, Rabone Chesterman, 1984)

Rabone, John, *Drawings of . . . rules, spirit levels, measuring tapes, etc. manufactured by J. Rabone & Son* (Birmingham, 1872)

Ransome's Agricultural Machinery

Ransomes of Ipswich: a history of the firm and a guide to its records (University of Reading, Institute of Agricultural History, 1975)

Spear & Jackson's Tools

Jones, P.d'A. and Simons, E.N., *Story of the Saw . . . Spear & Jackson Limited, 1760–1960* (Manchester, Newman Neame, 1961)

7 MEDICINES AND TOILETRIES

Allen & Hanbury's Medicines

Tweedale, Geoffrey, *At the sign of the plough: 275 years of Allen & Hanbury's and the British pharmaceutical industry, 1715–1990* (London, Murray, 1990)

Beecham's Pills

'"Best for me best for you": a history of Beecham's pills 1842–1998', *Pharmaceutical Journal*, 21–8 December 2002, vol. 269, no. 7229, 921–4

Burroughs Wellcome's Drugs

Macdonald, Gilbert, *One hundred years Wellcome* (London, Wellcome Foundation, 1980)

Joseph Crosfield's Soap

Musson, Albert Edward, *Enterprise in soap and chemicals. Joseph Crosfield & Sons, Limited, 1815–1965* (Manchester, Manchester University Press, 1965)

Elliman's Embrocation

Elliman Sons & Co., *The uses of Elliman's embrocation for horses, dogs, birds, cattle*, 5th edn (Slough, Elliman Sons & Co., 1906)

J.C. & J. Field's Toiletries

Beable, William Henry, *Romance of great businesses . . . Illustrated*, vol. 2 (London, Heath Cranton, 1926)

Gillette's Razors

Gillette, King C., *The Human Drift*, reprint of 1894 edn (New York, Scholars' Facsimiles and Reprints, 1976)

van Dulken, Stephen, *Inventing the 20th century* (London, British Library, 2000)

Glaxo Pharmaceuticals

Davenport-Hines, R.P.T. and Slinn, Judy, *Glaxo: a history to 1962* (Cambridge, Cambridge University Press, 1992)

Guerlain's Perfume

http://en.wikipedia.org/wiki/Guerlain

Lever's Soap

Williams, E., *Port Sunlight: the first hundred years, 1888–1988: the short history of a famous factory* (Kingston upon Thames, Lever Brothers, 1988)

Pears' Soap

bubbles.org/html/history/bubhistory.htm

Phillips' Milk of Magnesia

http://www.cslib.org/stamford/indhist.htm#n28

Victory V Lozenges

Room, Adrian, *Dictionary of trade name origins* (London, Routledge & Kegan Paul, 1983)

8 PASTIMES

John Dickinson's Stationery

Evans, Joan, *The endless web, John Dickinson & Co. Ltd, 1804–1954* (London, Jonathan Cape, 1955)

Ilford Film

Hercock, Robert J. and Jones, George A., *Silver by the ton: the history of Ilford Limited, 1879–1979* (London, McGraw-Hill, 1979)

Kodak Cameras and Film

http://www.kodak.com/US/en/corp/kodakHistory/

Reeves & Sons' Artist's Paints

http://www.npg.org.uk/live/artistsupp_r.asp

Wiggins Teape Paper

Mais, S.P.B., *Gateway House* (London, The Wiggins Teape Group, 1955)

W.D. & H.O. Wills' Cigarettes

Alford, B.W.E., *W.D. & H.O. Wills and the development of the UK Tobacco Industry 1786–1965* (London, Methuen, 1973)

INDEX

c1919